THE PALEO-CONSERVATIVES

New Voices of the Old Right

Joseph Scotchie, editor

"Paleoconservatism" as a concept came into circulation during the 1980s as a rejoinder to the rise of neoconservatism. It signifies a brand of conservatism that rose up in opposition to the New Deal, setting itself against the centralizing trends that define modern politics to champion the republican virtues of self-governance and celebrate the nation's varied and colorful regional cultures. This volume brings together key writings of the major representatives of "Old Right" thought, past and present.

The essays included here define a coherent intellectual tradition linking New York libertarians to unreconstructed Southern traditionalists to Midwestern agrarians. Part I is devoted to the founding fathers of the modern conservative movement. Essays by Frank Chodorov, Murray Rothbard, and James Burnham attack economic aspects of the New Deal, big government in general, and high taxes. Russell Kirk introduces cultural paleoconservatism, with its preference for social classes and distinctions of age and sex, while Richard Weaver explains why culture is more important to a civilization's survival than mere material conditions.

The second part covers the contemporary resurgence of the Old Right. Chilton Williamson, Jr. sets out the argument against large-scale immigration on cultural and economic grounds. The divisive issue of trade is covered. William Hawkins outlines a mercantilist trade policy at odds with the free trade libertarianism of Chodorov and Rothbard. On education, Allan Carlson goes further than

(Continued on back flap)

THE
Paleoconservatives

THE
Paleoconservatives

New Voices of the Old Right

Joseph Scotchie

EDITOR

Transaction Publishers
New Brunswick (U.S.A.) and London (U.K.)

Copyright © 1999 by Transaction Publishers, New Brunswick, New Jersey.

All rights reserved under International and Pan-American Copyright Conventions. No part of this book may be reproduced or transmitted in any form or by any means, electronic or mechanical, including photocopy, recording, or any information storage and retrieval system, without prior permission in writing from the publisher. All inquiries should be addressed to Transaction Publishers, Rutgers—The State University, 35 Berrue Circle, Piscataway, New Jersey 08854-8042.

This book is printed on acid-free paper that meets the American National Standard for Permanence of Paper for Printed Library Materials.

Library of Congress Catalog Number: 99-17346
ISBN: 1-56000-427-4
Printed in the United States of America

Library of Congress Cataloging-in-Publication Data

The paleoconservatives : new voices of the Old Right / Joseph Scotchie, editor.
    p. cm.
Includes bibliographical references and index.
ISBN 1-56000-427-4 (alk. paper)
    1. Conservatism—United States—History—20th century. I. Scotchie, Joseph, 1956–   .
JC573.2.U6P35   1999
320.52'0973'09049—dc21   99-17346
                                                              CIP

Contents

Acknowledgements   vii

Introduction: Paleoconservatism as the Opposition Party
Joseph Scotchie   1

Part I: Founding Fathers

1. Life in the Old Right
   Murray N. Rothbard   19

2. Taxation is Robbery
   Frank Chodorov   31

3. The Managers Shift the Locus of Sovereignty
   James Burnham   47

4. The Question of Tradition
   Russell Kirk   59

5. The Importance of Cultural Freedom
   Richard M. Weaver   79

Part II: A Resurgent Old Right

6. Promises to Keep
   Chilton Williamson, Jr.   97

7. The Anti-History of Free Trade Ideology
   William R. Hawkins   107

8. From Cottage to Work Station.... And Back Again:
   The Family and Home Education
   Allan Carlson   131

9. Is the American Experience Conservative?
   M.E. Bradford   145

10. Trollopes in the Stacks
    Thomas Fleming   153

11. Reconfiguring the Political Landscape
     Paul Gottfried   163

12. Restoring the Republic
     Clyde Wilson   179

13. Nationalism, Old and New
     Samuel Francis   189

     Contributors   201

     Bibliography   203

     Index of Names   209

Acknowledgements

Ch. 1. Murray N. Rothbard, "Life in the Old Right," originally published in *Chronicles*, August, 1994, pp. 15–19.

Ch. 2. Frank Chodorov, "Taxation is Robbery" from *Out of Step: The Autobiography of An Individualist* (New York: The Devin Adair Company, 1962): pp. 216–239. Also from *Fugitive Essays,* Liberty Fund, 1980, pp. 253–261. Reprinted with permission of Liberty Fund, Inc., 8335 Allison Pointe Trail, Indianapolis, IN.

Ch. 3. James Burnham, "The Managers Shift the Locus of Sovereignty," from *The Managerial Revolution* (Bloomington: University of Indiana Press, 1940): pp. 139–151. Copyright, 1941 by James Burnham. Reprinted by permission of HarperCollins Publishers, Inc.

Ch. 4. Russell Kirk, "The Question of Tradition" from *Prospects for Conservatives*, pp. 227–254. Copyright, 1989 by Regnery Publishing. All rights reserved. Reprinted by special permission of Regnery Publishing, Inc., Washington, D.C.

Ch. 5. Richard M. Weaver, "The Importance of Cultural Freedom," originally published in *Modern Age*, Winter 1961/62, pp. 21–33.

Ch. 6. Chilton Williamson, Jr., "Promises to Keep," originally published in *Chronicles*, July, 1991, pp. 20–23.

Ch. 7. William R. Hawkins, "The Anti-History of Free Trade Ideology" from *America Asleep*, published by United States Business and Industry Council Educational Foundation, 910 16th St., NW, Washington, D.C., 1991.

Ch. 8. Allan Carlson, "From Cottage to Work Station...And Back Again: The Family and Home Education," originally published in *The Family in America*, February, 1996, pp. 1–8.

Ch. 9. M.E. Bradford, "Is the American Experience Conservative?" from *The Reactionary Imperative: Essays Literary and Political*, (Peru, Ill.: Sherwood Sugden and Company, 1990): pp. 135–142. Originally delivered at the Heritage Foundation, Washington, D.C. in October 1986 as part of a series on "What Does It Mean to Be a Conservative?"

Ch. 10. Thomas Fleming, "Trollopes in the Stacks," originally published in *Chronicles*, April, 1993, pp. 12–15.

Ch. 11. Paul Gottfried, "Reconfiguring the Political Landscape," originally published in *Telos*, Spring, 1995, pp. 111–126.

Ch. 12. Clyde Wilson, "Restoring the Republic," originally published in *Chronicles*, June, 1992, pp. 22–24.

Ch. 13. Samuel Francis, "Nationalism, Old and New," originally published in *Chronicles*, June, 1992, pp. 18–22.

Thanks also to Susan Dalhstrom, Pat Eagleson and Donna Rinaldi for assisting with the typing, and my wife Anna for the research, proofreading and the extra special encouragement and patience.

Introduction:
Paleoconservativism as the Opposition Party

Joseph Scotchie

"Paleoconservatism" is a phrase that came into circulation during the 1980s, perhaps as a rejoinder to the rise of neoconservative influence on the American Right. More importantly, it is mean to signify a brand of conservatism whose roots reach back to before both the Cold War and even World War II. As such, paleoconservatives readily accept the much-used label "Old Right" so as to identify themselves in part with a conservativism that arose in opposition to the New Deal.

Paleoconservatism has been influenced by several European thinkers and epochs in history. Edmund Burke, the nineteenth-century English statesman whose preference for a rural, hierarchical order and in general, the nonmaterialistic things in life long inspired Russell Kirk and other traditionalists who came of age in the 1950s. Meanwhile, Kirk's friend, Richard Weaver, going back further in time, found a useable past in the chivalry of the Middle Ages, qualities that Weaver believed could be transported to the modern world.

Other major influences on the Old Right are classical. Russell Kirk's opus, *The Roots of American Order*, singles out the example of the ancient Hebrews, Greeks (notably Plato and Aristotle), Romans, and the England that emerged during the fourteenth century for molding the American character. Likewise, M. E. Bradford has cited the Roman republic, with its "durable and impressive social organisms" for exerting a great influence on the Founding Fathers. "A good Roman of the old school had personal pride and a considerable sense of honor," Bradford writes. "His was a shame culture, dominated by intense and personally felt loyalties to family, clan, and individual. Commitment to Rome had its roots in…these most primary attachments." Such were virtues that the Founders, especially George Washington, aspired to emulate.[1]

1

In modern times, such European Catholics and Anglo-Catholics as G.K. Chesterton, Joseph de Maistre, and T. S. Eliot have served as similiar inspirations for paleoconservatives. Also from the continent, the free market, antistatist "Austrian school" made famous by Friedrich Hayek, Ludwig von Mises, and Henry Hazlitt became the intellectual model for an economic and social alternative to New Deal state planning. By the 1990s, such labels as reactionary and, especially, traditionalist held more appeal to the Old Right that mere conservatism— since many of them wondered what exactly there was left to "conserve" from contemporary American culture.[2]

Many of the Old Right's antecedents have been American. Modern conservatism has always had a strong Southern influence: the decentralizing tenets of Thomas Jefferson, John Randolph of Roanoke, and John C. Calhoun are held up as eighteenth and nineteenth-century models of responsible statesmanship. The revolt of the Vanderbilt Agrarians (especially that of Andrew Lytle and Donald Davidson) against large-scale industrialization is also a cherished legacy for paleoconservatives.

In addition, "small-r" republicans, those opponents of a budding American empire have seen their reputations refurbished by paleoconservative writers. They include William Jennings Bryan, the fiery Midwestern populist; Idaho Senator William J. Borah, who fought Woodrow Wilson's League of Nations plan; and William J. Fulbright, the Arkansas solon who expressed grave reservations about the Johnson administration's escalation in Vietnam, while denouncing an "arrogance of empire" that had captured Washington policymakers and legislators alike. A post-Cold War foreign policy that combines a strong national defense and a nation free of such globalist organizations as the United Nations, the World Bank, the International Monetary Fund, and the World Trade Organization has been a good enough model for the Old Right.[3]

A defense of the nation's varied and colorful regional cultures animates the Old Right's opposition to the centralizing trends that defined most twentieth-century politics. Culture means celebrating American regionalism, for instance, Robert Frost's New England, the Old South of William Faulkner and the New South of Walker Percy, plus the West as portrayed in the novels of Edward Abbey to even such forgotten Midwestern novelists as Louis Bromfield and Glenway Westcott. On the grounds that America was not a "universal nation," but instead an extension of an Anglo-Saxon-Celtic civilization also influenced by Athens, Rome and Jerusalem, the Old Right first gained real notoriety by opposing massive Third World immigration into the United States.

II

Twentieth-century American political movements were often inspired by low-circulation journal of opinions that eventually exerted an important influence on a major political party. For the Left, there is the *New Republic* and the rise of the New Deal. On the post-World War II Right, *National Review* held a similiar influence on the Cold War politics of the Republican Party.

In 1979, two southern traditionalists, Thomas Fleming and Clyde Wilson, founded a publication orignally named the *Southern Partisan Quarterly Review*. A classicist and former academic, Fleming had long harbored ambitions of editing his own journal of opinion. Specifically, he hoped to edit a quarterly that focused on Southern culture, politics, literature, and history, a publication that would advance themes and ideas Fleming felt were ignored by such leading Southern-based journals as *Sewanee Review* and *Southern Review*. In Wilson, editor of the John C. Calhoun papers at the University of South Carolina, Fleming found a like-minded colleague from the usually inhospitable groves of academia.

The publication had a rocky beginning. Most fledging magazines fold within a year of their first number. This, too, was the case with *Southern Partisan* which ceased operation after only two issues. But two years later, the publication rose from the dead. Unbeknownst to Fleming and Wilson, the South Carolina-based Foundation for American Education (FAE) had hoped to start their own publication. Both the directors of the FAE and the founders of *Southern Partisan* shared a common goal, namely the restoration of Southern traditionalism in the face of a gaudy "New South" materialism. In 1981, FAE purchased *Southern Partisan's* mailing list and the magazine had a second life. Fleming stayed with *Southern Partisan* for two years before becoming managing editor of *Chronicles*, a conservative monthly published by the Rockford Institute in Rockford, Illinois. Leopold Tyrmand, a Polish emigré novelist, had founded *Chronicles* under the assumption that America's problems were not necessarily economic or political, but mostly cultural in nature. In 1986, Tyrmand died and Fleming succeeded him as editor.

Also in the early 1980s, Llewellyn Rockwell, formerly an aide to the libertarian congressman Ron Paul (R.-Tex.) left Washington to start the

Von Mises Institute in Auburn, Alabama. Named after the famed Austrian economist, the institute, as opposed to a libertarianism that, for instance, sees all religions as essentially "equal," championed both free markets and traditional Judeo-Christian values.

The think tank was bolstered by Rockwell's partnership with Murray Rothbard, the prolific libertarian author and teacher whose skepticism over America's Cold War foreign policy had long expelled him from the ranks of mainstream conservatism. By the late 1980s, Rothbard had traveled a long and colorful career path that saw him support Strom Thurmond's 1948 State's Rights third party, the ill-fated Robert A. Taft presidential candidacies of the 1950s and Norman Mailer's New York City mayoral campaign in 1969. Rothbard would also enthusiastically endorse Pat Buchanan's challenge to George Bush in the 1992 GOP presidential primaries. All the while, Rothbard claimed his "basic political views [had] not changed by a single iota." Indeed, all these political campaigns did fight, for various reasons and on various issues, the centralizing tide of the twentieth century. At Rockford and Von Mises, a fledging opposition to a post-Cold War globalism was born.

During the 1980s, conservatives were generally united behind Ronald Reagan's agenda of tax cuts, a slowdown (if not a reduction) in government spending, and a rollback of the Soviet Empire. Supreme Court appointees would presumably take care of the social agenda championed by religious conservatives whose numbers swelled the ranks of Republican voters. The Old Right was mostly quiet throughout the 1980s. Their largest presence was Paul Gottfried's editorial role at *The World and I*, a thick bimonthly published by the Washington Times Corporation.

In the political arena, the Old Right suffered a major defeat early on. After Reagan's landslide election in 1980, conservatives pushed M. E. Bradford to head the National Endowment for the Humanities. Along with Rothbard, Bradford was the major intellectual driving force behind a revived Old Right. A literary critic who specialized in Faulkner studies and the achievement of the Agrarians, Bradford was also a keen student of the U.S. Constitution. His 1979 collection on the founding era, *A Better Guide Than Reason* became a bible of sorts for young paleoconservatives. The back jacket of a 1990 collection, *The Reactionary Imperative*, contained, for instance, praise from Fleming, Wilson, Kirk, Sam Francis, Chilton Williamson, Jr., Tom Landess, and M. Stanton Evans. To Bradford, the Founders were not utopians hoping to build a "city on a hill," but somber republicans who preferred history—

with its stern lessons of man's failures and limitations—rather than mere reason to be their constitutional lodestar.

The NEH is a bureacracy mostly famous for funding part of Ken Burns's popular 1990 documentary on the Civil War. Some conservatives, however, thought Bradford's influence could reach the general public since the NEH, as a *Southern Partesan* editorial claimed, "to some extent shapes the direction of scholarly effort in this country." At the least, the appointment would recognize the importance of southern traditionalists to the potentially powerful Reagan coalition.[4]

It would never happen. Bradford's writings included a scathing, yet scholarly critique of the Lincoln legacy. In 1968 and 1972, Bradford also supported George Wallace's presidential bids. And so, a campaign against the nomination was put in motion. Such prominent conservatives as Heritage Foundation President Edwin Feulner, *Public Interest* editor Iriving Kristol, and syndicated columnist George Will joined the anti-Bradford forces. Their nominee was William Bennett, a then-unknown academic at the University of North Carolina. The battle reached the pages of the *New York Times, Washington Post, Los Angeles Times, Wall Street Journal,* and *Newsweek,* not to mention the CBS Evening News. Bradford had the support of William F. Buckley, Jr., Pat Buchanan, and numerous senators and congressmen, but when Chief of Staff James A. Baker came out against Bradford, the battle was over.

Old Right bitterness over the Bradford-Bennett showdown has never subsided. In 1986, Bradford was named president of the Philadelphia Society, a usually tame conservative debating club. That year, Bradford initiated a few sparks by lining up several speakers to criticize what they perceived as a growing complacency on the Right, if not an outright surrender, to liberal rhetoric and policy. The new establishment was charged with becoming "content with the welfare state," for being "global democrats and secularists, whose democratic universalism [was] reminiscent of Trotskyist utopianism." On the other side, Brigitte Berger praised East Coast conservatives for being "goal-rational" and interested in "achieving particular policy goals." The Old Right, Professor Berger contended, were "value-rational." Like liberals of the 1960s who cared more about "being left," the Old Right, presumably, was more interested in "being right" than in "achieving realizable goals." But for the most part, the targeted party refused to rise to the bait. The Old Right, most observers agreed, was a spent force with little clout inside an increasingly triumphant conservative movement.[5]

III

In November 1989, the Berlin Wall fell and the Cold War ended. American conservatives, needless to say, were delighted that the "twilight struggle" not only ended in their lifetime, but also saw a stunning victory for the West. However, it would not be long before a sense of uneasiness set in. A year later, William F. Buckley, Jr., still the chief arbiter of conservative discourse in America, published a *National Review* cover story, asking "What Now?" The essay covered familiar themes: trade, taxes, abortion, the environment, euthenasia, urban problems, and drugs. Buckley supported a interventionist, generally pro-human rights foreign policy. He also endorsed the idea of voluntary "national service" as a way to maintain a "sense of community" in a time when "high and illegal immigration and…factionalism…encourage centrifugal forces in our culture." The essay received its share of polite compliments, but the nervousness behind the title itself signified that American conservatives, at least its Washington/Manhattan elites, were entering an awkward era. With communism defeated abroad, the Right had to face the reality of continued liberal dominance of American culture at home.[6]

The end of the Cold War gave the Old Right an opportunity to fill a void in a movement unhappy with the administration of George Bush. Much of the Old Right's positions and ideas are smack in the conservative mainstream: privatizing social security; eliminating numerous cabinet positions, including Education, Commerce, Energy, Transportation; a pro-life stand on abortion, and opposition to affirmative action and quotas. But the Old Right would part company with Beltway conservatives on three major issues—immigration, trade and foreign policy—that in themselves constituted an entire worldview.

When Fleming was an editor at *Southern Partisan*, the immigration issue was addressed on a regular basis. But that was the early 1980s when anticommunism was the overriding concern on the Right. As editor of *Chronicles*, Fleming revisited the explosive issue in that publication's March 1989 number. There, Fleming proposed wide-scale immigration reform, but also supported increased migrations from Eastern Europe. For its stand on immigration, William F. Buckley, Jr. reportedly threatened to "excrete" *Chronicles* from the entire movement. While Norman Podhoretz, after the reading the same "Nation of Immigrants" number (which also included a laudatory piece on Podhoretz nemesis Gore Vidal), declared in a letter to Richard John Neuhaus: "I know the enemy when I see one and *Chronicles* is just that as far as I'm concerned." For their troubles, the Rockford Institute immediately lost a key Bradley Foundation grant (and any possible future grants) all for enunciating a position that *National Review* would essentially take for its own three years later. (In the summer of 1996, an essay in *Public Interest* nervously called for some restrictions on legal immigration, too.[7])

Similarly, the Gulf War, the North American Free Trade Agreement (NAFTA) with Mexico and the more ambitious General Agreement on Trade and Tariffs (GATT) allowed the Old Right to play a major opposition role to conflicts and policies supported not only by leaders in both political parties, but by the major newspapers and journals of opinions along the East Coast power corridor. On trade, paleos questioned the wisdom of an industrialized nation like the United States engaging in free trade with such third world countries as Mexico. While American workers may make up to $40 an hour building automobiles in Detroit, the same job can be done by Mexcians working for little over a dollar an hour. Such countries also lack America's stringent environmental laws not to mention the generous benefits secured over the years by the nation's trade unions. Libertarians and traditionalists alike opposed the creation of a World Trade Organization that, in time, would make repeated assaults on American sovereignity concerning trade practices and disputes among nations. However, as we shall see, libertarians remained strongly inclined to the idea of free trade.

Foreign policy also united libertarians and traditionalists. As powerful as America remains, its constant interference in the domestic affairs of other nations, especially in the form of trade sanctions, could come back to haunt it one day. Indeed, in 1998, European politicians considered an economic boycott of Texas on grounds that the Lone Star State used its death penalty too often. In general, paleos argue that a nation which is powerful and domineering abroad will treat its own citizens no less unkindly. "War sustains the Leviathan," maintains Lew Rockwell, "and so it is against the American people's interest." That claim is a broad one, but it sums up the opposition to post-Cold War adventures in Haiti, Somalia, and Bosnia.

The Old Right worldview is inward looking, even though it finds inspiration from other outposts of Western civilization throughout the world. Right-thinking Americans need to take control of their schools, town halls and other institutions—and, if necessary, to create new institutions, such as charter schools. They also need to rediscover their region's—and the nation's—history, culture, heritage, literature, its heroes, and mythologies. Or, in Fleming's words, "Our ancestors took on an entire continent, village by village, parish by parish, and that is exactly how we shall have to take it back." Paleoconservatism represents a ringing call for Americans to return to the nation's republican roots. As Sam Francis notes, understanding the difference between a republic and a democracy (at least a mass democracy) is crucial to the cause of liberty:

> A republic is...a form of government in which people govern themselves—not just periodic voting but by actually taking part in government at all levels all the time and also....by governing themselves in a private, non-political sense. A republic is not an easy form of government to maintain....It requires immense self-discipline....constant and continuous attention and involvement in public affairs, a high enough level of education that citizens can understand and take part in public affairs intelligently and—most of all—*independence*. Independence means being in a position to take responsibility for yourself and your family and your livelihood—supporting yourself, defending yourself, controlling yourself, governing yourself.[8]

IV

These essays hope to link writers from the "first Old Right" of the 1930s, 1940s, and 1950s to their successors in the final decades of the century. A diverse group to be sure, ranging from New York Jewish libertarians (Frank Chodorov, Murray Rothbard) to unreconstructed Southern traditionalists (Richard Weaver, M.E. Bradford, Thomas Fleming, Clyde Wilson, Samuel Francis) to Midwestern agrarians (Russell Kirk, Allan Carlson) all sharing the same devotion to the "Old Republic" of the eighteenth and early nineteenth centuries.

Iconoclastic and uncompromising, the essays represent the hell-for-leather approach that once characterized all conservative opposition to the liberal revolution. As Murray Rothbard's essay illustrates, it was the New Deal that created a conservative movement in the first place. For the original Old Right, the New Deal was not by any means the first blow against the American Republic. Some go back to the nation's founding, wondering if the anti-Federalists (whose leaders included Patrick Henry) may not have had a point when they opposed final ratification of the U.S. Constitution. The Articles of Confederation might have served decentralizing principles better than the Constitution of 1787.

That aside, the Civil War, most paleoconservatives agree, was the first real catastrophe sustained by the American Republic. Even such

New York paleolibertarians as Rothbard and Frank Meyer would join Bradford to bitterly criticize a war which not only resulted in 700,000 American dead, but also in a budding American empire abroad and the rise of a centralized state at home. During the 1860s, President Lincoln, among other things, shut down opposition newspapers, jailed political opponents, armed foreign mercenaries, and inaugurated the nation's first income tax to pay for the war effort. The Supreme Court struck down the income tax gambit as unconstitutional, but a breach had clearly been crossed.[9]

From the end of Reconstruction and into the twentieth century, a conservative coalition held sway in Congress, ushering in an era of minimal taxation and a significant degree of local government sovereignty. But the New Deal was such an ambitious, determined effort to—as one propagandist boasted—"remake America over" that a political and intellectual opposition was inevitable. "All socialism seemed to me monstrously coercive and abhorrent," Rothbard recalls. Added to that was a looming war that conservatives were certain would only increase the size and power of the centralized state. In short, America's entry into World War II would signify the final triumph of an increasingly endangered New Deal. An opposition party was born. Since FDR was a Democrat, the first paleocons gravitated toward the Republican Party. As Rothbard points out, many Republicans were militantly antistatist, but the party establishment was both globalist and completely beholden to Wall Street money. It also had the power to deny the 1952 presidential nomination to Ohio Senator Robert A. Taft, the premiere conservative politician of the immediate post-World War II era. The Right's long and unhappy marriage with the GOP had begun.

Essays by Frank Chodorov and James Burnham attack economic aspects of the New Deal and in general, "big government" and high taxation. Burnham's scathing critique of the "managerial revolution" brilliantly anticipated the rise of the dreaded bureaucracy—that ever-growing, lumbering apparatus whose power remains unchanged and undiminished with each passing Congress and administration.

Russell Kirk's "The Question of Tradition" introduces us to the cultural side of paleoconservativism. Not just a preference for a rural, agrarian life has been a defining element of Old Right traditionalism, but also a prejudice in favor of social classes and the distinctions of age and sex. Cultural conservatives opposed socialism, but many also expressed doubts about a free market ideology. What good does free markets and the idea of a totally "open society" do to the survival of traditional cultures?

An economic critique of the New Deal was important, but Kirk's eloquent emphasis on the "unbought grace of life" gave conservatism the strong metaphysical vision it needed to connect with traditionalist-minded Americans. Man's needs are more than material ones. Along with anticommunism, modern conservatism had its famous triad: small government, anticommunism, and the increasingly ambiguous (but through no fault of Kirk's) "traditional values."

Cultural issues have always excited paleoconservatives more than economics (famously dubbed by Kirk as the "dismal science"). In the 1980s and 1990s, the Old Right jumped headfirst into the cultural wars, a fact most clearly punctuated by Pat Buchanan's stemwinder at the 1992 Republican National Convention. Richard Weaver's magisterial "The Importance of Cultural Freedom," explains why culture is more important to a civilization's survival than mere material conditions:

> Culture in its formal definition is one of the fulfillments of the psychic needs of man. The human being is a focal point of consciousness who looks with wondering eyes upon the universe into which he is born a kind of stranger. No other being, as far as we can tell, feels the same amount of tension between himself and the surroundings in which he must pass his existence. His kind of awareness is accompanied by degrees of restlessness and pain, and it is absolutely necessary, as we must infer from the historical record, that he do something to humanize his vision and to cognize in special ways his relation to these surroundings. This he does by creating what is called culture.

A dramatic decentralization of nearly all government functions is the tenet that unites libertarians and traditionalists. If regional cultures were revived, then they would hardly need a cradle-to-grave social security state to guide its citizens through their lives. How would people live? As Allen Tate explained in the dark years following World War II: "It is my impression that [people] get fed and clothed incidentally to some other impulse, a creative power which we sometimes identify with religion and the arts." Thus culture drives economics, as it does politics. Healthy regional cultures might mean liberation from an over-bearing centralized state. Indeed, if it were up to the Rocky Mountain West, the nonurban South and Midwest, such a revolution may have already taken place.

V

The tone of the essays in "A Resurgent Old Right" is in most cases, much different from those in the preceding section. The mood and the style is often urgent, gloomy, sharp-elbowed, and apocalyptic. But the times have changed. In the 1980s and 1990s, the nation's cultural crisis was far more severe than whatever existed even during the Depression years. In this section, on issue after issue, both reigning conservative and liberal dogmas are laid to waste. The essayists all happily operate under the dictum that "sacred cows make the best meat."

While acknowledging that not all of the American experience has been conservative, M.E. Bradford, nonetheless, sharply lectures the Beltway Right on its fetish with "equality of opportunity." Declaring that such sentiments are a "misunderstanding of our heritage from the Declaration of Independence," an "undefined equality" also "threatens to swallow up our reverence for law, responsible character, moral principle, and inherited prescription." The doctrine of equality of opportunity, moreover, only clears the way for greater and more tyrannical state action (as Bradford and others have long contended, equality of opportunity *always* means equality of results). Instead, equality before the law is all conservatives should strive for.

As noted earlier, immigration was the issue that sent the open border Right on a search-and-destroy mission against paleoconservatives. Chilton Williamson, Jr. reiterates the familiar arguments against large-scale immigration on cultural and economic grounds. He also does so for environmental reasons—an issue long ignored by conservatives. The overall theme of the essay is a searing indictment of a utopian America, the millenial nation out to save the world, "a collective Christ figure redeeming the world by example and by purity of intention."

On the Left, opposition to immigration centers around economics: Large influxes of unskilled laborers takes jobs away from similiar low-skilled American workers. In many cases, such workers are inner-city blacks—the most loyal Democratic Party constituency. Conservatives make the same case, but they also add a cultural argument; namely what massive third world immigration has done to the nation's founding Western heritage. The triumph of multiculturalism illustrates how badly conservatives are losing the culture war. Yet, with the exception of *National Review*, the Beltway Right refuses to draw the connection between massive immigration, rapidly changing demographics, the rise of affirmative action, and the virtual disappearance of the "Western Civ" requirement on the nation's college campuses. Over the past decade, immigration has emerged as a key concern in the writings of all major paleoconservatives, especially Buchanan, Francis, Fleming, and Gottfried. In the context of the nation's lingering high poverty rates and the anti-Western cultural war, "Promises to Keep" can make its claim as one of this collection's most urgent and important contributions.

No issue divides paleoconservatives as much as trade. Chodorov and Rothbard, for instance, were both staunch free traders. Even though the paleolibertarian Von Mises Institute opposed both NAFTA and GATT on the grounds that those treaties created huge and unnecessary bureaucracies, Buchanan's trade policy, plus his quip that some conservatives spend too much time studying "dead Austrian economists" has lead to repeated criticisms of the commentator by libertarians who otherwise are sympathetic to Buchanan's America First platform.

Nevertheless, a mercantilist trade policy, such as the one outlined here by William Hawkins, has been championed by conservative intellectuals, mainly Anthony Harrigan, for several decades. Not only has it been a cornerstone of Buchanan's campaigns, but also Ross Perot's. Neither man, of course, has made it to the White House, but their candidacies took significant and decisive bites out of the old Nixon-Reagan coalition. The GOP's globalism has impressed Wall Street, but not its former blue-collar, working-class constituencies, especially in the urban Midwest, home to the swing-vote Reagan Democrats.

The sorry state of American education has bedeviled conservatives for decades. In the 1950s and 1960s, there was universal opposition to the specter of a "Federal Department of Education" dictating policy to the states. Indeed in 1980 presidential candidate Ronald Reagan promised, if elected, to abolish Jimmy Carter's Department of Education. That battle was (barely) fought and lost. After a half-hearted attempt to dismantle the DOE, the Reagan administration actually increased spending for a department conservatives claimed to loathe. And so the Beltway Right came to support vouchers, school choice, "magnet schools" and other reforms. Allan Carlson goes much further than the Beltway Right, giving a spirited defense of the home schooling revolution. If conservatives want to break the clock of a centralized regime, then withdrawing from its more culturally destructive functions is a good place to start.

VI

Since Ronald Reagan's election in 1980, conservatives have constantly declared victory. History is on their side, liberalism is finished, a glittering future dominated by the Republican Party lies ahead. In the 1980s, after-dinner testimonials repeated the grand story: Before Ronald Reagan, there was Barry Goldwater, before Goldwater, *National Re-*

view, before *NR*, William F. Buckley, Jr. and the dawning of a new era in American conservatism. After the 1994 election, the story was modified with Newt Gingrich taking his place among the pantheon of conservative heroes. As the decade and the century draw to a close, conservatives remain generally satisfied with the state of American civilization. A movement, as Pat Buchanan recalls, that always had room for pessimism, seems to be utterly lacking in a sense of tragedy, at least concerning the fate of their own country.

Paleoconservatives, on the other hand, cannot lie about victory. For them, the culture war is a grand battle royal waged between a mostly rural and small-town Middle America and their Washington-Manhattan-Hollywood tormentors. Essays by Paul Gottfried, Clyde Wilson, and Samuel Francis search for the roots of American populism and nationalism, the lessons to be learned from the past and how they may be applied in the future. They continue the decentralizing theme that runs through this volume—although Francis allows that the federal government can be used to advance "Middle American" interests. Paleos do not draw many distinctions between the Democratic and Republican parties. While the Beltway Right long ago cast its lot with the GOP, prominent paleos regularly vote for third party candidates and nearly all remain disappointed that Buchanan has not made his own third party stand.

But there are cultural phenomena that may be beyond the paleos—or for that matter, the mainstream Right's—control. Both Thomas Fleming and Paul Gottfried get to the heart of the problem. The dilemma of American decadence, an offspring of seventy years of welfare state policies, has emerged, under Fleming's editorship, as a leading theme on the pages of *Chronicles*. Here is another sentiment not shared by the Beltway Right. Most conservatives are happy to stay put with the Republican Party. Most, too, reject the idea that the masses may be terminally spoiled. Paleoconservatives are not so optimistic. Fleming notes that decent Middle American Christians may not want Madonna's latest literary offering at the local public library. However, these same Christians do not really care if their children are educated in the classics of Western civilization. Expressing sentiments similar to Carlson's, Fleming urges parents to skip the public route by "setting up their own libraries and filling them with the classics of Christendom."

While praising various populist movements which have sprung up in North America and Western Europe, Paul Gottfried expresses doubt that, at least in the United States, they may not be able to overcome "a century of managerial consolidation" and the "administrative-therapeutic regime that seeks to interfere with every aspect of [American] life." In addition, Gottfried has acknowledged the demographic obstacles placed before a rejuvenated populism. "With a mobile population, national communications network, and an international economy, it may be hard to recreate the kind of regional solidarity needed to curb federal administrators and federal judges," he has written elsewhere. Furthermore, while American populists talk of "cultural wars to be waged on behalf of Christian or biblical values," the majority of Americans, if public opinion polls are to be believed, "care more about material concerns than either national sovereignty or moral identity."[10]

If "gain-getting" remains more important to the public than cultural issues, then the paleoconservative rebirth of the 1990s may very well run out of steam by the early decades of the next century. It may simply represent a last stand of a dying civilization. Or its revival may lay the groundwork for real political triumphs. After all, in the spring of 1992, the populist-leaning candidacy of Ross Perot was poised to obliterate both parties while on its way to the White House. Four years later, Pat Buchanan, the leading paleo political figure, briefly had a real shot at winning the Republican Party's presidential nomination. Republicans elected to Congress in the 1990s are often sympathetic to Old Right concerns on trade, immigration and the entire globalist agenda. What remains undisputable is that an unapologetic paleoconservatism has represented an authentic opposition voice to the dominant cultural and political forces of our times.

Notes

1. See Russell Kirk, *The Roots of American Order* (Washington, D.C.: Regnery-Gateway, 1991). Also M.E. Bradford, "A Teaching for Republicans: Roman History and the Nation's First Identity," from *A Better Guide Than Reason: Federalists and Anti-Federalists* (New Brunswick, N.J.: Transaction Publishers, 1994), pp. 3–27.
2. Rather than trying to "conserve" what passes for contemporary culture, the Old Right is sympathetic to the advice given here by Sam Francis: "The first thing we have to learn about fighting and winning a cultural war is that we are not fighting to 'conserve' something; we are fighting to overthrow something. Obviously, we do want to conserve something—our culture, our way of life, the set of institutions and beliefs that distinguish us as Americans. But we must understand clearly…that the dominant authorities in the United States—in the federal government and often in state and local government…not only do nothing to conserve…our traditional way of life, but actually seek its destruction or are indifferent to its survival. If our culture is going to be conserved, then, we need

to dethrone the dominant authorities that threaten it." Samuel Francis, "Winning the Culture War," *Chronicles*, December 1993, pp. 12–15.

3. For kinds words about Borah and Fulbright, see Bill Kaufman, *America First! Its History, Culture, and Politics* (Amherst, N.Y.: Prometheus Books, 1995).
4. "Report From the Capitols," *Southern Partisan*, Fall 1981, pp. 4–5.
5. Jeffrey Hart, "Gang Warfare in Chicago," *National Review,* June 6, 1986, pp. 32–33.
6. William F. Buckley, Jr., "An Agenda for the Nineties," *National Review*, February 19, 1990, pp. 34–40.
7. Buckley's comment and the conservative wars in general are recounted in Thomas Fleming, "A Philanthropic Journalist," *Chronicles*, October, 1994, pp. 12–15. On immigration and shifting attitudes among the Beltway Right, see Peter Brimelow, "Time to Re-Think Immigration," *National Review*, June, 1992, pp. 30–46 and Norman Matloff, "How Immigration Harms Minorities," *The Public Interest*, Summer 1996, pp. 61–72.
8. "Partisan Conversation: Samuel Francis. *Southern Partisan*, Third Quarter, 1996, p. 35.
9. For the most penetrating Old Right criticism of the 16th president, see M.E. Bradford, "The Lincoln Legacy: The Long View," from *Remembering Who We Are: Observations of a Southern Conservative*, (Athens: University of Georgia Press, 1985): pp. 143–156.
10. Paul Gottfried, "Whither the Populist Wave?" *Chronicles*, July 1996, pp. 22–24.

Part I

Founding Fathers

1

Life in the Old Right

Murray N. Rothbard

One problem with labeling ideological movements "old" or "new" is that inevitably, with the passage of time, the "new" becomes an "old" and the markers get confusing. In the modern, post-World War II right wing, there have been a number of "news" and "olds" over the past half-century. But what I call the "Old Right" has an excellent claim to that label; for it was the original, oldest right, and it was in many ways radically different from all the rights that have followed after its demise.

The original right of which I speak, and of which I am one of the few survivors, stretched from 1933 to its approximate death, or fading away, upon the advent of *National Review* in 1955. The Old Right began in 1933 in response to the coming of the New Deal. It was "reactionary" in the best and most generous sense: it was a horrified reaction against the Roosevelt Revolution, against the Great Leap Forward toward collectivism that enraptured socialist intellectuals and enraged those who were devoted to the institutions and the strict limitations on centralized government power that marked the Old Republic.

Last fall, David Lauter, writing a think-piece in the *Los Angeles Times* about the Clinton health plan, wittingly or unwittingly echoed Maoist terminology about this Great Leap Forward, declaring that "every so often…the government collectively braces itself, takes a deep breath, and leaps into a largely unknown future." The Clinton health plan is such a leap, Lauter noted; the previous Great Leap was the civil rights laws of the 1960s; and before that, in perhaps the primordial leap, was the New Deal of the 1930s, when the nation agreed "to give the federal government a whole new set of responsibilities—from providing social security for the elderly to establishing a new system of national regulatory agencies to monitor the economy."

A fairly good summation, except that instead of the "nation" agreeing to give powers to the government the New Deal proceeded in the manner of all nonviolent revolutions: it was the federal government and its new rulers that seized power, drove through a flurry of socialisitic measures, and then won "agreement" by using the levers of propaganda and opinion-molding in society, as well as by relying on the sheer force of inertia and habit once the new institutions were in place.

The Old, original, Right realized the horrors of the New Deal and predicted the collectivist road on which it was setting the nation. The Old Right was a coalition of ideologies and forces that did not have one single, common, positive program, but "negatively" it was solidly united: all opposed the New Deal and were committed to its total repeal and abolition—lock, stock, and barrel. The fact that its unity was "negative" did not make it any less strong or cohesive: for there was total agreement on rolling back this collective excrescence and on restoring the Old Republic, the true America.

The Old Right coalition consisted of the following elements. Most "extreme" were the libertarian and individualist writers and intellectuals: H.L. Mencken, Albert Jay Nock, Rose Wilder Lane, Garet Garrett, all people who had resisted what they believed to be the mounting statism of the Republican regime of the 1920s and who called for an ultraminimal government that would have rolled back the statism of the Progressive period, the Civil War and Reconstruction eras, and perhaps the judicial despotism of Chief Justice John Marshall. Next came now virtually forgotten remnants of the conservative, states' rights Democrats of the nineteenth century, largely from the South, whose views were almost as libertarian as the first group's. These men were led by Governor Albert Ritchie of Maryland, who was a candidate for the Democratic presidential nomination in 1932, and Senator James A. Reed from Missouri. The third group consisted of conservative Republicans who were outraged at New Deal democracy and who largely came from the Midwest. Former Progressives and statists, who believed that the New Deal was going much too far, formed the final group; its leader was former President Herbert Hoover, who, though he had launched many New Deal measures in microcosm in his own administration, denounced the New Deal for going too far into "fascism." It was the first group that set the tone, since individualist and libertarian rhetoric provided the only general concepts with which New Deal measures could be opposed. The result, however, was that hack Republican politicians found themselves mouthing libertarian and antistatist slogans that they did not really believe—a condition that set the stage for later "moderation" and abandonment of their seemingly cherished principles.

Unity in our hostility and hatreds, however, combined with diversity of positive principle, had a healthy effect on the Old Right. It meant that we could unite and act together in denouncing and moving against the New Deal enemy, while disagreeing and arguing in friendly fashion among ourselves about the kind of America we would ultimately like to achieve. How much government did we wish to roll back? Stop at 1932, or press onward to repeal Progressive measures or even the centralization of the nineteenth century? We were all committed to states' rights, but how far did we want to carry this view? A few libertarian extremists wanted to go *all the way* back to the Articles of Confederation, but the great bulk of the right was committed to the United States Consitutition—but a Constitution construed so "strictly" as to outlaw much twentieth-century legislation, certainly on the federal level.

In those days, it was a pleasure to pore over the voting records of right-wing Republicans in Congress, especially in the harder-core House, for the common garden-variety rightists of the pre-1955 era make the most right-wing congressmen today seem impossibly leftist and socialistic. My two favorite congressmen were Howard Buffett of Nebraska and Frederick C. Smith of Ohio, both of whom would invariably draw "zero" ratings from the Americans for Democratic Action and other leftist groups. I remember being disappointed that once in a while they might deviate by favoring a federal anti-lynching bill; did they not know that the federal government is not supposed to have any police powers?

Friendly disagreement on positive principles meant genuine and healthy diversity and freedom of discussion within right-wing circles. As Thomas Fleming noted with astonishment when researching the Old Right, there was no party line, and there was no organ or central GHQ that excommunicated "unrespectable" members. There was a wide spectrum of positive views: ranging from pure libertarian decentralization to Hamilitonian reliance on strong government within rigid limits to various wings of monarchists. And in all this diversity and range of discourse, no one would react in shock and horror to any "extreme" views—so long as the "extremism" did not mean selling out the fight against the New Deal. There was also a great deal of disagreement on specific policies that had been open questions in the Old, pre-New Deal, Republic: tariffs vs. free trade; immigration restrictions vs. open borders; and what constitutes a military or foreign policy truly consistent with American national interests.

The Old Right experienced one big sea change. Originally, its focus was purely domestic, since that was the concentration of the early New Deal. But as the Roosevelt administration moved toward world war in the late 1930s, the Old Right added intense oppostion to the New Deal's war policies to its systemic opposition to the domestic New Deal revolution. For they realized that, as the libertarian Randolph Bourne had put it in opposing America's entry into World War I, "War is the health of the State" and that entry into large-scale war, especially for global and not national concerns, would plunge America into a permanent garrison state that would wreck American liberty and constitutional limits at home even as it extended the American imperium abroad. As anti-foreign interventionism was added to the anti-New Deal mix, the Old Right lost some adherents and gained even more. For Eastern Establishment anti-New Dealers, such as Lewis Douglas, William L. Clayton, Dean Acheson, and the Morgan Bank, embraced the entire New Deal package once it came wrapped in the enticing trappings of American Empire. On the other hand, antiwar progressives, originally New Dealers, men such as Senators William Borah and Gerald Nye, intellectuals and writers such as John T. Flynn and Harry Elmer Barnes, began to realize that there was something very wrong with a strong state that could expand into foreign adventures, and so they gradually became anti-New Dealers in every sense of the word.

World War II added foreign policy to the mix, so that by the end of the war, the Old Right was opposed to big government on every front, foreign and domestic. All parts of the right were opposed to global crusading, to what Clare Booth Luce wittily labeled "globaloney." They were opposed to what the former New Deal historian-turned-noninterventionist Charles A. Beard labeled the foreign policy of "perpetual war for perpetual peace."

There have been many memoirs about being Jewish and growing up in New York in the 1930s and 1940s. Although I am a few years younger than most of the memoirists—Irving Howe, Irving Kristol, Alfred Kazin, etc.—my experience was in many ways the same. It was great being a Walker in the City in that bygone era. New York street life was vital and fun. There was no harassment, no sense of crime lurking around every corner. Whites would go up to the Apollo Theater in Harlem to watch Pearl Bailey and other great entertainers with no sense of fear whatsoever. There were no bums or aggressive beggars on the street; if anyone wanted to see a bum, they could go to a short street downtown called the Bowery, where bums or "winos" hung out. And even they were not strictly "homeless," as they lived in very cheap Bowery hotels. The streets teemed with fascinating characters hawking their nostrums and ideologies. Soapboxes in Union Square or Columbus Circle featured any speaker who wanted to get up and address the crowd. I remember with affection one elderly guy working the streets in the Wall Street area, earnestly hawking the idea that lemonade or lemon juice was the panacea for all bodily ills. And at that time, New York was studded with inexpensive cafeterias, where one could sit nursing a cup of coffee for hours and either read or discuss ideas undisturbed. One guy came to be called "Senator Mendel," from spending most of his hours in the Senator Cafeteria on the Upper West Side. Nowadays, of course, such cafeterias would be filled with aggressive bums and muggers, and quiet or discourse would be impossible.

Looking back on it all, the discussions and arguments I got into, whether in street, neighborhood, family, or school, were marked by an instinctive civility and courtesy. Even though there were lots of communists around, there were no angry squads of enforcers of political correctness or threats to send you to brainwashing or sensitivity training sessions. And even though I was, with the exception of my father, virtually the only rightist I knew personally, I was uniformly treated not with hostility but rather with reactions ranging from astonishment to amused affection.

The one important aspect in which my growing up differed from these other Jewish memoirists, of course, is that they were some species of communist or socialist, whereas I was a right-winger and bitterly antisocialist from the very beginning. I grew up in a communist culture; the middle-class Jews in New York whom I lived among, whether family, friends, or neighbors, were either communists or fellow-travelers in the communist orbit. I had two sets of Communist Party uncles and aunts, on both sides of the family. But more important, the one great moral question in the lives of all these people was: Should I actually join the Communist Party and devote the whole of my life to the cause, or should I remain a fellow-traveler and "selfishly" devote only a fraction of my energy to communism? That was it; any species of liberalism, let alone conservatism, was nonexistent. And, contrary to the fond memories of Kristol, Howe, Kazin et al., I never heard of a Trotskyist in this period. Trotskyism was confined to a few intellectuals and future academics; for middle-class New York Jewry, the political world revolved around the C.P. (In later years, there was a reality-based joke on the left: "Whatever happened to the Old Left? The Trotskyites went into academia, and the Stalinists went into real estate.")

The one exception to this communist milieu was my father, David. My father emigrated to the United States from a Polish *shetl* in 1910, impoverished and knowing not a word of English. Like most immigrants of that era, he had resolved "to become an American" in every sense. And that meant, for him, not only learning English and making it his language, but also abandoning Yiddish papers and culture and purging himself of any foreign accent. It also meant devotion to the basic American Way: minimal government, belief in and respect for free enterprise and private property, and a determination to rise by one's own merits and not via government privilege or handout. Russian and Polish Jews before World War I were swept with communist, socialist, and Zionist ideologies and movements, or blends of the three. But my father never fell for any of them. An individualist rather than a socialist or tribalist, he believed his loyalty was to Amerca rather than to Zionism or to any Zionist entity in the Middle East.

I grew up in the same spirit. All socialism seemed to me monstrously coercive and abhorrent. In one family gathering featuring endless pledges of devotion to "Loyalist" Spain during the Civil War, I piped up, at the age of eleven or twelve, "What's wrong with Franco, anyway?" It didn't seem to me that Franco's sins, however statist, were any worse, to put it mildly, than those of the Republicans. My query was a conversation-stopper, all right, but I never received an answer.

When I shifted in early grades from the debasing and egalitarian public school system to a private school that I enjoyed a great deal, I found myself in another odd ideological climate. In those days, girls of the wealthier classes were protected, and so they were sent to a day school in New York, whereas upper-class boys were sent out of town to boarding school. The private day school I attended was coed, but it had difficulty attracting boys and was in danger of falling into all-girls status. As a result, they gave scholarships to bright, middle-class boys. The result was socially anomalous: the girls were all wealthy, driven to and from school in chauffered limousines, whereas at least half the boys were scholarship lads such as myself. Another fascinating note was that the students were mostly, though not solely, Jewish, whereas the staff and instructors were all WASPs. None of the Jewish students felt oppressed by this situation; indeed, none of us felt aggrieved when every Friday we attended chapel, nondenominational to be sure, but singing glorious Christian hymns. None of the Jewish students felt anything but happily assimilated into what America—which was, after all, a WASP and Christian country—was all about.

But while none of my fellow high school students was a communist, they were all left-liberals, what came to be called in New York "Park Avenue" or "limousine" liberals—all too literally in their case. I soon became established as the school conservative, arguing strongly in the eighth grade against Roosevelt's introduction of the capital-gains tax in 1938 and later against Mayor Fiorello LaGuardia's left-wing policy of coddling criminals.

My reputation as the high school rightist came in handy. In my junior year in high school, I was the supporter, in one of those meaningless school elections, of my friend Lloyd Marcus for school president or speaker or whatever the post was called. We thought we would be up-to-date politicos, so we happily had handbills printed up: "Lloyd Marcus: Charges and Facts." All the "issues" were trivial. There was nothing ideological about them; only personal friendships were at stake. But tough old Miss Birch, the school founder, scented "communism" and "strike" at the very sign of a handbill. (Lloyd Marcus was the son of the fabulously wealthy Bernard K. Marcus, who had gone to jail as part of the Bank of the United States scandal. Lloyd was indeed a "Park Avenue leftist," but the difference between the pro-Marcus and anti-Marcus camp was trivial and irrelevant to the election.) The ringleaders in the Marcus camp were called into Miss Birch's office one by one and quizzed sternly about "communism" and whether we were affiliated with the American Student Union, the communist student front at that time. I assured Miss Birch that no "strike" or Student Union thought was in any of our minds. In the event, all of the Marcus ringleaders (including the now-distinguished concert pianist and music historian Charles Rosen) were expelled, except myself. The idea that the school rightist was a commie was unthinkable.

When I entered Columbia during World War II for college and graduate school, the universe of people I met expanded, but the political ambience remained the same. Everyone was either a communist or a social democrat, or a variety of each. The only other Republican student at Columbia was an English major, and so we had little in common, as I was increasingly steeped in economics, both for its own sake and because it seemed to me that the knottiest political problems and the strongest arguments for socialism and statism were economic, dwelling on the alleged failures of free-market capitalism. The more I engaged in debates and discussion with fellow students and professors, who were all some variety of leftist, the more conservative I became.

I was so far out of it politically on campus that sometimes I served as a kind of father-confessor. One time, someone I knew only slightly came to see me and poured out a tale of woe. He was later to become a sociologist.) "Murray, you know I have been active in many liberal causes. Well, today, I was stunned, I don't know what to do. All my friends whom I thought were regular liberals came to me and invited me to join their cell of the Communist Party. I had no idea they were communists! What should I do? Should I join?"

What can you say to a mere acquaintance who spills out this kind of confession? I do not remember how I reacted, probably with some sort of cliche like "to thine own self be true" or "don't let anyone intimidate you." I never knew what he decided, but I am reasonably certain that he decided not to be sucked into the C.P.

During this peroid, I knew that there was a right-wing movement out there, but my knowledge was confined to such grand newspaper organs as the Hearst press, the marvelous *New York Sun*, and reports about Congress. For a while, after the war, I was perhaps the only New Yorker outside of libraries to suscribe to my favorite newspaper, the *Chicago Tribune*, which, in the grand old Colonel Robert McCormick era, was hard right throughout, not just in its editorial pages but in its reportorial staff as well. I had not yet, however, met any other rightist.

Finally, in 1946, I discovered the Old Right personally by finding the new Foundation for Economic Education (FEE) at Irvington-on-Hudson, New York, where I met the movement intellectuals and activists and was introduced to wonderful Old Right literature I had never heard of—libertarians Albert Jay Nock and H.L. Mencken, Frank Chodorov, John T. Flynn, and Garet Garrett—and all this very rapidly converted me from a free-market economist to a purist libertarian. This literature also converted me to hard-core isolationism in foreign policy. I had never really thought much about foreign policy, being steeped in economics, but now I realized that a non-interventionist foreign policy was part and parcel of a devotion to freedom and resistance to statism.

Libertarians in the post-World War II right naturally thought of themselves as "extreme right-wingers" amid the right-wing spectrum. There was no enmity between us and the less extreme or less pure; we were all happy to work together in the anti-New Deal cause: we were trying to get our less extreme allies to be more consistent; they were trying to get us to be more "pragmatic." Even in party politics, a purist libertarian like Congressman Howard Buffet (R-NE), whom I got to know personally, rose to become Senator Taft's Midwestern campaign manager at the ill-fated 1952 Republican Convention. I became a member of the Young Republican Club of New York in 1946 and wrote its policy paper blasting Harry Truman's price controls on meat, which he was forced to repeal during the 1946 campaign. I was astonished in later years to see "conservatives" hail Harry Truman as a model president: on the contrary, we opposed Truman hip and thigh, for his domestic statism as well as for his interventionist foreign policy. Indeed, one of my happiest political moments came when the Republicans swept both houses of Congress in the November 1946 election on the slogan, "controls, corruption, and communism." My first foray into print was a letter I sent to the Scripps Howard *New York World Telegram* celebrating the Republican victory, saying "Hallelujah!" and naively expecting the Republican Congress to promptly repeal the entire New Deal. Well they *said* they would, didn't they?

The first disillusion of many set in quickly. The National Association of Manufacturers, before that pledged to repeal the entire socialistic and pro-union Wagner Act, caved in, at their winter 1946 meeting, to the "responsible" corporate elements (read the "enlightened" Rockerfeller-type forces) and changed their tune to call for what finally did occur: not repealing but *extending* the powers of the federal government to apply criteria of "fairness" to unions as well as employers. In short: to extend government power over labor relations instead of removing it completely. And with the NAM acquiescence, the Republicans, led by Senator Taft (a brilliant man but someone who was, disastrously, *philosophically*—and not just tactically—devoted to compromise), went along with this new sell-out position and passed the amending Taft-Hartley Act instead of abolishing the entire Wagner Act. Politically, repeal might have succeeded, since the public was fed up with unions and strikes in 1946, and they had, after all, elected a right-wing Republican Congress. Also in this 80th Congress, the Republicans largely abandoned their "isolationist," noninterventionist principles, led by their foreign affairs committee head, renegade isolationist Senator Arthur Vandenberg (R-MI), who managed to establish the first, disastrous "bipartisan foreign policy," i.e., global interventionism, in the post-World War II era.

Old Right Republicans, the soul of the party, always managed to lose the presidential nomination, perpetually stolen from them by the Eastern Establishment-Big Banker-Rockerfeller wing of the party, who used their media clout, as well as hardball banker threats to call in the delegates' loans, to defeat majority sentiment in the party. In 1940, a Morgan bank blitz manged to steal the presidential nomination for the unknown utility magnate and leftist Republican Wendell Wilkie from Old Right isolationist Senator Taft and Tom Dewey, all his political life a Rockerfeller stooge, who in 1940 followed what was then the isolationist Rockerfeller line. In 1944, Dewey, now an internationalist following the Rockefellers' shift, won the Republican nomination. He was renominated in 1948, beating out the Old Right isolationist Senator John W. Bricker (R-OH) for the nomination, Bricker getting the consolation post of vice president.

As far as I was concerned, Dewey's nomination completed the congressional sellout, and even though I was unhappy that Truman ran a demagogic leftist campaign against the 80th Congress, I could not bring myself to support Dewey. Hence, once again naively, I embraced the new states' rights or "Dixiecrat" ticket of Strom Thurmond for president and Fielding Wright of Mississippi for vice president. I actually believed that the States' Rights Party would continue to become a major party and destroy what was then a one-party Democratic monopoly in the South. In that way, an Old Right, Midwestern Republican coalition with States' Rights Democrats could become the majority party!

At Columbia graduate school, I found a Students for Thurmond group. I showed up at the first meeting, which consisted of a group of Southern students and one New York Jew, myself. There were a brace of other New York Jews there, but they were all observers from the Henry Wallace Progressive Party, puzzled and anxious to find out to what extent fascism and the Ku Klux Klan had permeated the fair Columbia campus. They were especially bewildered when I got up at the meeting and made a fiery stump speech on behalf of states' rights and against centralized socialism. What was a nice Jewish boy doing in a place like this?

I have been asked many times whether the Old Right was rife with anti-Semitism. Left-wing undercover operators and smear artists such as "John Roy Carlson" had written a best-selling work, *Under Cover*, tarring all anti-New Dealers and America Firsters with the anti-Semitic and "neo-Nazi" brush, and the reputation of the Old Right has grown worse over the years, since, as usual, the interpretation of history has been solely in the hands of the internationalist winners.

The answer to this question, however, is a resounding No. In my decade on the Old Right, I never once encountered any anti-Semitic hostility. It is true there were unfortunately very few Jews on the Old

Right, but those that were there—notably the great libertarian Frank Chodorov—were widely admired and encountered no ethnic hostility. It is true that there was a general unhappiness with the fact that most Jews seemed to be leftists, as well as widespread opposition to the Zionist program of driving Palestenian Arabs out of their lands and homes, but these were attitudes that I myself fully shared.

The Old Right finally began to fade away over the issue of the Cold War. All Old Rightists were fervently anticommunist, knowing full well that the communists had played a leading role in the later years of the New Deal and in getting us into World War II. But we believed that the main threat was not the foreign policy of the Soviet Union, but socialism and collectivism here at home, a threat that would escalate if we engaged in still another Wilsonian-Rooseveltian global crusade, this time against the Soviet Union and its client states. Most Old Rightists, therefore, fervently opposed the Cold War, including the Truman Doctrine, the Marshall Plan, and the quasi-debacle of the Korean War. Indeed, while the entire left, with the exception of the Communist Party, got behind the Korean War as opposition to North Korean "aggression" under the cover of the United Nations, the Old Right, particularly its hard-core members in the House of Representatives, led by the *Chicago Tribune*, opposed all of these policies to the hilt. Howard Buffett, for example, was one of the major voices in Congress opposed to the Korean adventure.

By the mid-1950s, however, the Old Right began to fade away. Senator Taft was robbed of the Republican nomination in 1952 by a Rockefeller-Morgan Eastern banker cabal, using their control of respectable "Republican" media. In the early 1950s, Taft himself and the doughty Colonel McCormick passed away, and the veteran Old Right leaders faded from the scene. The last gasp of the Old Right in foreign policy was the defeat of the Bricker Amendment to the Constitution in 1954, an amendment that would have prevented international treaties from overriding American rights and powers. The amendment was sabotaged by the Eisenhower administration.

Finally, the Old Right was buried by the advent in late 1955 of the lively weekly *National Review*, a well-edited periodical that filled the ideological vacuum resulting from the deaths of McCormick and Taft and the retirement of other isolationist stalwarts. *National Review* set out successfully to transform the American right from an isolationist defender of the Old Republic to a global crusader against the Soviet Union and international communism. After *National Review* became established as the GHQ of the right, it proceeded to purge all right-wing factions that had previously lived and worked in harmony but now proved too isolationist or too unrespectable for the newly transformed Buckleyite right. These purges paved the way for later changes of line as well as future purges: of those who opposed anti-Stalinist, pro-welfare state liberals called "neoconservatives," as well as of those who persisted in opposing the crippling of property rights in the name of "civil" and other victimological "rights."

As time passed and Old Right heroes passed away and were forgotten, many of the right-wing rank-and-file, never long on historical memory, forgot and adapted their positions to the new dispensation. The last political manifestation of the Old Right was the third-party Andrews-Werdel ticket of 1956, which called for the repeal of the income tax and the rollback of the New Deal. Its foreign policy was the last breath of the pre-Cold War Old Right: advocating no foreign war, the Bricker Amendment, and the abolition of foreign aid. The betrayal of Senator Taft in 1952 had driven me out of the Republican Party, and after supporting the Andrews-Werdel ticket, I spent the following decades in the political wilderness, trying to join abortive third "Constitutional" parties and to separate libertarians out from a right wing that I no longer recognized and that seemed to me far closer to the hated New Deal, domestic and foreign, than to its Old Right enemy, which I had happily discovered and embraced in the years just after World War II.

2

Taxation is Robbery

Frank Chodorov

The *Encyclopedia Britannica* defines taxation as "that part of the revenues of a state which is obtained by the compulsory dues and charges upon its subjects." That is about as concise and accurate as a definition can be; it leaves no room for argument as to what taxation is. In that statement of fact the word "compulsory" looms large, simply because of its ethical content. The quick reaction is to question the "right" of the State to this use of power. What sanction, in morals, does the State adduce for the taking of property? Is its exercise of sovereignty sufficient unto itself?

On this question of morality there are two positions, and never the twain will meet. Those who hold that political institutions stem from "the nature of man," thus enjoying vicarious divinity, or those who pronounce the State the keystone of social integration, can find no quarrel with taxation per se; the State's taking of property is justified by its being or its beneficial office. On the other hand, those who hold to the primacy of the individual, whose very existence is his claim to inalienable rights, lean to the position that in the compulsory collection of dues and charges the State is merely exercising power, without regard to morals.

The present inquiry into taxation begins with the second of these positions. It is as biased as would be an inquiry starting with the similarly unprovable proposition that the State is either a natural or a socially necessary institution. Complete objectivity is precluded when an ethical postulate is the major premise of an argument and a discussion of the nature of taxation cannot exclude values.

If we assume that the individual has an indisputable right to life, we must concede that he has a similar right to the enjoyment of the products of his labor. This we call a property right. The absolute right to property follows from the original right to life because one without the other is meaningless; the means to life must be identified with life itself. If the State has a prior right to the products of one's labor, his right to existence is qualified. Aside from the fact that no such prior right can be established, except by declaring the State the author of all rights, our inclination (as shown in the effort to avoid paying taxes) is to reject this concept of priority. Our instinct is against it. We object to the taking of our property by organized society just as we do when a single unit of society commits the act. In the latter case we unhesitatingly call the act robbery, a *malum in se*. It is not the law which in the first instance defines robbery, it is an ethical principle, and this the law may violate but not supersede. If by the necessity of living we acquiesce to the force of law, if by long custom we lose sight of the immorality, has the principle been obliterated? Robbery is robbery, and no amount of words can make it anything else.

We look at the results of taxation, the symptoms, to see whether and how the principle of private property is violated. For further evidence, we examine its technique, and just as we suspect the intent of robbery in the possession of effective tools, so we find in the technique of taxation a telltale story. The burden of this intransigent critique of taxation, then, will be to prove the immorality of it by its consequences and its methods.

By way of preface, we might look to the origin of taxation, on the theory that beginnings shape ends, and there we find a mess of iniquity. A historical study of taxation leads inevitably to loot, tribute, ransom— the economic purposes of conquest. The barons who put up toll-gates along the Rhine were tax-gatherers. So were the gangs who "protected," for a forced fee, the caravans going to market. The Danes who regularly invited themselves into England, and remained as unwanted guests until paid off, called it Danegeld; for a long time that remained the basis of English property taxes. The conquering Romans introduced the idea that what they collected from subject people was merely just payment for maintaining "law and order." For a long time the Norman conquerors collected catch-as-catch-can tribute from the English, but when by natural processes an amalgam of the two peoples resulted in a nation, the collections were regularized in custom and law and were called taxes. It took centuries to obliterate the idea that these exactions served but to keep a privileged class in comfort and to finance their internecine wars; in fact, that purpose was never denied or obscured until constitutionalism diffused political power.

All that is long passed, unless we have the temerity to compare such ancient skullduggery with reparations, extraterritoriality, charges for maintaining armies of occupation, absconding with property, grabbing of natural resources, control of arteries of trade and other modern techniques of conquest. It may be argued that even if taxation had an unsavory beginning it could have straightened itself out and become a decent and useful citizen. So, we must apply ourselves to the theory and practices of taxation to prove that it is in fact the kind of thing above described.

First, as to method of collection, taxation falls into two categories, direct and indirect. Indirect taxes are so called because they reach the state by way of private collectors, while direct taxes arrive without bypass. The former levies are attached to goods and services before they reach the consumer, while the latter are in the main demands upon accumulations of wealth.

It will be seen that indirect taxation is a permission-to-live price. You cannot find in the marketplace a single satisfaction to which a number of these taxes are not attached, hidden in the price, and you are under compulsion either to pay them or go without; since going without amounts to depriving yourself of the meaning of life, or even of life itself, you pay. The inevitability of this charge on existence is expressed in the popular association of death and taxes. And it is this very characteristic that commends indirect taxation to the state, so that when you examine the prices of things you live by, you are astounded by the disproportion between the cost of production and the charge for permission to buy. Somebody has put the number of taxes carried by a loaf of bread at over one hundred; obviously, some are not ascertainable, for it would be impossible to allocate to each loaf its share of taxes on the broom used in the bakery, on the axle-grease used on the delivery wagon. Whiskey is perhaps the most notorious example of the way products have been transmuted from satisfactions into tax-gatherers. The manufacturing cost of a gallon of whiskey, for which the consumer pays around twenty dollars, is less than a half-dollar; the spread is partly accounted for in the cost of distribution, but most of the money which passes over the counter goes to maintain city, county, state, and national officials.

The hue and cry over the cost of living would make more sense if it were directed at taxation, the largest single item in the cost. It should be noted too that though the cost-of-living problem affects mainly the poor, yet it is on this segment of society that the incidence of indirect taxation falls most heavily. This is necessarily so; since those in the lower earning brackets constitute the major portion of society they must account for the greatest share of consumption, and therefore for the greatest share of taxation. The state recognizes this fact in levying on goods of widest use. A tax on sale, no matter how small comparatively, yields much more than a tax on diamonds, and is of greater significance socially and economically.

It is not the size of the yield, nor the certainty of collection, which gives indirect taxation preeminence in the State's scheme of appropriation. Its most commendable quality is that of being surreptitious. It is taking, so to speak, while the victim is not looking. Those who strain themselves to give taxation a moral character are under obligation to explain the State's preoccupation with hiding taxes in the price of goods. Is there a confession of guilt in that? In recent years, in its search for additional revenue, the State has been tinkering with a sales tax, an outright and unequivocal permission-to-live price; wiser solons have opposed this measure on the ground of political expediency. Why? If the State serves a good purpose the producers will hardly object to paying its keep.

Merely as a matter of method, not with deliberate intent, indirect taxation yields a profit of proportions to private collectors, and for this reason opposition to the levies could hardly be expected from that corner. When the tax is paid in advance of the sale it becomes an element of cost which must be added to all other costs in computing price. As the expected profit is a percentage of the total outlay, it will be seen that the tax itself becomes a source of gain. While the merchandise must pass through the hands of several processors and distributors, the profits pyramided on the tax can run up to as much as, if not more than, the amount collected by the State. The consumer pays the tax plus the compounded profits. Particularly notorious in this regard are customs duties. Follow an importation of raw silk, from importer to cleaner, to spinner, to weaver, to finisher, to manufacturer, to wholesaler, to retailer, each one adding his mark-up to the price paid his predecessor, and you will see that in the price milady pays for her gown there is much more than the tariff schedule demands. This fact alone helps to make merchants and manufacturers indifferent to the evils of protection.

Tacit support for indirect taxation arises from another by-product. Where a considerable outlay in taxes is a prerequisite for engaging in a business, large accumulations of capital have a distinct competitive advantage, and these capitalists could hardly be expected to advocate a lowering of the taxes. Any farmer can make whiskey, and many of them do; but the necessary investment in revenue stamps and various license fees makes the opening of a distillery and the organizing of distributive agencies a business only for large capital. Taxation has forced the individually owned and congenial grog-shop to give way to the palatial bar under mortgage to the brewery or distillery. Likewise, the manufacture of cigarettes is concentrated in the hands of a few giant corporations by the help of our tax system; nearly three-quarters of the retail price of a package of cigarettes represents an outlay in taxes. It would be strange indeed if these interests were to voice opposition to such indirect taxes (which they never do) and the uninformed, inarticulate and unorganized consumer is forced to pay the higher price resulting from limited competition.

Direct taxes differ from indirect taxes not only in the manner of collection but also in the more important fact that they cannot be passed on; those who pay them cannot demand reimbursement from others. In the main, the incidence of direct taxation falls on incomes and accumulations rather than on goods in the course of exchange. You are taxed on what you have, not on something you buy; on the proceeds of enterprise or the returns from services already rendered, not on anticipated revenue. Hence there is no way of shifting the burden. The payer has no recourse.

The clear-cut direct taxes are those levied on incomes, inheritances, gifts, land values. It will be seen that such appropriations lend themselves to soak-the-rich propaganda, and find support in the envy of the incompetent, the bitterness of poverty, the sense of injustice which our monopoly-economy engenders. Direct taxation has been advocated since colonial times (along with universal suffrage), as the necessary implementation of democracy, as the essential instrument of "leveling." The opposition of the rich to direct taxation added virulence to the reformers who plugged for it. In normal times the State is unable to overcome this well-knit, articulate and resourceful opposition. But, when war or the need for ameliorating mass poverty strains the purse of the State to the limit, and further indirect impositions are impossible or threaten social unrest, the opposition must give way. The State never relinquishes entirely the prerogatives it acquires during an "emergency," and so, after a series of wars and depressions direct taxation became a fixture of our fiscal policy, and those upon whom it falls must content themselves to whittling down the levies or trying to transfer them from shoulder to shoulder.

Even as it was predicted, during the debates on the income tax in the early part of the century, the soak-the-rich label turns out to be a wicked misnomer. It was impossible for the State to contain itself once this instrument of getting additional revenue was put into its hands. Income is income, whether it stems from dividends, bootlegging operations, gambling profits, or plain wages. As the expenses of the State mount, as they always do, legal inhibitions and considerations of justice or mercy are swept aside, and the State dips its hands into every pocket. So, in Philadelphia, the political power demands that the employer shall deduct an amount from the pay envelope and hand it over. The soak-the-rich principle has been applied on a large scale to the lowliest paid worker, not only by deductions from wages, but more so through the so-called social security taxes. These, by the way, show up the utter immorality of political power. Social security taxation is nothing but a tax on wages, in its entirety, and was deliberately and maliciously misnamed. Even the part which is "contributed" by the employer is ultimately paid by the worker in the price of the goods he consumes, for it is obvious that this part is merely a cost of operation and is passed on, with a mark-up. The revenue from social security taxes is not set aside for the payment of social "benefits," but is thrown into the general tax fund, subject to any appropriation, and when an old-age pittance is ultimately allowed it is paid out of the then current tax collections. It is in no way comparable to insurance, by which fiction it made its way into our fiscal policy, but it is a direct tax on wages.

There are more people in the low income brackets than in the high brackets; there are more small bequests than larger ones. Therefore, in the aggregate, those least able to meet the burden of soak-the-rich taxes bear the brunt of them. The attempt to offset this inequity by a system of graduations is unreal. Even a small tax on an income of one thousand dollars a year will cause the payer some hardship, while a fifty percent tax on fifty thousand dollars leaves something to live on comfortably. There is a vast difference between doing without a new automobile and making a patched-up pair of pants do more service. It should be remembered, too, that the worker's income is almost always confined to wages, which are a matter of record, while large incomes are mainly derived from business or gambling operations, and are not so easily ascertainable; whether from intent to avoid paying the full tax, or from the necessary legal ambiguities which make the exact amount a matter of conjecture or bookkeeping, those with large incomes are favored. It is the poor who are soaked most heavily by soak-the-rich taxes.

Taxes of all kinds discourage production. Man works to satisfy his desires, not to support the State. When the results of his labors are taken from him, whether by brigands or organized society, his inclination is to limit his production to the amount he can keep and enjoy. During the war, when the payroll deduction was introduced, workers got to figuring their "take home" pay, and to laying off when this net, after taxes, showed no increase comparable to the extra work it would cost; leisure is also a satisfaction. A prize fighter refuses another lucrative engagement because the additional revenue would bring his income for the year into a higher tax bracket. In like manner, every business man must take into consideration, when weighing the risk and the possibility of gain in a new enterprise, the certainty of a tax-offset in the event of success, and too often he is discouraged from going ahead. In all the data on national progress the items that can never be reported are: the volume of business choked off by income taxes, and the size of capital accumulations aborted by inheritance taxes.

While we are on the subject of discouragement of production by taxation, we should not overlook the greater weight of indirect taxes, even though it is not so obvious. The production level of a nation is determined by the purchasing power of its citizens, and to the extent that this power is sapped by levies, to that extent is the production level lowered. It is a silly sophism, and thoroughly indecent, to maintain that what the state collects it spends, and that therefore there is no lowering of total purchasing power. Thieves also spend their loot, with much more abandon than the rightful owners who would have spent it, and on the basis of spending one could make out a case for the social value of thievery. It is production, not spending, that begets production. It is only by the feeding of marketable contributions into the general fund of wealth that the wheels of industry are speeded up. Contrariwise, every deduction from this general fund of wealth slows down industry, and every levy on savings discourages the accumulation of capital. Why work when there is nothing in it? Why go into business to support politicians?

In principle, as the framers of the Constitution realized, the direct tax is most vicious, for it directly denies the sanctity of private property. By its very surreption the indirect tax is a back-handed recognition of the right of the individual to his earnings; the State sneaks up on the owner, so to speak, and takes what it needs on the grounds of necessity, but it does not have the temerity to question the right of the owner to his goods. The direct tax, however, boldly and unashamedly proclaims the prior right of the State to all property. Private ownership becomes a temporary and revocable stewardship. The Jeffersonian ideal of inalienable rights is thus liquidated, and substituted for it is the Marxist concept of state supremacy. It is by this fiscal policy, rather than by violent revolution, or by an appeal to reason, or by popular education, or by way of any ineluctable historic forces, that the substance of socialism is realized. Notice how the centralization hoped for by Alexander Hamilton has been achieved since the advent of the federal income tax, how the contemplated union of independent commonwealths is effectively dissolved. The commonwealths are reduced to parish status, the individual no longer is a citizen of his community but is a subject of the federal government.

A basic immorality becomes the center of a vortex of immoralities. When the State invades the right of the individual to the products of his labors it appropriates an authority which is contrary to the nature of things and therefore establishes an unethical pattern of behavior, for itself and those upon whom its authority is exerted. Thus, the income tax has made the State a partner in the proceeds of crime; the law cannot distinguish between incomes derived from production and incomes derived from robbery; it has no concern with the source. Likewise, the denial of ownership arouses a resentment which breaks out into perjury and dishonesty. Men who in their personal affairs would hardly think of such methods, or who would be socially ostracized for practicing them, are proud of, and are complimented for, evasion of the income tax laws; it is considered proper to engage the shrewdest minds for that purpose. More degrading even is the encouragement by bribes of mutual spying. No other single measure in the history of our country has caused a comparable disregard of principle in public affairs, or has had such a deteriorating effect on morals.

To make its way into the good will of its victims, taxation has surrounded itself with doctrines of justification. No law which lacks public approval or acquiescence is enforceable and to gain such support it must address itself to our sense of correctness. This is particularly necessary for statutes authorizing the taking of private property.

Until recent times taxation rested its case on the need of maintaining the necessary functions of government, generally called "social services." But, such is the nature of political power that the area of its activity is not self-contained; its expansion is in proportion to the lack of resistance it meets. Resistance to the exercise of this power reflects a spirit of self-reliance, which in turn is dependent upon a sense of economic security. When the general economy falls, the inclination of a people, bewildered by lack of understanding as to basic causes, is to turn to any medicine man who promises relief. The politician serves willingly in this capacity; his fee is power, implemented with funds. Obscured from public view are the enterprises of political power at the bottom of the economic malady, such as monopoly privileges, wars and taxation itself. Therefore the promise of relief is sufficient unto itself, and the bargain is made. Thus it has come about that the area of political power has gradually encroached upon more and more social activities, and with every expansion another justification for taxation was advanced. The current philosophy is tending toward the identification of politics with society, the eradication of the individual as the essential unit and the substitution of a metaphysical whole, and hence the elimination of the concept of private property. Taxation is now justified not by the need of revenue for the carrying on of specific social services, but as the necessary means for the unspecified social betterment.

Both postulates of taxation are in fact identical, in that they stem from acceptance of a prior right of the state to the products of labor; but for purposes of analysis it is best to treat them separately.

Taxation for social services hints at an equitable trade. It suggests a *quid pro quo*, a relationship of justice. But, the essential condition of trade, that it be carried on willingly, is absent from taxation; its very use of compulsion removes taxation from the field of commerce and puts it squarely into the field of politics. Taxes cannot be compared to dues paid to a voluntary organization for such services as one expects from membership, because the choice of withdrawal does not exist. In refusing to trade one may deny oneself a profit, but the only alternative to paying taxes is jail. The suggestion of equity in taxation is spurious. If we get anything for the taxes we pay it is not because we want it; it is forced on us.

In respect to social services a community may be compared to a large office building in which the occupants, carrying on widely differing businesses, make use of common conveniences, such as elevator transportation, cleaning, heating, and so on. The more tenants in the building, the more dependent are they all on these overall specialization, and at a pro rata fee the operators of the building supply them; the fee is included in the room-rent. Each of the tenants is enabled to carry on his business more efficiently because he is relieved of his share of the overall duties.

Just so are the citizens of as community better able to carry on their several occupations because the streets are maintained, the fire department is on guard, the police department provides protection to life and property. When a society is organizing, as in a frontier town, the need for these overall services is met by volunteer labor. The road is kept open by its users, there is a volunteer fire department, the respected elder performs the services of a judge. As the town grows these extra-curricular jobs become too onerous and too complicated for volunteers, whose private affairs must suffer by the increasing demands, and the necessity of hiring specialists arises. To meet the expense, it is claimed, compulsory taxation must be resorted to, and the question is, why must the residents be compelled to pay for being relieved of work which they formerly performed willingly? Why is coercion a correlative of taxation?

It is not true that the services would be impossible without taxation; that assertion is denied by the fact that the services appear before taxes are introduced. The services come because there is need for them. Because there is need for them they are paid for, in the beginning, with labor and, in a few instances, with voluntary contributions of goods and money; the trade is without compulsion and therefore equitable. Only when political power takes over the management of these services does the compulsory tax appear. It is not the cost of the services which calls for taxation, it is the cost of maintaining political power.

In the case of the overall services in the building the cost is met by a rent-payment, apportioned according to the size and location of the space occupied, and the amount is fixed by the only equitable arbiter of value, competition. In the growing community, likewise, the cost of social services could be equitably met by a charge against occupancy of sites within the community, and this charge would be automatically met because it is set by the higgling and haggling of the market. When we trace the value of these locations to their source we find that they spring from the presence and activity of population; the more people competing for the use of these locations the higher their value. It is also true that with the growth of population comes an increasing need for social services, and it would seem that the value arising from integration should in justice be applied to the need which also arises from it. In a polity free from political coercion such an arrangement would apply, and in some historical instances of weak political power we find that land rent was used in this social manner.

All history points to the economic purpose of political power. It is the effective instrument of exploitative practices. Generally speaking, the evolution of political exploitation follows a fixed pattern: hit-and-run robbery, regular tribute, slavery, rent-collections. In the final stage, and after long experience, rent-collections become the prime proceeds of exploitation and the political power necessary thereto is supported by levies on production. Centuries of accommodation have inured us to the business, custom and law have given it an aura of rectitude; the public appropriation of private property by way of taxation and the private appropriation of public property by way of rent collections become unquestioned institutions. They are our *mores*.

And so, as social integrations grow and the need for overall services grow apace, we turn to taxation by long habit. We know no other way. Why, then, do we object to paying taxes? Can it be that we are, in our hearts, conscious of an iniquity? There are the conveniences of streets, kept clean and lighted, of water supply, sanitation, and so on, all making our stay in the community convenient and comfortable, and the cost must be defrayed. The cost is defrayed, out of our wages. But then we find that for a given amount of effort we earn no more than we would in a community which does not have these advantages. Out at the margin, the rate per hour, for the same kind of work, is the same as in the metropolis. Capital earns no less, per dollar of investment, on Main Street than on Broadway. It is true that in the metropolis we have more opportunities to work, and we can work harder. In the village the tempo is slower; we work less and earn less. But, when we put against our greater earnings the rent-and-tax cost of the big city, do we have any more in satisfactions? We need not be economists to sense the incongruity.

If we work more in the city we produce more. If, on the other hand, we have no more, net, where does the increase go? Well, where the bank building now stands there was in olden times a pigsty, and what was once the site of a barn now supports the department store. The value of these sites has risen tremendously, in fact in proportion to the multiplicity of social services which the burgeoning population calls for. Hence the final resting place of our increased productivity is in the sites, and the owners of these are in fact the beneficiaries of the social services for the maintenance of which we are forced to give up our wages.

It is the landowner then who profits from the taxation. He does indeed own the social services paid for by production. He knows it, makes no bones about it, tells us so every time he puts his lot up for sale. In his advertisements he talks about the transit facilities it enjoys, the neighborhood school, the efficient fire and police protection afforded by the community; all these advantages he capitalizes in his price. It's all open and above board. What is not advertised is that the social services he offers for sale have been paid for by compulsory dues and charges collected from the producing of the public. These people receive for their pains the vacuous pleasure of writing to their country cousins about the wonders of the big city, especially the wonder of being able to work more intensely so that they might pay for the wonders.

We come now to the modern doctrine of taxation—that its justification is the social purpose to which the revenue is put. Although this has been blatantly advertised as a discovery of principle in recent years, the practice of taxation for the amelioration of social unrest is quite ancient; Rome in its decadence had plenty of it, and taxes to maintain the poor house were levied long before the college-trained social worker gave them panacea proportions. It is interesting to note that this doctrine grew into a philosophy of taxation during the 1930s, the decade of depression. It stamps itself, then, as the humanitarian's prescription for the malady of poverty-amidst-plenty, the charitarian's first-aid treatment of apparent injustice. Like all proposals which spring from the goodness of heart, taxation-for-social-purposes is an easy top-surface treatment of a deep-rooted illness, and as such it is bound to do more harm than good.

In the first place, this doctrine unequivocally rejects the right of the individual to his property. That is basic. Having fixed on this major premise, it jumps to the conclusion that "social need" is the purpose of all production that man labors, or should labor, for the good of the "mass." Taxation is the proper means for diffusing the output of effort. It does not concern itself with the control of production, or the means of acquiring property, but only with its distribution. Strictly speaking, therefore, the doctrine is not socialistic, and its proponents are usually quick to deny that charge. Their purpose, they assert, is reform not revolution; even like boys whose innocent bonfire puts the forest ablaze.

The doctrine does not distinguish between property acquired through privilege and property acquired through production. It cannot, must not, do that, for in so doing it would question the validity of taxation as a whole. If taxation were abolished, for instance, the cost of maintaining social services of a community would fall on rent—there is no third source—and the privilege of appropriating rent would disappear. If taxation were abolished, the sinecures of public office would vanish, and these constitute in the aggregate a privilege which bears most heavily on production. If taxation were abolished, the privilege of making profits on customs levies would go out. If taxation were abolished, public debt would be impossible, to the dismay of the bondholders. Taxation-for-social-purposes does not contemplate the abolition of existing privilege, but does contemplate the establishment of new bureaucratic privileges. Hence it dare not address itself to the basic problem.

Furthermore, the discouragement of production which must follow in the wake of this distributive scheme aggravates the condition which it hopes to correct. If Tom, Dick, and Harry are engaged in making goods and rendering services, the taking from one of them, even if the part taken is given to the others, must lower the economy of all there. Tom's opulence, as a producer, is due to the fact that he has served Dick and Harry in a way they found desirable. He may be more industrious, or gifted with superior capabilities, and for such reasons they favor him with their custom; although he has acquired an abundance he has not done so at their expense; he has because they have. In every equitable trade there are two profits, one for the buyer and one for the seller. Each gives up what he wants less for what he desires more; both have acquired an increase in value. But, when the political power deprives Tom of his possessions, he ceases, to the extent of the peculation, to patronize Dick and Harry. They are without a customer in the amount of the tax and are consequently disemployed. The dole handed them thus actually impoverishes them, just as it has impoverished Tom. The economy of a community is not improved by the distribution of what has already been produced but by an increase of the abundance of things men live by; we live on current, not production. Any measure, therefore, which discourages, restricts or interferes with production must lower the general economy, and taxation-for-social purposes is distinctly such a measure.

Putting aside the economics of it, the political implications of this eleemosynary fiscal policy comes to a revolution of first magnitude. Since taxation, even when it is clothed with social betterment, must be accompanied with compulsion, the limits of taxation must coincide with the limits of political power. If the end to be achieved is the "social good" the power to take can conceivably extend to total production, for who shall say where the "social good" terminates? At present the "social good" embraces free schooling up to and including postgraduate and professional courses; free hospitalization and medical services; unemployment insurance and old age pensions; farm subsidies and aid to "infant" industries; free employment services and low-rent housing; contributions to the merchant marine and projects for the advancement of the arts and sciences; and so on, approximately ad infinitum. The "social good" has spilled over from one private matter to another, and the definition of this indeterminate term becomes more and more elastic. The democratic right to be wrong, misinformed, misguided or even stupid is no restraint upon the imagination of those who undertake to interpret the phrase; and whither the interpretation goes there goes the power to enforce compliance.

The ultimate of taxation-for-social-purposes is absolutism, not only because the growing fiscal power carries an equal increase in political power, but because the investment of revenue in the individual by the State gives it a pecuniary interest in him. If the State supplies him with all his needs and keeps him in health and a degree of comfort, it must account him a valuable asset, a piece of capital. Any claim to individual rights is liquidated by society's cash investment. The State undertakes to protect society's investment, as to reimbursement and profit, by way of taxation. The motor power lodged in the individual must be put to the best use so that the yield will further social ends, as foreseen by the management. Thus, the fiscal scheme which begins with distribution is forced by the logic of events into control of production. And the concept of natural rights is inconsistent with the social obligation of the individual. He lives for the State which nurtured him. He belongs to the State by right of purchase.

Taxation's final claim to rectitude is an ability-to-pay formula, and this turns out to be a case of too much protesting. In the levies of goods, from which the state derives the bulk of its revenue, the formula is not applicable. Whether your income is a thousand dollars a year or a thousand dollars a day, the tax on a loaf of bread is the same; ability-to-pay plays no part. Because of the taxes on necessaries, the poor man may be deprived of some marginal satisfaction, say a pipe of tobacco, while the rich man, who pays the same taxes on necessaries, will hardly feel impelled to give up his cigar. In the more important indirect taxes, then, the magic formula of social justice is nonexistent.

It is applicable only in levying taxes on incomes before they are spent, and here again its claim to fairness is false. Every tax on wages, no matter how small, affects the worker's measure of living, while the tax on the rich man affects only his indulgences. The claim to equity implied in the formula is denied by this fact. Indeed, this claim would be valid only if the state confiscated all above a predetermined, equalitarian standard of living; but then, of course, the equity of confiscation would have to be established.

But no good can come of ability-to-pay because it is inherently an immorality. What is it but the highwayman's rule of taking where the taking is best? Neither the highwayman nor the tax-collector give any thought to the source of the victim's wealth, only to its quantity. The State is not above taking what it can from known or suspected thieves, murderers or prostitutes, and its vigilance in this regard is so well established that the breakers of other laws find it wise to observe the income tax law scrupulously. Nevertheless, ability-to-pay finds popular support—and that must be recognized as the reason for its promulgation—because of its implied quality of justice. It is an appeal to the envy of the incompetent as well as to the disaffection of the mass consigned by our system of privileges to involuntary poverty. It satisfies the passions of avarice and revenge. It is the ideal leveler. It is Robin Hood.

Supporting the formula is the argument that incomes are relative to the opportunities afforded by the State, and that the amount of the tax is merely payment for these opportunities. Again the *quid pro quo*. This is only partially true, and in a sense not intended by the advocates of this fiscal formula. Where income is derived from privilege—and every privilege rests on the power of the State—it is eminently fair that the state confiscate the proceeds, although it would be fairer if the state did not establish the privilege in the first place. The monopoly rent of natural resources, for instance, is income for which no service is rendered to society, and is collectible only because the state supports it; a hundred percent tax on rent would therefore be equitable. The profits on protective tariffs would be fair game for the tax-collector. A levy on all subsidized businesses, to the full amount of the subsidies, would make sense, although the granting of subsidies would still require explanation. Bounties, doles, the "black market" profits made possible by political restrictions, the profits on government contracts—all income which would disappear if the state withdrew its support—might properly be taxed. In that event, the State would be taking what it is responsible for.

But that is not the argument of ability-to-pay energumens. They insist that the State is a contributing factor in production, and that its services ought properly to be paid for; the measure of the value of these services is the income of its citizens, and a graduated tax on these incomes is only due compensation. If earnings reflect the services of the State, it follows that larger earnings result from more services, and the logical conclusion is that the State is a better servant of the rich than of the poor. That may be so, but it is doubtful that the tax experts wish to convey that information; what they want us to believe is that the State helps us to better our circumstances. For the tax he pays does the farmer enjoy more favorable growing weather? Or the merchant a more active market? Is the skill of the mechanic improved by anything the State does with what it takes from him? How can the State quicken the imagination of the creative genius, or add to the wisdom of the philosopher? When the State takes a cut from the gambler is the latter's luck bettered? Are the earnings of the prostitute increased because her trade is legalized and taxed? Just what part does the State play in production to warrant its rake-off? The State does not give; it merely takes.

All this argument, however, is a concession to the obfuscation with which custom, law and sophistry have covered up the true character of taxation. There cannot be a good tax nor a just one; every tax rests its case on compulsion.

3

The Managers Shift the Locus of Sovereignty

James Burnham

Any organized society patterns its life according to certain rules—customs, laws, decrees. These rules may not be written down, may not be explicitly formulated even in verbal terms, but they must exist or there would be no sense in calling the society organized. The origin of many of the rules, at any given moment, is lost in a remote past; but there must be within the society some mechanism for enforcing those taken over from the past, and, since the rules are always changing and being added to or dropped, for stating and enforcing new or changed rules. A social group which makes and enforces its own rules for itself, and does not recognize rules made for it by an agency outside the group, is called "autonomous" or "sovereign"—as the capitalist nations all claimed to be and the chief of them in fact were.

The "sovereignty" of the group, by virtue of which rules are made, cannot, however, simply float in the group air. It must *be localized,* concretized, in some human institution which is accepted as the institution from which rules (in complex society called "laws") come. In practice, this institution never includes all the members of the group: it might, for example, in a comparatively small and simple society, include all persons above a certain age meeting in "council," but it would exclude at least infants. In complex and large societies, the institution is always relatively small, sometimes a single person—a king, for instance, who publishes laws as personal royal decrees.

In large societies the situation is more complicated than might be suggested by the preceding paragraph. The particular institution (king or parliament or council of elders) where sovereignty is localized does not, in a broader sense, "possess" full sovereignty. Basic social power and privilege are possessed by the ruling class; the small institution is able to act as sovereign, promulgate laws, and have them enforced—not by virtue of the individual strength of its individual members (or member) but because, on the whole, it represents the interests of the ruling class and is, besides, able to gain acceptance or, at least, sufferance from a sufficient percentage of the population outside of the ruling class. Nevertheless, the question of the localization of sovereignty is by no means trivial in the history of societies. Some institution must be the public maker of the rules, the laws. Histories can be, and have been, written which center their attention on just this problem of where sovereignty is to be localized, and the many struggles which have as their political form the disputed claims to sovereignty of different institutions.

History shows that there are many kinds of institutions which can serve the social purpose of the localization of sovereignty. However, within any given type of society there are fairly strict limitations to the possible varieties. One of the most obvious and important of these limitations is *technical:* the sovereign body must be able to handle its work, at least not too badly. It is technical limitation which excludes infants—infants do not know enough to be lawmakers, even poor lawmakers—or which necessitates abandoning assemblies of all adults after a society gets beyond a certain size: there would be no place where they all could assemble, much less transact business if assembled. Moreover, a tribe that does nothing much else but hunt or fish has got to have a sovereign body that can handle at least those political problems that come up in connection with hunting or fishing.

But there are different sorts of limitation as well. For instance, the sovereign body must have a certain appropriateness of form in terms of the patterns of social thought, the ideologies. If it does not, it will be hard for it to get publicly accepted as sovereign. Furthermore, a new type of society will almost certainly have a different type of sovereign institution from that in which sovereignty was localized in the preceding society. This follows because the old institution becomes, over a long period, hardened in the ways of the old society, not sufficiently flexible to readapt itself to the new; and because mass hatred is directed against the old institution as representative of the old order. Though this is the case, the institution where sovereignty is shifted will usually have existed in the old society, though not as the sovereign institution. What will be new will be its possession of sovereignty, not its existence. This tends to be the case because social institutions in actuality change slowly, cannot be built up artificially overnight; and because the institution to which sovereignty shifts really represents in the old society those forces tending toward the new.

In an earlier chapter I have referred to the shift in the localization of sovereignty that occurred in connection with the transition from feudal to capitalist society. The result of this shift was to localize sovereignty more and more fully in "parliaments" (by whatever name they were, in different nations, called). History is not as tidy as a geometrical theorem; there is not a perfect equation between the development of capitalist society as a whole and the development of the sovereignty of parliament; but that there is a general correspondence, that in capitalist society sovereignty is *typically* localized in "parliament," could hardly be denied.[1]

There is, certainly, a historical and structural propriety in this fact. Parliaments (the commons or "third estate" only is in question here) existed in the late Middle Ages. They were simply the representative assemblies of the burgesses (the early capitalists) of the towns. They were called together, as infrequently as possible, by prince or king or great feudal lord, primarily when the prince wanted to get money from the burgesses, in return for which the burgesses would demand certain rights. Through this bargaining, the social power of the burgesses, and thus, on the political side, the sovereignty of their representative institutions, the parliaments, were built up. Historically there is no doubt about the status of parliaments as the typical political institution of the capitalists. In spite of changes and of the extension of the vote to sections of the population other than the capitalists, parliaments have retained the social marks of their origin. Constitutions, written and unwritten, and above all the control of basic power and privilege by the capitalists, have kept parliaments securely within the framework of capitalist society.

But in make-up and structure also, parliament has been a most appropriate institution for the localization of sovereignty under capitalism. Consider who are the members of parliaments. From the beginning probably a majority of them have been lawyers that is, persons trained in the economic and juridical relations of capitalist society. They have been the kind of person you meet in businessmen's clubs—not clubs of the first rank, perhaps, but whose members are all the sounder and surer capitalist loyalists for the very reason of their second-ratedness. In addition, there has been, especially in earlier days, a minority of powerful and brilliant political figures who identified the advance of their own political careers with the fate of capitalist society.

These persons, the members of parliaments, met, discussed, and concluded in circumstances very similar to those of many gatherings of capitalists in the economic field. When we read descriptions of the sixteenth-century meetings of parliaments, we cannot help being struck with the resemblance between them and the meetings of the bourses (exchanges) which were then starting in Antwerp and Lyons. The resemblance has continued. A law comes out of a parliament in a way not at all unlike that in which a price comes out of the bargaining on an exchange or other market.

Moreover, these men who were the members of parliaments, and the parliamentary methods of conduct, were fitted, well enough, for doing the law and policy-making business of the "limited" capitalist state. This business, though often of the highest importance, did not as a rule need advanced technical, engineering, or scientific training. Nor, except on rare occasions, was there much loss from the fact that the procedure was slow and cumbersome. In what the parliaments had to do, time out for party disputes, faction wrangling, speeches from dozens of persons, compromises and attempts at compromise, could usually be afforded. The economic process went on, in any case, at its own pace and under its own direction, largely outside the parliamentary province. States moved ponderously in their own element.

It is no news to anyone to point out that during the generation since the first world war, sovereignty has been slipping away from parliaments. No development of this period is more obvious and indisputable; yet, for some reason, it has received far less attention than its unquestionably major importance deserves. It is a remarkable comment on men's unwillingness to face the facts of their own time that, though in recent decades hundreds of books and articles have been written on the history of how parliaments won sovereignty, there is scarcely a handful of serious studies of how, today, parliaments are losing it or of the implications of this loss.

In four of the major nations of the modern world (Germany, Russia, Italy, France) sovereignty has already altogether departed from parliament; in two (Japan and England) parliament retains a small shred; and even in the last refuge, the United States, parliamentary (Congressional plus Supreme Court) sovereignty is more than half way into its grave.

In Germany, Russia, Italy, and France, it is true that a parliament, in form, is retained as part of the state apparatus. These parliaments occasionally meet and even pass a few motions unanimously, of course. But, even juridically, not to speak of *de facto,* these parliaments are no longer regarded as possessing the attribute of sovereignty. The rules (laws) for the societies do not issue from them. Their meetings are simply propaganda devices, like a parade or a radio and press campaign. Often the parliaments meet only to hear a speech or two: they provide a sounding board, in a ritualistic way symbolizing the nation. Sometimes they take a vote "approving" or accepting" the speech. But they never initiate any measure; their acceptance is always of something already done by another agency. However, even this nominal, *ex post facto* acceptance is rare. The parliaments take no part of any kind in almost all the actions of the regimes.

The example of Russia is particularly instructive, because revolutionary Russia made an attempt to continue parliamentary sovereignty: not a sovereignty localized in the Duma, the parliament of the old regime, but in the Congress of Soviets, which was thought to be the fitting representative of the new order. The Congress of Soviets, in 1917, was made up of representatives of local soviets which, in turn, were elected primarily by workers and peasants in the various local districts. In the Congress of Soviets which met at the beginning of November, 1917, the Bolshevik party had a majority. This Congress then declared itself to be "the government": that is to say it claimed *sovereignty* and declared that sovereignty was no longer possessed by the Kerensky government which was based upon the remnants of the old Duma. The Soviet Congress then proceeded to enact the chief initial measures of the new regime and to elect an executive—the Council of Commissars.

It would seem, then, that sovereignty was still localized in a parliament; and, for a short time, this was more or less the case. But this state of affairs did not last. Parliamentary sovereignty proved inappropriate for a nation that rapidly developed in the direction of *managerial society.* Within a few years, well before the death of Lenin and the subsequent exile of Trotsky, the Soviet Congress had lost, one by one, all the attributes of sovereignty. Its nominal rehabilitation in the "Stalinist" Constitution of 1937 changed nothing and left the Soviet Congress the mere minor propaganda instrument which it continues to be.

The development was indicated at least as early as the so-called "Kronstadt revolt," which took place in 1921. The opposition platform of the sailors and populace of the Kronstadt area had as its key plank, "new elections to the soviets." This demand was in reality an effort to return sovereignty to the soviets and the Soviet Congress and an implicit recognition that these institutions no longer possessed sovereignty. The demand was rejected by the true sovereign institutions of the Soviet state, and the dissidents answered by armed suppression. I am not here raising any question about who was "justified" in this famous dispute—a problem which has been so hotly and so often debated. I mention the incident to bring out only the point that it revealed the loss of sovereignty by the Soviet Congress, that is, the parliament.

In this shift of sovereignty away from parliament in Russia, which seems to have taken place without any very clear intentions on anyone's part, several important factors were involved. Experience shows that localization of sovereignty in parliament presupposes the existence of more than one legal political grouping (political party or some organized group comparable to a party). When there is more than one party, even if one of the parties is an overwhelming majority, parliament has always at least a minimum real function, since it provides a forum where the majority defends its policy against minority criticism. But where there is only one party, there is really nothing much left for parliament to do, and its political significance cannot be more than propagandistic. The politically significant body will be the controlling institution of the one political party, whatever that institution may be. The decisions of the party institution, when the one party monopolizes political life, complete the political job. The parliament can only reflect these decisions to whatever extent is thought propagandistically expedient. Even in this minor work, the parliament's sphere will dry up, since there is no use in merely having parliament duplicate tasks that are actually done elsewhere. From one point of view, and for certain types of activity, sovereignty shifts into the hands of the key party institutions.

But this is not the whole story. We are not asking here who or what in some ultimate sense "runs things" in a society (as a matter of fact, as we have seen, in the more general sense things are run by and for the ruling class). Often in a society where sovereignty is localized in a parliament, the decisions later adopted by parliament are actually made by some institution of a firm majority party. Nevertheless, the phenomenon which I have called the "localization of sovereignty" is understood within a society, even if not by that name. Whoever may run things ultimately, some given institution or group of institutions is commonly recognized and accepted as the public lawmaker, the proclaimer of the rules for society. A political party or parties must work *through* this institution or group of institutions, at the least. In capitalist society the typical institution of this sort is the parliament. We are asking what institution or group of institutions replaces parliament in this matter of the localization of sovereignty. We are not concerned here with where "real" power may be. History has shown the enormous *symptomatic* importance of shifts in the localization of sovereignty, and that is all that is necessary for our present purposes.

In the case of Russia, as of Germany and Italy, the rules, regulations, laws, decrees, have more and more issued from an interconnected group of administrative boards, commissions, bureaus—or whatever other name may be used for comparable agencies. Sovereignty becomes, *de facto* and then *de jure* also, localized in these boards and bureaus. They become the publicly recognized and accepted lawmaking bodies of the new society. When you want to know what the law is, you look up the records not of parliament but of a Four Year Plan Commission or Commissariat of Heavy Industry or Bureau for the Colonies. Similarly, the place of "committees of parliament" is filled by subcommissariats and subsidiary bureaus. Sovereignty has shifted from parliament to the administrative bureaus.

There are many who think that this development is the special result of the activities of communist and fascist politicians who by means of "subversive" activities have overthrown the old parliamentary order. As soon as we turn our eyes back to the United States we should begin to realize the incompleteness of such a view. Exactly the same process has been going on in the United States as everywhere else, though it is today at a different stage from that reached in Russia or Germany. This fact is enough to show that the process has deeper historical roots than the deliberate schemes of revolutionaries.

In the United States, sovereignty may still be chiefly located in Congress (together with the Supreme Court), it may still be the principal "lawmaking" body; but no one with eyes open during the past generation and especially the past decade will believe that its claims are today undisputed. "Laws" today in the United States, in fact most laws, are not being made any longer by Congress, but by the NLRB, SEC, ICC, AAA, TVA, FTC, FCC, the Office of Production Management (what a revealing title!), and the other leading "executive agencies." How well lawyers know this to be the case! To keep up with contemporary law, it is the rulings and records of these agencies that they have chiefly to study. How plainly it is reflected in the enormous growth of the "executive branch" of the government—which is no longer simply executive but legislative and judicial as well—in comparison with that of the other two branches. Indeed, most of the important laws passed by Congress in recent years have been laws to give up some more of its sovereign powers to one or another agency largely outside of its control.

The process is, naturally, not yet completed in the United States. Congress is not yet the same as Hitler's Reichstag or Stalin's Soviet Congress. But it has gone much further than Congress itself would be willing to realize. Congress still occasionally "revolts," still now and then "disciplines" an administrative agency or even abolishes it; but these acts are like the petty tyrannies of an already close-to-powerless old man. Very little control over the state is actually, today, possessed by Congress. The last year has shown that even the question of making war, most crucial of all the attributes of sovereignty, is, in spite of the Constitution, in reality beyond the power of Congress. Wars, also, are no longer conducted according to the parliamentary code.

In the new form of society, sovereignty is localized in administrative bureaus. They proclaim the rules, make the laws, issue the decrees. The shift from parliament to the bureaus occurs on a world scale. Viewed on a world scale, the battle is already over. The localization of sovereignty in parliament is ended save for a lingering remnant in England (where it may not last the next few months), in the United States, and certain of the lesser nations.

There is no mystery in this shift. It can be correlated easily enough with the change in the character of the state's activities. Parliament was the sovereign body of the limited state of capitalism. The bureaus are the sovereign bodies of the unlimited state of managerial society. A state which is building roads and steel mills and houses and electric plants and shipyards, which is the biggest of all bankers and farmers and movie producers, which in the end is the corporate manager of all the major instruments of economic production, can hardly be run like the state which collected a few taxes, handled a leisurely diplomacy, and prosecuted offenders against the law. Nor can the same kind of men run it. The new agencies and new kinds of agency are formed to handle the new activities and extensions of activity. As these activities overbalance the old, sovereignty swings, also, over to the new agencies. If a state is running steel plants, this is a more influential activity than punishing murderers; and the institution directing the steel plants has more social weight than that which makes laws about murderers.

In theory, even under these circumstances, the locus of sovereignty might remain in parliament. Parliament might continue to exercise representative sovereignty rights with respect to the great issues of general policy, providing a basic guide for all the agencies and bureaus. But this, which might well prove awkward in any case, is ruled out in practice for other reasons.

The shift in the locus of sovereignty is only a symbol of the shift in basic social relations, the shift from the rule of the capitalists to the rule of the managers. As has happened in the other comparable historical transitions, managerial society does away with the representative political institution of the old society, not merely because a new type of institution is technically better for the new society, but precisely because the old institution represents the old society; it becomes despised and hated, and the resentment of the masses is turned against it (look at France in the early summer of 1940); psychologically, ideologically, it is not suited for the new rule.

Equally important, the administrative bureaus have the same kind of general appropriateness for localizing *managerial* rule as the parliaments had for localizing capitalist rule. For that is the real significance of the shift in sovereignty toward the bureaus: it is simply one of the phases, in the field of political structure, of the transition from capitalist to managerial society.

The old-line parliamentarians do not do well in the bureaus. One or two of them may be present, as figureheads, for decorative purposes. But the actual directing and administrative work of the bureaus is carried on by new men, a new type of men. It is, specifically, the *managerial* type, the type we noticed also when considering the structural developments in "private enterprise." The active heads of the bureaus are the managers-in-government, the same, or nearly the same, in training, functions skills, habits of thought as the managers-in-industry. Indeed, there is less and less distinction between the two: in Russia, managers-in-industry and managers-in-government are one and the same, since there is no (important) industry apart from government. In all countries, as government expands, it incorporates the tasks and fields which were before left to private industry.

Moreover, even before the state has swallowed all of the economy, the way in which the new administrative agencies conduct their affairs is, by the nature of the case, close to the way in which the managers act elsewhere—certainly far closer than a parliament's way, which is at an opposite extreme from the managers' habits. In structure, mode of functioning and personnel, the administrative agency, board, or commission appears as the typical institution for the localization of sovereignty in managerial society, as parliament did in capitalist society.

It is clearly to the advantage of the managers that the localization of sovereignty should be shifted to the administrative bureaus. These institutions are of a sort with which the managers can most easily collaborate; in fact, these bureaus have, in their leading staffs, got to be peopled primarily by managers—it is a managerial function that the bureaus are performing. Thus the social rule of the managers as a class can be best assured when sovereignty is recognized as pertaining, *de facto* and to a considerable extent *de jure* as well, to the bureaus. The social position of the managers is buttressed in the bureaus both against the claims of the capitalists and also against the pressure of the masses, neither of which groups can function effectively through the bureaus.

Here, as before in the case of government ownership, the practical attitude of the capitalists is most revealing. Just as, in their overwhelming majority, the capitalists oppose every extension of government ownership, so do they oppose the setting up of new bureaus, boards and commissions or the extension of the powers of those already set up. They inspire a constant stream of propaganda against them, including a continual effort to belittle their accomplishments and to picture them as ridden with graft, red tape, and inefficiency compared with "private business"—which, when it is true (as it usually is not), is most often so because the bureau work has been interfered with by private capitalists. Following the customary pattern, when the agencies are nonetheless set up and functioning, the private capitalists then try to keep control of their activities in order to benefit primarily themselves. So long as the transition is in its early stages, so long as the dominant sectors of the economy still are those of private enterprise, this can be done. But when the balance swings, when the greater amount of economic life is subject to the bureaus' control, the base of leverage is lost, the capitalists' vantage point is undermined, and the managers through the bureaus swing into dominance. For just as the capitalists cannot continue as the ruling class, cannot continue even to exist, under a system of state ownership and control of the economy, so they cannot rule through a structure where sovereignty is localized primarily in the bureaus.

It would, I think, be difficult to exaggerate the significance of this shift in the localization of sovereignty. It is, perhaps, a secondary phenomenon in the entire social revolution through which we are going. But it is a secondary phenomenon of a symptomatic character. Just as, in the case of the outward and evident symptoms of so many diseases, the nature of the disease is most plainly grasped by observing the symptom, minor in itself, so does this historical symptom reveal plainly to us the nature of the social revolution we are studying.

Note

1. In the United States, under the interpretation of the Constitution which became accepted during the early years of the nineteenth century, sovereignty has been, by and large, shared by Congress and the Supreme Court. Some historians would, indeed, hold that the Supreme Court alone has been the sovereign institution. This United States deviation from "pure" parliamentary sovereignty does not, however, affect the main course of my analysis, particularly since the aim of this analysis is to clarify the present shift of sovereignty *away from* those institutions where it has been typically localized in capitalist society to a type of institution which was, on any account, not sovereign within capitalism.

4

The Question of Tradition

Russell Kirk

When I was a very small boy, I used to lie under an oak on the hillside above the mill-pond, in the town where I was born, and look beyond the great willows in the river-valley to a curious and handsome house that stood on the opposite slope, away back from the road, with three or four graceful pines pointing the way to it. This was an octagonal house, its roof crowned with a glass dome—a dignified building, for all its oddity.

Long since, the county planners have chopped down the old willows and converted the land about the old mill-pond into what the traffic engineers and professional town-planners think a "recreational area" should look like: a dull sheet of water with some dwarf evergreens to set it off. And the octagon-house was bought by a man with more money than he knew how to spend, who knocked the house down (that costing him a good deal more money than he had expected, for the place had been built like a fortress), and erected on its site a silly "ranch-type" dwelling vaguely imitated from Californian styles. I record with some satisfaction that later this man, an officer of the Teamsters' Union, was convicted of crimes and sent to prison—though his having committed an architectural atrocity was not incorporated in his indictment.

As Thoreau used to buy in his fancy all the farms round Walden Pond, so I had made myself, from time to time, in my mind's eye, proprietor of the octagon-house. It still is mine in memory—which is not a wholly satisfactory form of possession.

This brutal destruction of fine old houses and of the very landscape, in this age of the bulldozer, constitutes a belligerent repudiation of what we call tradition. It is a rejection of our civilized past—and a rejection out of which sharp characters may make a good deal of money. Of course this physical destruction is only one aspect of a general assault upon traditional beliefs, customs, and institutions—a campaign of annihilation that has been carried on, with increasing force, for two centuries.

Every genuine conservative retains some affection for things traditional. So I set down here some observations on America's traditions, and on their sources.

Formerly the word *tradition* signified oral communication, as distinguished from books or documents; in the twentieth century, however, *tradition* has been widely employed to mean, also, prescriptive wisdom expressed in literature—and, by extension, to include old ways, beliefs, and even material objects that constitute a part of the modern age's cultural patrimony. The Latin verb *tradere*, meaning to "hand down" or "hand over," is the root of our word. *Tradition* implies acceptance, preservation, and passing on. It gives permanence to customs and ideas; it confers upon change the element of continuity, keeping the alteration of society in a regular train. Everything which the living possess has roots in the spiritual and intellectual achievements of the past. Everything man has—his body, his mind, his social order—is in large part an inheritance from people long dead. The passage of times brings new acquisitions; but unless men know the past, they are unable to understand distinctions between what is permanent and what is transient in their lives. Man always is beset by questions, of which the largest is the question of his own existence. He cannot even begin to think about his existence, and lesser questions, until he has acquired the command of means that come to him from the past, such as the names that people customarily use with reference to modes of being and acting.

Man inherits a physical world, a biological world, and a cultural world. Tradition is concerned principally with his cultural world—which, nevertheless, is closely joined to his physical and biological worlds. Tradition is the means by which man comes to understand the principles of his own nature and of society; it joins the individual with the generations that are dead and the generations that are yet to be born. In short, tradition is a way of preserving the wisdom of our ancestors and a means by which we can give some significance and application to our own private reason.

In every age, philosophers have spoken of the power of tradition. Cicero, in his *Republic* and his *Offices*, shows how the Roman commonwealth was dependent upon custom and inherited belief for justice, order, and freedom. Fulbert of Chartres, in the eleventh century, observed that "We are dwarfs mounted upon the shoulders of giants," able to see so far only because of the stature of the wise men who have preceded us in time. The present moment, in the eyes of men attached to tradition, is merely a film upon the deep well of the past, an illusory line of demarcation between history and futurity. It is upon tradition that the future must be built. The long essential continuity of culture and human intelligence can be maintained only if the past is conserved through living tradition. The man who respects tradition, then, is not a reckless reformer who would alter society and human nature upon some utopian design, but a thinker who tries to reconcile the best in tradition with the constant necessity for change. Burke said that his model of a statesman was one who combined the disposition to preserve with the ability to reform. A healthy society, he suggested elsewhere, is never wholly old or wholly new, but, like any living thing, is forever casting off its old fabric and acquiring new tissue. Prescription, or tradition, is the means by which this healthy society preserves the wisdom of our ancestors and applies that wisdom to the new problems which it faces.

The process of growth always involves the process of reform—the process by which the acorn becomes the oak. This process is always at work in human affairs. The problem which thinking men always face is the difficulty of distinguishing between necessary and desirable alteration, and unnecessary and undesirable destruction. Tradition is a guide to the permanent qualities in society and thought and private life which need to be preserved, in one form or another, throughout the process of inevitable change.

True progress, improvement, is unthinkable without tradition, as Vazquez de Melia suggests, because progress rests upon addition, not subtraction. Change without reference to tradition runs the risk of aimless alteration for alteration's sake, terminating in anarchy or nihilism. Real progress consists in improvement of private and public morality, private and public intelligence, the increase of justice, order, and freedom, and of those material conditions which contribute to human happiness. It is scarcely possible to judge of what humanity wants, or of what measures are calculated to make men better or happier, without knowledge of what benefits have been gained in the past, and of what mistakes have been made. Tradition is the means by which humanity filters out its mistake from its progressive discoveries. Every great institution among civilized men seems to have tried to recapture or preserve the values of the past. This is especially true of the Christian

Church, sifting the pre-Christian inheritance of Western culture and "baptizing" whatever might be adapted to Christianity.

Tradition works in the sciences also. The essence of tradition is the preservation of continuity in the midst of change. The modern physical sciences rely continuously on certain abiding principles, despite the fact that modern science is always reviewing, and sometimes revising, those principles in the light of newly acquired knowledge or theory. A.N. Whitehead, in the first chapter of *Science and the Modern World*, makes some observations on this theme. It is often argued that the essential characteristic of the physical sciences is dependence on weighing, measuring, counting, and the like. Whitehead, however, sees that the essential characteristic is the idea of oneness, of unity, which is a view not far removed from that of the medieval Scholastics. The medieval age was a period of practice in the use of Aristotelian logic, examining its relation to the idea that the truth about the universe is necessarily one truth. The principle upon which Aristotelian logic depends, the principle that Aristotle named as the principle of greatest certainty—the law of contradiction—is the central principle in physical science. This principle, unlike the weighing, counting, and measuring that frequently are regarded as most important in the physical sciences, is basic to all knowledge. It illustrates the idea of identity in continuity, and is clearly joined to the idea of one God, one truth. Thus tradition—the preservation of continuity, the retaining of unifying principle despite the acquisition of new knowledge—operates in the sciences.

Yet there can be error in tradition, and even a tradition made up of errors. Man always is compelled to choose among conflicting traditions, and to sort out from the mass of inherited precept the maxims and customs which truly apply to his present situation in the world. This is a problem which cannot be solved by any hard-and-fast rule. There would be no problem of tradition if men were not in some important senses free. When men let their moral and intellectual freedom sink altogether into desuetude, and rely uncritically upon pure tradition, their society is liable to pass into decay, or at least find itself unable to resist the pressure of livelier societies: such appears to have been a condition in the civilization of ancient Egypt and of Peru. Routine without change, and change without routine, appear to be almost equally perilous.

Yet it does not follow that *all* traditions are evanescent. At the core of the body of traditions of any society is to be found a number of customs and precepts, described by some as natural law formulated into traditions, which that society ignores at its peril. And, far from being peculiar to a savage or barbarian condition of society, this seems to be especially true of complex civilizations, which are the more dependent upon certain underlying assumptions about man and society, the more complicated their activities become. Some of these traditions appear to be almost universal in essence, although they are formulated in various ways. The Decalogue expresses some of the more important of these, in the Judeo-Christian culture. The distinctions between good acts and evil acts; the duties within the family; the duties toward other men; the relationship between God and man: these concepts ordinarily are defined and maintained in any society by the force of ancient traditions, accepted almost without question from time out of mind. And when they are doubted or denied by the doctrinaire skeptic, any society is in peril of losing these moral sanctions which make the civil social order possible. Whether regarded as revealed truths or as necessary fictions (Polybius, in the Hellenistic world, took the latter view, as have various cultural relativists since his time), the traditions which govern private and social morality are set too close about the heart of a civilization to bear much tampering with. Skeptics like Hume, and rationalists like Voltaire, have acknowledged the necessity for conventions and traditions to make life in society tolerable.

The religious and ethical convictions which, however weakened in some quarters, still govern Western civilization in large part, are composed of Hebraic, Greek, Roman, and Christian elements; and are sanctioned and sheltered by a complex body of traditions. Shorn of tradition, our modern attitude toward the meaning of life would be meager and feeble. The Christian attitude toward the importance of tradition is suggested in the second epistle of Paul to Timothy, Chapters III and IV: "But continue thou in the things which thou has learned and hast been assured of, knowing of whom thou has learned them.... For the time will come when they will not endure sound doctrine; but after their own lusts shall they heap to themselves teachers, having itching ears. And they shall turn away their ears from the truth, and shall be turned unto fables." To the Christian, conformity to religious tradition is not superstition, but the part of wisdom; it is the doctrines of presumptuous private rationality and interest that are fables. Tradition, in short, to the religious man, is transcendent truth expressed in the filtered opinions of our ancestors.

What purported revelations are true, and what are false; whether revelation still is possible in human experience, or whether it has ceased to work among men; whether a new revelation could undo a major tradition, and by what tests such a revelation ought to be judged—these grave questions, and certain others, are not easily answered. But much of life always remains veiled in mystery, and the simple existence of a tradition, accepted for many generations by a people, logically creates a presumption that such a tradition has purpose and significance, unless proof to the contrary is very strong.

Traditions also have been defended upon empirical grounds. That a society seems to have thrived when it obeyed the dictates of tradition, and seems to have suffered when it sought to substitute some new moral or social scheme for prescriptive wisdom—this test has been applied again and again by philosophers and moralists. The decay of tradition is the theme of the Roman satirists and historians: they judge the importance of tradition by the consequences of the disregard of tradition. And this argument is advanced by the Hebrew prophets and the early Christian fathers. Unfortunately for a society which neglects tradition, this proof can be afforded only when the decay of traditional belief has brought society near to catastrophe, if not actually to positive ruin. A society may for a great while appear to be thriving, despite its rejection of tradition, when in reality that society is decaying, and moving toward dissolution; an outward prosperity may mask a cultural and moral decay, the end of which is as sudden as its progress toward disaster has been gradual. The respecter of tradition argues that to abandon tradition— that is, to abandon respect for prescriptive wisdom, what Chesterton calls "the democracy of the dead," the voice of the wise men who have lived in ages past—is to commit a society inevitably to such dissolution.

The lamentations of Jeremiah very frequently are justified by the event, however much a complacent generation may have mocked at the adherents to traditions allegedly outworn. Yet sometimes such lamentations are merely splenetic or misguided, and some traditions actually do wear out. Each generation is compelled to judge for itself just how far to obey the letter of tradition, and just how far to modify tradition by the admission of salutary change. This faculty of distinguishing between needful and imprudent alteration seems to be granted only to a few persons in each generation. In general, the attitude of the respecter of tradition is that of the farseeing Lord Falkland, in the English Civil Wars: "When it is not necessary to change, it is necessary not to change." The fact that humanity has lumbered along tolerably well in obedience to a tradition creates a legitimate presumption, in short, in favor of retaining that tradition; the burden of proof rests upon the innovator.

Most men and women are good only from habit, or out of deference to the opinions of their neighbors, the friend to tradition argues; and to deprive them of their habits, customs, and precepts, in order to benefit them in some novel way, may leave them morally and socially adrift, more harmed by their loss of ethical sanctions than helped by the fancied new benefit.

Tradition cannot suffice to guide a society, nevertheless, if it is not understood and expounded and, if need be, modified by the better intelligences and consciences in every generation. It is not possible for the living to see with the eyes of the dead. Whatever wisdom exists in any generation is, in a sense, born with that generation; and that generation's wisdom seeks sustenance in tradition, but cannot be kept alive merely by tradition. Wisdom has to be born over and over again; tradition is the element of continuity which enables each generation's wisdom to profit from the wisdom of preceding generations. The past exists only in the living; yet whether the living are aware of it or not, most of their experience and their apprehension of their own experience is determined by their legacy from the past. This is a condition peculiar to man. The vegetable, unaware of its inheritance, is unable to use its inheritance for its own improvement. Man cannot be like the vegetable, for he has reason, conscience, and consciousness, and he inherits an awareness of his ancestors. He is either better or worse than a vegetable, and whether he is better or worse depends upon his relationship to the sources of his being. It is tradition which makes it possible for him, short of mystical experience, to know his part in the "contract of eternal society" that joins him to those who are dead and those who are not yet born, and also to a nature that is more than material and more than human.

If tradition sinks into mere unquestioning routine, it digs its own grave; for man then approximates vegetal nature, disavowing reason and conscience as correctors and restorers of tradition. It was one of the more eloquent apologists for tradition, Chateaubriand (in his *Memoires d'outre-tombe*) who lamented "the mania for adhering to the past, a mania which I never cease impugning.... Political stagnation is impossible; it is absolutely necessary to keep pace with human intelligence. Let us respect the majesty of time; let us reverentially contemplate past centuries, rendered sacred by the memory and the footsteps of our fathers; but let us not try to go back to them, for they no longer possess a vestige of our real nature, and if we endeavored to seize hold of them, they would fade away." This is the traditionalist of elevation, appealing to his generation to hold by living tradition, but not to be governed by a letter from which the spirit has departed.

There exists no danger nowadays that Americans might sink into a social antiquarianism. The expectation of change has come to exceed the expectation of continuity nearly everywhere in the United States. For the annihilation of America's traditional architecture and town patterns moves on apace, though not so swiftly as it did during the administration of President Lyndon Johnson, when purported "urban renewal" became obliteration of nearly everything worth preserving or restoring in America's cities. And so it goes in nearly all lands. In T. S. Eliot's sentence, we are "destroying our ancient edifices to make ready the ground upon which the barbarian nomads of the future will encamp in their mechanized caravans." It is so in things of the mind and the spirit, as well as in bricks and mortar, and the consequences are immeasurable, but ruinous. It might be possible to establish a direct ratio between the decline of order in the twentieth century, and the widespread decline of belief in the truth of tradition.

A consciousness of our spiritual inheritance, Gabriel Marcel writes in *The Decline of Wisdom*, is possible only in an atmosphere of diffuse gratitude: and gratitude not merely to the generations that have preceded us in this life, but gratitude toward the eternal order, and the source of that order, which raises man above the brutes, and makes art man's nature. *Pietas*, in short, the veneration of man's sacred associations and of the wisdom of man's ancestors—this spirit survives only in holes and corners of modern society; and for lack of piety, modern men are bored, impatient, and ready enough to subvert the civil social state which is the source of their own material prosperity.

Now "the contract of eternal society," that phrase which describes the concept of social obligation presently decaying among us, is the idea which forms the kernel of Burke's *Reflections*. Society is indeed a contract, Burke says, but not a contract in any mere historical or commercial sense. It is a partnership between those who are living, those who are dead, and those who are yet to be born. It is a contract, too, between God and man, "linking the lower with the higher natures, connecting the visible and invisible worlds, according to a fixed compact sanctioned by the inviolable oath which holds all physical and all moral natures, each in their appointed place." We have no right to break this contract of eternal society; and if we do, we are cast out of this world of love and order into the antagonist world of hate and discord. Burke does not believe that wisdom began with the eighteenth century. He employs the words "contract" and "compact" in their most venerable meaning, the bond between God and man. "I do set my bow in the cloud, and it shall be for a token of a covenant between me and the earth." This is the thirteenth verse of the ninth chapter of the book of Genesis. This contract, this covenant, is the free promise of God, and its terms are obeyed by man in gratitude and in fear. Far from being a grandiloquent transcendence of real meaning, as some of Burke's critics have protested, Burke's employment of "contract" has the sanction of the Bible, the Schoolmen, and the whole body of ethical conviction which carries us back to Job and beyond Job.

Burke, then, spoke with the authority of a profound and practical intellect, not merely with the enthusiasm of an accomplished rhetorician, when he described the great primeval contract of eternal society; and I believe that our modern blindness to the reality of this contract, and to the sobriety of Burke's phrases, has mightily impeded any alleviation of our present discontents, our maladies of spirit and of the body politic. What Burke illuminates here is the necessity to any high and just civilization of a conscious belief in the value of continuity: continuity in religious and ethical conviction, continuity in literature and schooling, continuity in political and economic affairs, continuity in the physical fabric of life. I think we have neglected the principle of continuity to our present grave peril, so that with us, as Aristophanes said of his own generation, "Whirl is king, having overthrown Zeus." Men who do not look backward to their ancestors, Burke remarks elsewhere, will not look forward to their posterity.

If we retain any degree of concern for the future of our race, we need urgently to reexamine the idea of an eternal contract that joins the dead, the living, and those yet unborn. Even if we have lost most of that solicitude for posterity, still we may need to return to the principle of continuity out of simple anxiety for self-preservation. We live in a time when the fountains of the great deep are broken up; half the world has been drowned already, so far as the life of spirit and liberty and liberal learning is concerned; yet we are complacent, many of us, with Cyrus at the very gates. I think that these ideas of Burke's, rather than being vestiges of what Paine called "the Quixote age of chivalry nonsense," are even more pertinent in our time than they were to his own society.

Burke wrote before the modern proletariat had become a distinct force in society, although even then its dim lineaments could be discerned in England and France. Yet in passage after passage, with his prophetic gift, Burke touches upon the terrible question of how men ignorant of tradition, impatient of any restraint upon appetite, and stripped of true community, may be kept from indulgence in a leveling envy that would fetch down in ruin the highest achievements of mind and spirit, and kept from releasing that congenital violence in fallen human nature which could reduce to ashes the venerable edifice of the civil social state. Once most men should forget the principle of continuity, once they should break the eternal contract, they would be thrown on the meager resources of private judgment, having run recklessly through the bank and capital that is the wisdom of our ancestors. Under this newfangled system, "laws are to be supported only by their own terrors, and by the concern which each individual may find in them from his own private speculations, or can spare to them from his own private interests....Nothing is left which engages the affections on the part of the commonwealth. On the principles of this mechanic philosophy, our institutions can never be embodied, if I may use the expression, in persons; so as to create in us love, admiration, or attachment. But that sort of reason which banishes the affections is incapable of filling their place."

For, after all, abstract rationality cannot persuade us to observe the contract of eternal society. It is possible for Reason to persuade us to profit from the wisdom of our ancestors, true enough, even if pure Reason cannot teach us real veneration. But simple rationality, guided by self-interest, never can succeed in inducing us to look forward with solicitude to the interests of posterity. Men who are governed only by an abstract intellectuality will violate their obligations toward their ancestors by the destruction of tradition and the very monuments of the past, since we cannot learn veneration from mere logic; and such men will violate also their obligations toward posterity, for with them immediate appetite always must take precedence over the vague claims of future generations; and immediate appetites, if indulged without restraint, are insatiable in any society, however prosperous. Moreover, these men will snap that connection between the higher and the lower natures which is the sanction of the Eternal Contract, and thus will expose society to that conflagration of will and appetite which is checked, at length, only by force and a master. When men have repudiated the divine element in social institutions, then indeed power is everything.

Why, when all is said, do any of us look to the interest of the rising generation, and to the interest of the generations which shall exist in the remote future? Why do we not exhaust the heritage of the ages, spiritual and material, for our immediate pleasure, and let posterity go hang? So far as simple rationality is concerned, self-interest can advance no argument against the appetite of present possessors. Yet within some of us, a voice that is not the demand of self-interest or pure rationality says that we have no right to give ourselves enjoyment at the expense of our ancestors' memory and our descendants' prospects. We hold our present advantages only in trust. A profound sentiment informs us of this; yet this sentiment, however strong, is not ineradicable. In some ages and in some nations, the consciousness of a sacred continuity has been effaced almost totally. One may trace in the history of the Roman empire the decay of belief in the contract of eternal society, so that fewer and fewer men came to sustain greater and greater burdens; the unbought grace of life shrank until only scattered individuals partook of it—Seneca, Marcus Aurelius, here and there a governor or a scholar to knit together, by straining his every nerve, the torn fabric of community and spiritual continuity; until, at length, those men were too few, and the fresh dedication of Christian faith triumphed too late to redeem the structure of society and the larger part of culture from the ruin that accompanies the indulgence of present appetites in contempt of tradition and futurity.

Respect for the eternal contract is not a mere matter of instinct, then; it is implanted in our consciousness by the experience of the race and by a complex process of education. When the disciplines which impart this respect are imperiled by violence or by a passion for novelty, the spiritual bond which joins the generations and links our nature with the divine nature is correspondingly threatened. Christopher Dawson, in his little book *Understanding Europe*, expresses this well:

> Indeed the catastrophes of the last thirty years are not only a sign of the bankruptcy of secular humanism, they also go to show that a completely secularized civilization is inhuman in the absolute sense, hostile to human life and irreconcilable with human nature itself. For…the forces of violence and aggressiveness that threaten to destroy our world are the direct result of the starvation and frustration of man's spiritual nature. For a time Western civilization managed to live on the normal tradition of the past, maintained by a kind of sublimated humanitarian idealism. But this was essentially a transitional phenomenon, and as humanism and humanitarianism fade away, we see societies more and more animated by the blind will to power which drives them on to destroy one another and ultimately themselves. Civilization can only be creative and life-giving in the proportion that it is spiritualized. Otherwise the increase of power inevitably increases its power for evil and its destructiveness.

For the breaking of the contract of eternal society does not simply obliterate the wisdom of our ancestors: it commonly converts the future into a living death also, since progress, beneficent change, is the work of men with a sense of continuity, who look forward to posterity out of love for the legacy of their ancestors and the dictates of an authority more than human. The man who truly understands the past does not detest all change; on the contrary, he welcomes change, as the means of renewing society; but he knows how to keep change in a continuous train, so that we will not lose that sense of gratitude which Marcel describes. As Burke puts it, "We must all obey the great law of change. It is the most powerful law of nature, and the means perhaps of its conservation. All we can do, and that human wisdom can do, is to provide that the change shall proceed by insensible degrees. This has all the benefits which may be in change, without any of the inconveniences of mutation."

The outward fabric of our world must alter, as do our forms of society; but to demolish all that is old, out of a mere contempt for the past, is to impoverish that human faculty which yearns after continuity and things venerable. By such means of measurement as we possess—by such indices as suicide-rate, the incidence of madness and neurosis, the appetites and tastes of the masses, the obliteration of beauty, the increase of crime, the triumph of force over the law of nations—by these signs, it seems clear, all that complex of high aspiration and imaginative attainment which makes us civilized men is shrinking to a mere shadow of a shade. If indeed society is governed by an eternal contract, then we may appeal to the Author of that covenant; but words without thoughts to Heaven never go, and the continuity which pertains directly to society must be repaired by those means which still are within the grasp of man.

This brings us back to my hill above the mill-pond. The eternal contract, the sense of continuity among men, has been made known to succeeding generations, from the dawn of culture, by the agency of tradition. Tradition is the process of handing on beliefs, not so much through formal schooling, or through books, as through the life of the family and the observances of the church. Until the end of the eighteenth century, no one thought it conceivable that most men could obtain most of their knowledge in any other way than this; and though cheap books and eleemosynary schooling have supplanted to some extent the old functions of traditionary instruction, still tradition remains the principal source of our moral beliefs and our worldly wisdom. Young persons do not acquire in school, to any considerable extent, the sense of continuity and the veneration for the eternal contract which makes possible willing obedience to social order; children acquire this sense from their parents and other elders, and from their gradual introduction to religion, if they obtain any; the process is illative, rather than deliberate. Now let us suppose that parents cease to impart such instruction, or come to regard tradition as superstition; suppose that young people never become acquainted with the church—what happens to tradition? Why, its empire is destroyed, and the young join the crowd of the other-directed whom David Riesman describes.

In a looser sense, by "tradition" we mean all that body of knowledge which is bound up with prescription and prejudice and authority, the accepted beliefs of a people, as distinguished from "scientific" knowledge; and this, too, is greatly weakened in its influence among the rising generation by a growing contempt for any belief that is not founded upon demonstrable "fact." Almost nothing of importance really can be irrefutably demonstrated by finally ascertained "fact"; but the limitations of science are not apprehended by the throng of the quarter-educated who think themselves emancipated from their spiritual heritage. When we confront these people, we are dealing not merely with persons ignorant of tradition, but actively hostile toward it.

Now cheap books and free schooling are not the principal reasons for this decay of the influence of tradition. The really decisive factors are the industrialization and urbanization of modern life. Tradition thrives where men follow naturally in the ways of their fathers, and live in the same houses, and experience in their own lives that continuity of existence which assures them that the great things in human nature do not much alter from one generation to another. This is the mood of Ecclesiastes. But the tremendous physical and social changes that have come with the later stages of our industrial growth, and the concentration of population in raw new cities, shake men's confidence that things will be with them as they were with their fathers. The sanction of permanence seems to have been dissolved. Men doubt the validity of their own opinions, founded upon tradition, and hesitate to impart them to their children—indeed, they may thrust all this vast obligation upon the unfortunate school-teacher, and then grow annoyed when the teacher turns out to be incapable of bestowing moral certitude, scientific knowledge, and decent manners upon a class of fifty or sixty bewildered and distracted children. Most natural keepers of tradition, in short, abdicate their function when modern life makes them doubt their own virtue.

Though of course I did not understand all this at the time, it was this decay of the force of tradition which was sweeping away the old mill-pond almost before my eyes, as I lay on the hill under my oak. For my part, I still was a tradition-guided boy; but the planners who altered the landscape, presently, were Benthamites confident in the sufficiency of pure rationality, and the man who demolished the octagon-house was an other-directed individual who positively dreaded identification with anything dead and gone, and longed to be associated, however vaguely, with the milieu of Beverly Hills. The Utilitarians and the other-directed people were using up the moral and intellectual capital which had been accumulated by a traditionary society, I came to realize much later; and that process has been in the ascendant, with an increasing velocity, throughout the United States, for two generations now.

It cannot continue forever. Our guardians of tradition have been recruited principally, although not wholly, from our farms and small towns; the incertitude of the cities disturbs the equanimity of the tradition-guided man. And our great cities have been swelling at the expense of our country and village population, so that the immense majority of young people today have no direct acquaintance with the old rural verities. Our reservoir of tradition will be drained dry within a very few decades, if we do not deliberately open up once more the springs of tradition. The size of the United States, and the comparative gradualness of industrial development in many regions, until now saved us from a complete exhaustion of tradition, such as Sweden seems to have experienced. At the beginning of this century, Sweden had seven people in the country for one in the city; now that ratio is worse than inverted; and one may obtain some hint of what the death of tradition means to a people from the fact that the Swedes, previously celebrated for their placidity and old-fashioned heartiness, now endure remarkably high rates of abortion and suicide, dismayed at the thought of bringing life into this world or even of enduring one's own life.[1]

I do not wish our traditions to run out, because I do not believe that formal indoctrination, or pure rationality, or simple imitation of our contemporaries, can replace traditions. Traditions are the wisdom of the race; they are the only sure instruments of moral instruction; they have about them a solemnity and a mystery that Dr. Dryasdust the cultural anthropologist never can compensate for; and they teach us the solemn veneration of the eternal contract which cannot be imparted by pure reason. Even our political institutions are sustained principally by tradition, rather than by utilitarian expediency. A people who have exhausted their traditions are starved for imagination and devoid of any general assumptions to give coherence to their life.

Yet I do not say that tradition ought to be our only guide, nor that tradition is always beneficent. There have been ages and societies in which tradition, stifling the creative faculty among men, put an end to variety and change, and so oppressed mankind with the boredom of everlasting worship of the past. In a healthy nation, tradition must be balanced by some strong element of curiosity and individual dissent. Some people who today are conservatives because they protest against the tyranny of neoterism, in another age or nation would be radicals, because they could not endure the tyranny of tradition. It is a question of degree and balance. But I am writing of modern society, especially in the United States; and among us there is not the slightest danger that we shall be crushed beneath the dead weight of tradition; the danger is altogether on the other side. Our modern affliction is the flux of ceaseless change, the repudiation of all enduring values, the agonies of indecision and the social neuroses that come with a questioning of everything in heaven and earth. We are not in the plight of the old Egyptians or Peruvians; it is not prescription which enslaves us, but the lust for innovation. A young novelist, visiting George Santayana in his Roman convent in the last year of the philosopher's life, remarked that he could not endure to live in America, where everything was forever changing and shifting. Santayana replied, with urbane irony, that he supposed if it were not for kaleidoscopic change in America, life there would be unbearable. A people infatuated with novelty presently cannot bear to amble along; but the trouble with this is that the pace becomes vertiginous, and the laws of centrifugal force begin to operate.

I know there are people who maintain that nothing is seriously wrong with life in the United States, and that we need not fret about tradition one way or the other; but I confess, at the risk of being accused of arrogance, that I take these people for fools, whether they call themselves liberals or conservatives. They have a fondness for pointing to the comfortable routine of our suburbs as a demonstration of our mastery over the ancient tragedy of life. Now I am not one of those critics of society who look upon residence in suburbia a stain worse than the mark of the beast; but neither am I disposed to think that a commuter's ticket and a lawn-sprinkler are the proofs of national greatness and personal exaltation. And I am convinced that, if the reservoir of our traditions is drained dry, there will not be ten thousand tidy little suburbs in America, very long thereafter; for the suburbs are dependent upon an older order of social organization, as well as upon an intricate modern apparatus of industrial technology, for their being.

When tradition is dissipated, men do not respond to the old moral injunctions satisfactorily; and our circumstances and national character differing from Sweden's, I do not think we would experience the comparative good fortune to slip into an egalitarian boredom. The contract of eternal society forgotten, soon every lesser form of contract would lose its sanction. I say, then, that we need to shake out of their complacency the liberals who are smug in their conviction of the immortality of Liberal Democratic Folkways in the United States, and the conservatives who are smug in their conviction of the abiding superiority of the American Standard of Living. Political arrangements, and economic systems, rest upon the foundation of moral prejudices which find their expression in tradition.

Men who assail smugness cannot hope to be popular, in any climate of opinion; so the conservative ought not to expect to be thanked for reminding his age of the contract of eternal society. When he protests against the reduction of the mass of men to a condition below the dignity of true humanity, he will be attacked as an enemy of democracy, and ridiculed as a snob—when, in truth, he is endeavoring to save a democracy of elevation, and to put down the snobbery of a rootless new managerial elite. Wyndham Lewis, in *Rude Assignment*, refers to the abuse which many professors and publicists heap upon anyone who presumes to suggest that there is something wrong with modern minds and hearts: "To keep other people in mental leading-strings, to have *beneath* you a broad mass of humanity to which you (although no intellectual giant) can feel agreeably superior: this petty and disagreeable form of the will-to-power of the average 'smart' man counts for much in the degradation of the Many. And there is no action of this same 'smart' man that is more aggravating than the way in which he will turn upon the critic of the social scene (who has pointed out the degradation of the Many) and accuse him of 'despising the people.'" Nothing is more resented than the truth, and, as Lewis says, "people have deteriorated. They have neither the will nor common sense of the peasant or guildsman, and are more easily fooled. This can only be a source of concern and regret, to all except 'the leader of men.'"

Wherever human dignity is found, it is the product of a conviction that we are part of some great continuity and essence, which elevates us above the brutes; and wherever popular government is just and free, it is in consequence of a belief that there are standards superior to the interest of the hour and the will of a temporary majority. If these things are forgotten, then indeed the people will become despicable. The conservative, in endeavoring to restore a consciousness among men of the worth of tradition, is not acting in contempt of the masses; he is acting, instead, out of love for them, as human persons, and he is trying to preserve for them such a life as men should lead. The conservative does not believe that learning must be debased "because the people want it," or that a country's aspect must be made hideous "because the people want it," or that literature must vanish before the comic-book "because the people want it." He does not entertain so low an opinion of the people. The proletariat, shorn of tradition and roots, may crave such a degradation; but the conservative hopes to restore the lonely crowd who make up the faceless proletariat to character and individuality once more. And perhaps the first step in that restoration must be a renewed attention to the claims of tradition.

Is it possible to revive a sense of traditions among a crowd who have forgotten the whole concept of tradition? The thinking conservative believes so. The work must be slow and subtle; but I suggest here some of the aspects of the undertaking:

1. A reaffirmation of the truth that lies in tradition. The conservative will contend against the presumption of "intellectuals" who think that all wisdom comes from pure rationality and formal schooling. He will assure men, with Pascal, that the heart has reasons which the reason knows not, and that the immemorial customs and beliefs of a people ordinarily have meaning and value in them, whether or not we can explain them by pure reason.

2. A defense of the classes and regions in which tradition still is a living force. The conservative will do everything in his power to prevent the further diminution of our rural population; he will recommend decentralization of industry and deconcentration of population; he will seek to keep as many men and women as possible close to the natural and customary world in which tradition flourishes. This will not be an artificial reaction against a natural process of consolidation, for our intensive industrialization and urbanization, from the days of Hamilton to the Vietnamese War, have been deliberate policies, encouraged by state and national governments and by great corporate bodies. If we were to apply half as much energy and thought to the preservation of rural life and the old structure of community as we have put to consolidation, we might be as well balanced in these relationships as is Switzerland.

3. A humanization of urban life, bringing to the city man a sense of continuity. It is not impossible for urban people to have their traditions,

though tradition finds the country more congenial. In America, our towns have thrown all their influence behind a deliberate disruption of old ways and old things, commonly. In an Idaho town, recently, it was proposed that the trees in the public square be sawed down and a parking-lot established there. Someone protested; and a member of the city council, a shopkeeper, was astounded that there should be any objection: "Why, some of those trees are as much as thirty years old!" Whatever had roots and age, in this energumen's view, ought to be extirpated, as antiprogressive. Half the battle for the tradition of townsfolk would be won by a simple change of attitude. The preservation of old houses and neighborhoods, for instance, is a buttress of tradition in general; but most city-planners and traffic-engineers desire to sweep away every vestige of past generations. With the physical past, they abolish the sense of continuity, very commonly.

4. The returning to family and church and voluntary association of their old responsibilities as transmitters of tradition. The arrogant claim of many educationalists that they have a right to "train the whole child," and to form his character and opinions regardless of the prejudices of his family and his church and all the older agencies for education, must be denied by the conservative. Parents ought to be encouraged to instruct their children in moral traditions, in the disciplines of private conduct, and in the ways of the world; churches ought to be supported in their endeavors to make religious knowledge the most important part of any educational system. The formal agencies of the state cannot convey to young people, in any satisfactory degree, a sense of continuity and the eternal contract; and we ought to confess this, and restore to other and older agencies the duties which should never have been taken from them. A dismal compulsory salute to the flag, and mumbled collective pledge of allegiance to an abstract state, is a wretched substitute for the feeling of loyalty which grows out of love of family and love of local community.

In the defense of tradition, as with the several other problems I have touched upon in this book, the conservative must not be daunted by the probability that he will be misunderstood by most people, and assaulted by everyone whose material interest seems to be bound up with the continued degradation of the masses. The doctrinaire liberal will call him names, and the unreflecting present possessor of property and power will give him no support. And the conservative must face the fact that he may very well be beaten; unlike the Marxist, the conservative does not profess a fanatic belief in an ultimate inevitable triumph of his cause.

But the conservative, despite all this, will not surrender to the contagion of mass-opinion or the temptations of material aggrandizement and power. Convinced that he is a party to the contract of eternal society, he will abide by the sanctity of that contract, and do his appointed part under that compact. His back is to the wall, in our day, so that if he hopes to conserve anything at all, he must make his stand unflinchingly. He is not now defending mere ornaments and details of the civil social existence; he is not arguing simply about the Corn Laws, or the strict interpretation of the Constitution, or the mode of electing senators, or the regulation of wages and hours. All these were important questions in their time, but the modern conservative has Medusa to contend with, and lesser matters shrink to insignificance beside the dilemma of humanity in this century.

The grand question before us is really this: Is life worth living? Are men and women to live as human persons, formed in God's image, with the minds and hearts and individuality of spiritual beings, or are they to become creatures less than human, herded by the masters of the total state, debauched by the indulgence of every appetite, deprived of the consolations of religion and tradition and learning and the sense of continuity, drenched in propaganda, aimless amusements, and the flood of sensual triviality which is supplanting the private reason? Are they to be themselves, endowed with personality and variety and hope, or are they to be the vague faces in the Lonely Crowd, devoid of all the traditional motives to integrity? The radical and the liberal, I think, have failed dismally to show us any road to the redemption of mankind from modern boredom and modern decadence. The conservative is to become our guide, whether he likes it or not, and regardless of the will of the crowd. He may not succeed in covering the dry bones of this program with flesh and blood. If he is unequal to the task, the clock will strike, and Faustus will be damned.

Great civilizations do not fall at a single blow. Our civilization has sustained several terrible assaults already, and still it lives; but that does not mean that it can live forever, or even endure through another generation. Like a neglected old house, a society whose members have forgot the ends of society's being and of their own lives sinks by degrees almost imperceptible toward its ruin. The rain comes in at the broken pane; the dry-rot spreads like the corpse of a tree within the wall; the plaster drops upon the sodden floor; the joists groan with every wind; and the rat, creeping down the stair at midnight, gnaws his dirty way from the desolate kitchen to the mildewed satins of the parlor. We men of the twentieth century have this house only, and no other: the storm outside, in the winter of our discontent, will allow of no idle building of dream-castles; the summer indolence of the age of optimism is long gone by. The conservative, if he knows his own tradition, understands that his appointed part, in the present forlorn state of society, is to save man from fading into a ghost condemned to linger hopeless in a rotten tenement.

Note

1. A Scottish friend of mine invited young Swedish connections to his country house every summer; and what interested him most in their behavior was their pleasure at being emancipated from the boredom of the terrestrial paradise called the Third Way. The silent tyranny of democratic conformity, to which they had been always subjected at home, was lifted as soon as they arrived in Fife; at first they were surprised and suspicious, looking for someone to reprove them for their indulgence of individuality; but once they had grown accustomed to the freedom of a society in which some elements of variety, tradition, and even irrational emotion are not eradicated, they loathed the notion of going home to the superior comforts, the abundant food, and the everlasting monotony of social-democratic Sweden.

5

The Importance of Cultural Freedom

Richard M. Weaver

Culture in its formal definition is one of the fulfillments of the psychic needs of man. The human being is a focal point of consciousness who looks with wondering eyes upon the universe into which he is born a kind of stranger. No other being, as far as we can tell, feels the same amount of tension between himself and the surroundings in which he must pass his existence. His kind of awareness is accompanied by degrees of restlessness and pain, and it is absolutely necessary, as we must infer from the historical record, that he do something to humanize his vision and to cognize in special ways his relation to these surroundings. This he does by creating what is called a culture.

A culture nearly always appears contemporaneously with the expression of religious feeling. However, the two expressions must be distinguished as follows: religion is man's response to the totality and to the question of his destiny. Through religion he reveals his profoundest intuition regarding his origin, his mission on earth, and his future state. Culture is sometimes auxiliary to this expression, but characteristically it is man's response to the various manifestations of this world as they impinge upon his mundane life. He alters these to forms that reflect meaning; he fills interstices which appear unbearable when left void; he dresses with significance things which in their brute empirical reality are an affront to the spirit. In doing this he makes extensive use of symbolism, and because symbolism is supranatural, we can say that cultural expression is a vestibule between man's worldly activities and the concept of a supranature which lies at the core of most religions. Anyone who engages in cultural activity, however unconscious he may be of this truth, is testifying to a feeling that man is something more than a part of nature. And only when man has begun to create a culture does he feel that he has found a proper way of life.[1]

II

Little more needs to be said about the value of culture (a value which has on some occasions been challenged). But something does need to be said about the right of a culture to its self-constitution and self-direction. In surveying the history of cultures, we may be tempted to describe any given culture as a perfectly spontaneous and unregulated expression of the human spirit which can know no law except delight in what it creates. But when we study the phenomenology more critically, we become aware of a formal entelechy. A fact strikingly evident in the history of cultures is that any given culture is born, rises, and flourishes as an integer; that is to say, an entity striving to achieve and maintain homogeneity. It is this cohesive wholeness which enables us to identify it as different from other cultures, to give coherent descriptions of it, and to make predictions on the basis of these descriptions. Culture by its very nature tends to be centripetal, or to aspire toward some unity in its representational modes.

The reason for this is that every culture polarizes around some animating idea, figment, or value, toward which everything that it produces bears some discoverable relation. Everyone perceives that cultures are marked by characteristic styles; and the style will have its source in some idea, feeling, or projection that exists as a fountain feeding the various streams that flow down even into those areas where cultural expression is but slight. A culture lives under the aegis of an image, almost a tyrannizing image, which imposes something of its form upon all the numerous and varied manifestations of its activity. This but underlines the truth that a culture is a shared thing, which cannot exist without consensus. The members of a culture are in a manner of speaking communicants of that culture, and they look toward the center as to some source of authority for an imperative. Thus culture always appears as a creation integral and self-forming, which maintains a coherency amid things which may be neutral, foreign, or destructive.[2]

The above feature deserves stressing because today culture is being threatened by some who do not understand—and who would oppose if they did understand—this principle of cultural integrity. A chief danger to cultural freedom in our time comes from certain political fanaticisms which are trying to break down this cultural integrity by assuming or attempting to prove that it has no right to exist. Sometimes this proceeding is against cultures which have existed independently under one political sovereignty; sometimes it is against the traditional or naturally evolved culture within one nation because it is argued that the institutions of that culture are obstacles to "progressive" reform. In the first case the movement is against culture pluralism, out of a hostility to independent centers of influence; in the second it may be this also, but it may be more directly interested in subordinating culture to ends of the state which have been conceived out of speculation rather than out of consultation with history.

The fomenters of such movements are trying to make political schemata prevail, and they are prone to regard anything that stands in the way of these—even cultural creations of the highest power to gratify artistically—as "reactionary." Both would deny to culture its rightful measure of autonomy, the one trying to pour it into the mould of the supervening national state, the other attempting to bring it into line with political abstractions which may have no relation to the spirit out of which the culture was born. Both are opposed to culture as expressive of a region, but there is ample ground for asserting that all cultures are necessarily regional.

We are not equipped to oppose their attempts without a fuller understanding of the essential nature of culture. For this reason I return to the point that a culture has to retain a high degree of integrity in order to survive, and that in order to maintain that integrity it has to practice a principle of exclusiveness. A culture is born expressive of a place and a time, and a mood which say implicitly, "We hold these values." It is these particularities which give it character, and as a matter of nature character and integrity go together. A culture is like an organic creation in that its constitution cannot tolerate more than a certain amount of what is foreign or extraneous. Certain outside values may be assimilated through transformation or reworking, but fundamentally unless a culture can maintain its own right to its choices—its own inclusions and exclusions—it will cease. It may be simply suppressed, or the cessation may take the form of a decline into eclecticism, cosmopolitanism, Alexandrianism, or those politically fostered modes which have been an emergence of our time—all of which conditions are incapable of profound cultural creation.

For the freedom of cultures as wholes, two rights must be respected: the right of cultural pluralism where different cultures have developed, and the right of cultural autonomy in the development of a single cul-

ture. In a word, cultural freedom on this plane starts with the acknowl-
edgment of the right of a culture to be itself. This is a principle deduced
from the nature of culture, not from the nature of the state. Culture
grows from roots more enduring than those of the political state. It also
offers satisfactions more intimate than those of the political state; and
hence it is wrong to force it to defer to political abstractions; the very
fact that it has not chosen to embody those abstractions is evidence that
they are extraneous. Culture emerges out of climatic, geographical,
ecological, racial, religious, and linguistic soils; a state may have to
deal with all these factors, but it does not deal with them at the level
where they enter into cultural expression. That is the reason for saying
that the policy of a state toward the culture or the cultures within it
should be *laisser faire*, except at those points where collisions may be
so severe that they imperil the minimum preservation of order with
which the state is charged.

Abstraction in the form of the political dictate is the great foe of what
must develop physiognomically. Cultural freedom is in special danger
today because so much of our life has been politicized in recent decades.
We need not concern ourselves with the repression which was practiced
in National Socialist Germany and is being practiced in Soviet Russia
today. We know these forms for what they are; they are part and parcel of
such regimes, and the case against them is largely one with the case
against those regimes. It is otherwise with governments which are popular and free, but which allow political sanction to pressures building up
against types of cultural expression. Sometimes we do not find it easy, in
these cases, to distinguish between society and government; but we can
be clear as to the direction of the pressure. It moves to condemn on grounds
which are social and political, and its desire is for uniformity, standardization, consolidation, and all the other features of *Gleichschaltung*, as it
moves to protect from criticism and even from realistic depiction something over which people have become politically excited. In our American experience, these pressures have been social largely, but sometimes
they have been sufficient to manipulate local official bodies, such as
boards and legislatures, to effect their will. Moreover, the occurrences
have been occasional rather than systematic, but if they are allowed to
happen often enough, the occasions could harden into a precedent.

A current trend which throws into clear relief this danger is the practice of condemning books because they give an unflattering picture or
apply supposedly derogatory terms to minority groups. Ethnic groups
have been especially militant against this kind of expression, and even

that American classic *Huckleberry Finn* has been challenged and actually withdrawn from circulation in some places because the author applied to the Negro a form of the name widely used in his time. But the principle if accepted could be invoked by any minority which had had its feelings hurt or which merely happened to be politically or socially ambitious. Applied in extreme form it could require us to remove Boswell from the shelves because of Dr. Johnson's derogatory remarks about Scotsmen and Americans.

I hope there is no need to argue that it would be culturally fatal to regard in this way any individual or group as being above artistic intuition or critical evaluation. I call this an example of political fanaticism invading the realm of culture because the primary role of culture is neither to carry into effect the specific laws of the state or to give force to political ideologies which have won a temporary ascendancy. In these instances it is being asked to bow before a dogmatic equalitarianism. The truth to be recognized is that the cultural mission is to symbolize reality as this is reflected in men's attitudes, and there can be no *a priori* dictation to it to flatter or disparage. Creations that do one or the other must come out of honest perceptions and feelings, which are at some point in time expressive of a consensus. An artist may use as his subject matter attitudes of a past time, of a present time, or of a future time.

There exist, and I hope there will always continue to exist a large number of minorities of different kinds. Inevitably these will be the objects of varying attitudes, and the attitudes themselves will undergo changes. Whatever the level of expression, any such restraint of treatment would cut artistic effort off from the possibility of doing what it is supposed to do, and the situation would be far worse if the minority were allowed to prescribe the treatment. In short, it is wholly unpermissible to censor work of culture for presenting a subject as less attractive than one would like it to be. The right to represent freely is an inherent prerogative of culture; corrections will have to be left to change of attitude, to improvement of taste, to supplementation—or to better art.[3] The principle is simple: an artist cannot be bound to present only images of the innocuous. If he is a profound artist, he may be presenting images of what the majority will like a generation hence, for what the artist sees and what the generality of men see are at times two different things.

III

These forces of repression raise the question of whether there exists any significant relation between the various forms of government and the liberty of culture to flourish. Many would like to assume that there is a steady relation between the degree of democracy and the degree of cultural freedom, but this assumption is open to historical challenge. The most brilliant phase of Greek culture occurred under a democracy, but a democracy which, according to Thucydides, was a "rule by the first citizen." The Augustan age of Rome, in the first century of the Empire, was by no means culturally poor. No would one call England in the latter half of the sixteenth century a period in which culture was stifled by a strong Tudor government. The high point of French drama was reached under Louis XIV, not to speak of the flourishing of many other arts at that time. Descending to later periods, we find that Imperial Germany in the later part of the nineteenth century was enormously creative. Even Czarist Russia, despite its many repressions, was very productive of literature.

On the other hand, there have been governments of the monarchial kind which have been discouraging to cultural endeavor. George Savile, Lord Halifax, in that remarkable political testament called "The Character of a Trimmer," while declaring himself biased in favor of monarchy, confessed that "in all overgrown monarchies reason, learning, and inquiry are hang'd in effigy for mutineers."[4]

Two extremes emerge from this examination. There are some despotic governments so filled with a feeling of insecurity that they regard the free life of culture as a threat to their existence (according to an informant of mine, contemporary Spain is an example). Others out of simple barbarousness or selfishness may do the same. A highly centralized government which is fearful of the structure of its power may be unfavorable to cultural activity except in so far as culture can be manipulated in the government's vindication.

On the other extreme is the kind of popular government which is so distrustful of all forms of distinction that it sees even in the cultivated individual a menace to its existence. Such states are likely to maintain a pressure which discourages cultural endeavor, although the pressure may be exerted through social channels. But apostrophes to universal enlightenment and culture do little good if the state renders odious or impossible the forms in which these have to manifest themselves concretely. Everyone recognizes that there has been a strain of this in American life, although we have been spared the harshness of Jacobinism. Democracies tend to be jealous of exemptions from their authority. Yet there is certainly something to Machiavelli's statement that a popular form of government elicits more of the energies of the people. It is important to note that Jacobinism has always been hostile to culture.[5] When the scientist Lavoisier was brought to trial during the French Revolution, his contributions to knowledge, which were of the first order, were pleaded as a reason to spare his life. The plea is said to have been answered by the President of the Revolutionary Tribunal with the statement: *"La Republique na pas besoin de savants,"* and Lavoisier was sent to the guillotine. The extreme radical François Babeuf, in his "Manifesto of the Society of Equals," exclaimed, "Let all the arts perish if only we can have equality." The nihilist Pisarev declared that he would rather be a Russian shoemaker than a Russian Raphael. In Hitler's Germany, which was a pathological deviation of the right as this extremism was of the left, there was contempt for cultivation well epitomized for posterity in the saying, "When I hear the word 'culture,' I reach for my revolver."

The reason is simply that these are viruses, and that culture does not survive in the presence of a virus.

Modern communism is full of the spirit of Jacobinism; and its influence upon culture, wherever it has made headway, has been much the same. The story of Pasternak needs no retelling. Mikhail Sholokov is, I believe, under a kind of limited dispensation; he is allowed to portray the local and the traditional, but not to the point of impugning party doctrine. Communism is by its very nature intolerant of independent projections of reality. And there is the further consideration that no one can take culture seriously if he believes that it is only the uppermost of several layers of epiphenomena resting on a primary reality of economic activity.

IV

These are political interferences, but no discussion of cultural freedom would be complete without some notice of the right to moral censorship claimed by the political state. Whatever its form, virtually every state has at one time or another used its apparatus of coercion to forbid certain cultural expressions on the ground of their pernicious moral tendency. This is essentially an intrusion, to be distinguished from that cultural coercion which the spirit of a culture exercises in defense of its integrity. The ever latent temptation to invoke the right of moral censorship makes it desirable to study the question in principle.

The idea that a society can be absolutely open either politically or culturally seems to be untenable. But it can be more open culturally, and the reason for saying this is that cultural or artistic creation exists in the province of the imagination. That is not a completely isolated province, but since cultural works are not immediately translated into moral consequences, they should get the longest hearing before it is determined whether "nature imitating art" they are going to prove deleterious.

Usually, it seems to me, we approach the problem from the wrong end. Granted that an ultimate right of censorship is defensible, still a society which is culturally or physically in good health will not often need to invoke it. This does not mean that in the life of such a society cultural expression will never touch upon matters of obscenity or depravity. On the contrary, in such societies these subjects may receive quite frank treatment, as they did in the comedy of Aristophanes, the poetry of Chaucer, the plays of Shakespeare, some eighteenth-century novels, and many other forms. The point is that in such artistic expressions these matters are not the dominant foci of interest; they are there simply as filling out the normal range of human activity and interest. The culture is healthy enough to take them in its stride, to incorporate them, to hold them in their place, and to pass on to more important matters. They are not offered to excite pruriency; they are present rather because their absence would be an evidence of the infidelity of the artist to the complete artistic picture.[6] The Elizabethans and Jacobeans, for example, did not grow worried over "indecent" allusions; they saw no reason why one should not be frank about all the facts of life. They had a vision which was steady and whole, and they were interested in serious themes, which become less serious in proportion as things are suppressed because they might incite the perverse or the immature to harmful acts. Frankness is of course allied in meaning with freedom, which connotes maturity and poise.

The conclusion is that a society will not feel the need for much censorship unless it is somehow out of joint itself. The exploitation of cultural media for purposes which could be called morbid shows not that there are naughty people around but that the society itself has developed weaknesses. (I cannot deal here with the problem of how the state should protect minors from things they are not yet ready to cope with.) There may be occasions on which a society shows itself to be in such poor health that too many people are going to obvert things—are going to turn the products of culture toward ends that supply a different sort of gratification. Then some public restraint on the principle of *salus rei publicae suprema lex* may be necessary. Yet this is a stopgap procedure; the real reform must come from the other end, with the symmetrical development of the individual, so that he is his own sufficient guardian.

Our situation in the United States is complicated by a special historical inheritance. We are still suffering from the Puritan gnosis, which operates by rejecting totally certain parts of reality and then reacts hysterically when these parts come slipping back in the forms of artistic representation. Unless it could be established that Puritanism is the consensus of our culture, we can only say that in the various rebellions against Puritanical suppression we are witnessing not a tendency toward evil, but a normal effort of the cultural spirit to express itself without crippling hindrance. The remedy for this situation is educating more people to see life and art in their true relations.

V

The question of the freedom of the creator in relation to his own cultural tradition is of special interest to our time. No other period has seen so many instances of artists in apparently violent revolt, of creative workers of all kinds departing radically from the tradition or seeming to attack its deepest presuppositions. In modern poetry, in painting, in music, in sculpture, and in other forms, the story has been much the same. The new artists are new in a sense which could imply total dissociation from the past. If modern culture has produced some works which are aesthetically gratifying (and I for one would contend that it has) how can this wholesale revolt be explained meaningfully within a pattern of consensus and freedom?

Here one has to proceed with additional circumspection, because it is not given to us to lay down laws to poets, regarding either their subject matter or their forms. Still, we can insist that they be judged against a requirement that cultural creation must satisfy certain psychic needs which we have earlier connected with the birth of culture.

Within the fairly recent past the matter of artistic goals has become complicated by circumstances which artists in other ages have not had to face, at least in anything like such severe form. In most of the recognizable periods of art in the world's history, we can see clearly enough how the artist was held to performance in a tradition by an overriding *mythos*—a story about man or creation which provided the basic themes for his creations. The classical world had its mythology; the Islamic world had its religion, and our culture until recent times had the Christian story of man's life on earth and the Christian eschatology. This was a constructive symbol which gave the artist a starting point and a resolution of his values, even when the latter was only implicit.

But in the last century or two there has occurred a fragmentation of belief which has largely swept away this resource. In consequence, the artist of modernity has been faced with a true dilemma. He could choose on the one hand to symbolize the traditional values in the traditional forms for a public which no longer had a live belief in those values and thus suffer the fate of being regarded as merely quaint; or he could attempt to revitalize the tradition, beginning with audiences sophisticated and serious, who are aware of what has happened to man and to art. The most likely way to kill a tradition is to overformalize it, which is to carry it on in the same way after everyone has ceased to defer to it. The way to revive it is to show that it has grown out of and is still related to our most cherished values. But this requires radical insight and the stripping away of many things which are mere accretions.

It is a mistake to suppose, as some apparently do suppose, that all modern artists who have employed highly novel forms have been in revolt for revolt's sake. The truth is that they have been in revolt against some of the products of our civilization. The past century has seen such an increase in popular education, with accompanying accent on the peripheral, such availability of printing, so much cheap reproduction and growth of the means of communication that there has been introduced into our culture a factor of vulgarity which touches many things and which works powerfully against the discipline of respect. The dominant trend of journalism and popular art has been in the direction of the non-serious. However, true culture and art cannot flourish unless people believe that life presents some issues which are momentous. The tide of the trivial has been overwhelming, and it has seemed impossible to artists to oppose the sweep through its own channels; that is, by fighting back through the very media that have engulfed them. It has seemed equally impossible to oppose it by chanting the old values in the old ways, for this would truly be incantation. No one today can write a successful Shakespearean tragedy because our age in general does not possess a sense of the tragic ambivalence of man. No one today could produce a *Paradise Lost* because the paradigm on which this epic depends does not exist in the minds of the people. This is the kernel of truth in Walt Whitman's remark that "To have great poets there must be great audiences too." The only remaining strategy is to recover for man that sense which tells him that he needs this kind of play and this kind of poem. In his effort toward revivification of this sense, the modern artist has not infrequently retired into himself; he has accepted isolation or even alienation. We hear much complaint about the self-alienation of the artist from society, yet we must ask ourselves whether this is not sometimes defensible or even necessary. Sometimes the good has to underground, as it were. C. S. Lewis points out that in the time of Domitian, humanity itself had to become an underground movement.

At any rate, the "revolutionary" artist of whom I speak has had the aim of saving himself from the surrounding forces of sentimentality and vulgarity. In the nature of the case it is impossible to make a deal with these forces, and we should not be surprised if in striking back the artist has done so in ways even intended to be offensive. He has sometimes shown defiance and contempt toward those who would deny his level of seriousness.

All of this can be pointed up by remarking that we live in a post-1914 world. Most of the problems which men thought had been buried by two centuries of progress and a century of peace have been resurrected into life, some of them with a more frightening power to produce violence and chaos than ever before. As W. E. Hocking has observed: "The world-turmoil cannot fail to bring with it so wide a loss of order and predictable circumstances that *no art today can bear to speak simply in terms of beauty and affirmation.*"[7] That is why much modern art is signalized by an offensive warfare against the complacent and the stereotypical. The artist with his superior insight has perceived that we cannot *afford* such addictions.

And art, with its usual prescience, anticipated 1914 somewhat. The new movements were stirring by the beginning of the nineteenth century (in limited forms somewhat before), but the one which I select as an illustration erupted rather suddenly around 1912, the date conventionally taken for the beginning of modern poetry.

The modern poet, at war with the complacent and the stereotypical, has been spoken of as a revolutionary, but for reasons that will appear it would be just as meaningful, and it would better enable us to understand the object he has in view, to call him a reactionary. He is reacting through revolutionary means towards a vision of the world which earlier epochs, not affected by the kind of degradation ours has been through, possessed more fully. Not all poets of course have done this in equal degree, but it is safe to say that no poet today can get a hearing among serious readers of poetry unless his work somehow reflects the torturing experiences, with the resulting complexity of attitude, which distinguish our age.

Looking over the characteristics of the genre, we see the poet trying to break through superficies of falsehood and inadequacies of sensibility by avoiding all stock devices and patterns of imagery, of phrasing, and sometimes of syntax, which might be expected to evoke a complacent response. He has spoken boldly through symbol and metaphor, avoiding the more leisurely simile and full predication; through unexpected combinations, violent antitheses, juxtapositions of the colloquial with the traditionally poetic or literary, and other means of surprise and shock which he hoped would awaken the reader into an awareness that there is a reality to be intuited aesthetically behind the sentimental, romantic, and often vulgar encrustation of the last century or so.

As a leading example of this, and an example very instructive on points which lack general understanding, I shall use T. S. Eliot. If we follow Eliot through "The Love Song of J. Alfred Prufrock," "The Waste Land," and "The Hollow Men," and then on through his later poems, we shall see what might be called the evolution of a conservative, or a conservator of our tradition. He has pursued this evolution while remaining one of the most experimental of our creative writers.

The first of the works named, which appeared in 1915, has been subjected to varying interpretations; but I am satisfied to regard it as an extraordinary intuition of the frustration, lack of direction, and helplessness which can be felt by a modern man at the height of our materially flourishing civilization. Space will not allow me to support this proposition with texts, but those familiar with the poem will recall enough of its method. They will realize that for a reader brought up in the preceding tradition of poetry, which means roughly the Victorian tradition, the poem teems with images which are vivid, but which shock, tease, or puzzle by their incongruity.

The wonder created by "Prufrock," however, was exceeded by that which met "The Waste Land" upon its appearance in 1922. This is admittedly a difficult poem, with its ransacking of legend and literature for images, its sudden breaks in surface continuity, and its odd juxtapositions of the noble and the beautiful with the cheap and the tawdry. Now, after the lapse of half a century, when the poetry of Eliot and some others has to some extent passed into the public mind and has itself become a tradition of a sort, the novelty of the method does not seem as striking as it did then. But then such affronts to the established idea of what a poem should be were taken as proofs positive that the poet had deserted his office, that he had contemptuously alienated himself from the whole tradition of poetry, that he was a man talking to himself, and so on. The feeling was not lessened by the appearance of "The Hollow Men," where the poet pursued the theme of emptiness through images of the barren and the repulsive.

But with the later appearance of "The Journey of the Magi," "Ash Wednesday," and the "Four Quartets," it began to be seen that Eliot was doing something very nearly the opposite of what had been alleged. He was in fact working to restore the tradition in so far as that depends upon a positive and coherent belief about man and his duty or destiny. "Prufrock" could indeed be called negative in the sense that its emphasis is upon a theme of deprivation. But "The Waste Land," for all its images of chaos and its mood of resignation to the breakdown of modern society, in fact prepared us for a turning toward affirmation, so much so that it has been described by one critic as "the rehabilitation of a system of beliefs."[8] "The Hollow Men" presents some of the philosophical difficulties, or difficulties of reintegrating the sensibility, which will be encountered in the work of this rehabilitation. With the publication of "Ash Wednesday" (1927–29) it became evident that Eliot was perhaps the foremost Christian poet of our time, who had won his way through a dark night of the soul to an affirmative position very much in line with our tradition. For this poem, in the words of one interpreter, "describes states of despair, self-abnegation, moral recovery, resurgent faith, need of grace, and renewal of will toward both world and God."[9] His beautiful "Four Quartets," coming somewhat later, has been called a meditation upon what it means to be a Christian.

I am not here supposing that art has to be Christian in order to be good; my point is that Eliot through his revolutionary techniques (still revolutionary in the "Four Quartets") is not simply presenting a picture of fragmentation or anarchy or supplying an impulse toward antinomianism; but is arriving at something like the consensus which underlay the mythic structure of Western culture. What needs stressing is that he could not have done this in any other way; at least he could not have done so as a creative poet. Only by bringing the elements of our modern experience together in these arresting combinations could he have given the reading public a feeling that here is something momentous which must be heard seriously.

Much the same lesson can be found in the career of another great modern poet, William Butler Yeats. Yeats was of course writing before the outburst of modern poetry, but then these movements should not be too neatly periodized. While not as outwardly revolutionary as Eliot, he felt increasingly as he grew older an impulse to make an overt rejection of modern nihilism and to give his poems continuing reference to a system of belief. Conscious in a similar way that the old system had fallen into disbelief, he went the length of inventing his own system of mythology. This was published in 1925 as *A Vision*. An elaborate construction, it gives "a picture of history, an account of human psychology, and an account of the life of the soul after death."[10] Now there is hardly anything more radical than to invent a mythology, but the use to which this one was put was orthodox and traditional: it was to supply a unifying framework for the creations of the artist. Images from the system constantly recur in his subsequent poems and give them a depth of meaning they would not have otherwise.

Both of these poets have produced most affecting pictures of the maladies of modernism; but they are not breaking the world in pieces; rather they are at least striving to put it back together again. Their method is a response to the condition of the modern sensibility. A poet who cannot show that he has felt the disillusionments of his own time as poignantly as other people cannot speak to his time. This is the point from which the poet must begin the road back to more humane traditions.[11] F. O. Mathiessen notes that James Joyce, faced with a similar artistic difficulty, used the narrative structure of the *Odyssey* to give his novel *Ulysses* a framework.[12]

The only conclusion possible is that a cultural worker must remain free whether he is giving expression to his cultural tradition or seeking by some strategy to recover it. Experimentation and innovation on the part of the artist are not necessarily signs of ignorance or irresponsibility. "An art that merely reports or reenacts the human load of footlessness, dismay, or despair—as what we call modern art tends to do—may be a loyal art, refusing romantic honors to the headless powers of the time."[13] It is true that inadmissible heresies will sometimes arise, but the policing of these will have to be left to the forces of the culture itself.

Finally let us bear carefully in mind that art is a form of cognition of reality; one of its functions is thus epistemic, and the epistemic is almost never bound or limited except to our loss. True, the consensus speaks to the artist, but it does not tell him exactly what he must do. Or, if he allows it to tell him exactly what he must do, he is not an artist of the first rank. It rather says, "Tell the story, but tell it in a new way." The Greek tragedians, bound as they felt themselves to be to the traditional stories, felt the need of this second injunction. That is all the coercion we can allow in the case of the artist. He is a man deeply affected by the momentousness, uniqueness, and truthfulness of various aspects of the pageant of existence. He must be culturally free to do what he can do with his own special gifts and insights. Where the sanction descends, it descends in the name of art, identifying but not forcibly suppressing, the faulty, which may be meretricious, didactic, or ideologically inspired. What is true for art thus narrowly conceived is true for culture as a whole regarded as an art, up to the limits where physical and moral survival raise problems of a more immediate kind.

In brief, cultural freedom as an integral part of the free society requires that distinctive cultures be allowed to preserve their homogeneity; that creators of cultural works should not be hobbled by political and sociological dogmas; and that in a given culture a tradition should be left free to find its own way of renewing itself. Violation of any of these shows a fundamental ignorance of what culture is and of how it ministers to the life of the spirit.

Notes

1. It may be asked whether in the following discussion I am dealing with cultures empirically, recognizing any formalized and elaborated human activity as a culture, or whether I am supposing a normative, axiological definition. An attempt to define the limits of cultural freedom naturally implies the second approach. Every marked development of formal activity is a sign that the cultural impulse is present; in this sense the first datum is anthropological. But it is ridiculous to maintain that all cultures are equal and of infinite worth; whether a culture or a cultural activity is better or worse must be judged by the amount of satisfaction it provides for the higher faculties. That judgment can be reached only on the basis of a true philosophy of the human spirit. The point of view in this essay is, therefore, cultural pluralism but not cultural relativism. It is inevitable and right that there should be different cultures, but any culture may be viewed critically if the viewer has a definition of man.
2. Even anthropologists concede the impulse of a culture to integrate itself. For a discussion of this subject from the anthropological point of view, see Ruth Benedict, *Patterns of Culture* (New York: Houghton, Mifflin, 1934), Ch. III.
3. A substantial part of American folklore has consisted of jokes about "the Irish." One may doubt that the Irish were ever done much harm by these, and today the situation has changed so that their application to the Irish seems to lack point.
4. *Complete Works of George Savile, First Marques of Halifax*, ed. Walter Raleigh (Oxford: The Clarendon Press, 1912), p. 63.
5. Matthew Arnold makes this point in his *Culture and Anarchy*, and he adds the further important consideration that Jacobinism has a fierce hatred of the past. This thought could be elaborated: no government and no ideology which try to cut a people off from its past can be friendly to culture.
6. Sir Herbert Read has stated the principle (*Truth is More Sacred: A Critical Ex-*

change on Modern Literature, by Edward Dahlberg and Sir Herbret Read [New York: Horizon Press, 1961] pp. 216–217): "No censorship can be imposed on the imagination, and the truth we should hold sacred....it is truth to the divine promptings of the Muse—promptings which may take a poet into a lady's bedroom or a brothel as easily and as frequently as into the vernal woods or the market place."

7. "The International Role of Art in Revolutionary Times," *Modern Age*, Vol. IV (Spring, 1960), p. 132.

8. Cleanth Brooks, *Modern Poetry and the Tradition* (Chapel Hill: University of North Carolina Press, 1939), p. 171.

9. George Williamson, *A Readers' Guide to T.S. Eliot* (New York: Noonday Press, 1953), p. 184.

10. Brooks, *op. cit.*, p. 177.

11. I wish that the same hope could be expressed for architecture, which seems the most disoriented of the modern arts. Bruno Zevi has made an apt statement of its situation (*Architecture in America: A Battle of Styles*, ed. William A. Coles and Henry Hope Reed, Jr. [New York: Appleton-Century-Crofts, 1961] p. 133): "The moment of ostentatious novelty and avant-garde manifestoes has passed and modern architecture must now take its place in architectural tradition, aiming above all at a critical revision of this tradition. It has become evident that an organic culture cannot, in dealing with the past and specfically with architectural history, use two standards of judgment, one for modern and another for traditional architecture, if it is, as it must be, designed to provide modern disoriented and rootless man with a base and a history, to integrate individual and social needs which manifest themselves today as an antithesis between freedom and planning, theory and practice. Once we are able to apply the same criteria in evaluating contemporary architecture and that of previous centuries, we shall be taking a decisive step forward in this direction."

12. F.O. Mathiessen, *The Achievement of T.S. Eliot* (New York: Oxford University Press, 1947), p. 45.

13. Hocking, *op. cit.,* p. 129.

Part II

A Resurgent Old Right

6

Promises to Keep

Chilton Williamson, Jr.

The modern temper shows a fatal tendency to break large moral and historical questions into smaller technocratic ones and to tinker with each of these as a separated "policy problem." Unfortunately for advocates of this approach, the immigration debate presents us with what is essentially a moral problem, requiring the use of the moral—even of the prophetic—imagination to put the parts together and, viewing them whole, to recognize that the subject is part of another whole that is larger still.

Many of the proponents of continuing immigration into the United States at current or increased levels insist that immigrants are good for our economy, since their numbers help to make up for a declining birthrate among the native population and because the more highly educated of them bring skills that are no longer being developed in sufficient quantity in this country. This is the kind of talk that got the Morrison bill passed by Congress last year—insofar, that is, as talk and ideas had anything to do with its passage at all. (Ben Wattenberg actually suggested that federal taxes paid by would-be immigrants could by themselves liquidate the federal deficit!) Advocates of liberal immigration policies remind us that we are "a nation of immigrants" and that it is therefore un-American—by which they mean "immoral"—to cut off, or even drastically to reduce, the flow of foreigners to this country. We are, and have been for two centuries, they say, the opportunity and hope of the world, and so we should deny ourselves to nobody. (Hollywood is, and has been for decades, full of beautiful women who have thought the same way.) Five billion people, they imply, have a natural and God-given right to share in the benefits of American citizenship (even if, having moved here, they decide not to avail themselves of it): "California or bust!" is an old slogan with new life in it. Not just millions but billions of people can reside comfortably with us, Julian Simon insists. And, since we are already a nation of well-assimilated strangers (we all wear Reebok shoes, eat at Burger King, and listen to Bon Jovi on Sony Walkmans) we obviously can assimilate the entire world, if need be. We have become *Homo economicus* and all of us, including the rawest newcomers to these shores, understand the morality, as well as the practical desirability, of playing the game on a level table. Finally, the pro-immigrationists say, we are living in what George Bush (who stated that he looked forward "eagerly" to signing the Morrison legislation into law) calls the New World Order, which I imagine as a kind of universal extension of Columbia University's International House in Morningside Heights on New York City.

One reason to distrust these arguments is that they are usually formulated and delivered by a variety of special interest groups—the U.S. Chamber of Commerce, truck gardeners and fruit growers in California and Florida, refugee welfare associations, ethnic organizations, human rights activists, and every sodality of professional ideologue— that have no interest in the larger reality lying behind their own narrow and parochial concerns. The more important reason, though, is that even if correct they are incidental to the much larger and more critical concerns raised by our existing immigration policies. Having read at least a portion of the pertinent material, I am, for example, persuaded by my opinion (as St. Paul said) that immigrants *do* take jobs from native-born Americans; that a great many of them do not pay taxes or, anyway, their fair share of them; and that—particularly in cities like Los Angeles—they are a tremendous tax burden on the already oversubscribed natives. The work of Donald Huddle, professor of economics at Rice University, seems to me to substantiate conclusively these statements.

Nevertheless, if Professor Huddle's findings were discredited tomorrow, and the writings of Julian Simon bathed simultaneously in a bright transforming light, I would, while conceding a point, remain opposed to a liberal American immigration policy on the grounds that all economic arguments are extraneous to the larger questions. You could "prove" to me that, without the immediate transference of the entire population of Hong Kong to the state of California, the United States would be in a major economic depression by the middle of next year, and I would still be against transferring it there. Or you could "prove" to me that yes, the United States *can* support comfortably all of the earth's five-billion-plus people, and my response would be (a) what does "comfortably" mean? and (b) who wants to live with five billion people where formerly there were a quarter billion? If we really do require all these immigrants from many lands to goose our economy and to strengthen our anemic blood with their robust red corpuscles, their breeding habits that are better suited to laboratory mice than to human beings, and their rejuvenating cultural "diversity," then indeed it is later than I think. When we arrive at the point where the United States must rely upon massive transfusions of human as well as of financial capital from abroad to restore us to what we were in 1789—an energetic, canny, thrifty, resourceful, interesting, brave, and above all confident civilization—then quite frankly there no longer *is* a United States of America in any save the legalistic sense, and I for one don't give a hang what becomes of the formalist (though alas not empty) shell that remains.

We ought, I propose, to forget about economic considerations and the economy (which seems to get along on its own anyhow) when we think about immigration, and divert our attention instead to what Herbert Croly called "the promise of American life" and what today is known in more general terms as "the quality of life," even if all too few people who use the phrase have any fair idea of what it is they are talking about. Although Bill McKibben assures us that mankind has arrived at the point where it must choose the "humble" path over the "defiant" one in making its future way through the natural world, contemporary environmental argument is for the most part restricted to gaudy and generalized crises like the greenhouse effect and the global population explosion. The fragmentation of contemporary "thought" causes such mega-subjects to be detached from more restrictive and subordinate topics and problems, set apart from them and elevated into towering abstractions that become the objects of a peculiar sort of counter-idolatry. As a result, a variety of "opinion-makers" in the United States today are running around yelling their heads off that the sky is going to fall tomorrow because the population of China reached one billion yesterday, while hardly one of them (with a few brave exceptions like Georgie Anne Geyer) dares—or perhaps even thinks—to say that the American land is going to be overrun and despoiled in fifty or a hundred years because of the folly, greed, and dishonesty with which Congress has responded to the immigrant invasion during the past twenty-five years.

It is considered "humanitarian" to fret about population growth and its effects on the natural environment at the global (which is to say, at the abstract) level; but "racist," "xenophobic," "uncompassionate," and "un-American" to worry about the population crisis as it immediately effects the United States, the only place in the world where we are in a position to be able to do anything about it. A few years ago, the late Edward Abbey agreed to write an article on the subject of immigration, legal and otherwise, for the *New York Times'* op-ed page, at the invitation of its editor. The editor held the piece for two months before requesting that the author, who had written to specification, reduce it by about 50 percent. This Abbey proceeded to do. Another month passed before a different editor wrote to say that the article could not be printed owing to a lack of space. The *Times* never paid Abbey a kill fee or even bothered to return the manuscript to him; later he published it as "Immigration and Liberal Taboos" in a collection of his essays. One of his sentences asks: "How many of us, truthfully, would prefer to be submerged in the Caribbean-Latin version of civilization?" The *Times* editors weren't telling, but stories about the hazards of nuclear-waste disposal, the horrors of air pollution and strip-mined hills, and the destruction of the Brazilian rain forests continued to make it into the Sunday editions of the paper, as did reports of famine in Chad and Ethiopia and almost monthly head counts of the population of China.

The few "conservative" writers (I suppose we *are* conservatives; it's getting hard to distinguish between the players these days) who outspokenly oppose substantial immigration into the United States have long known better than to play the environmental card when making their bid to their fellow "conservatives," all too many of whom equate conservatism with unrestrained capitalism, although five or six centuries of industrial capitalism have probably done more to destroy traditional and humane ways of life than a century and a half of militant Marxist-Leninism. On this subject, however, the time has arrived for plain speaking: the environmentalist argument, plus the cultural one, provides the essential overriding case against the waves of immigrants now cresting along the borders of the continental United States. Contrary to "conservative" opinion, America is *not* "underpopulated" (whatever that might mean). Advocates of immigration at present or elevated levels repeat *ad nauseam* that immigration is "an American tradition." Well, so are spacious skies, amber waves of grain, wide-open spaces, the open range, and the wilderness of mountain, desert, and plain. Can anyone really imagine America without them? (Pause for reflection.) Can anyone really imagine America without another thirty million Mexicans, six million more Iranians, ten million additional people from the Caribbean, and three or four million future refugees from the Soviet Union? (I thought so.) As for the environmentalists themselves, they need a little—much more than a little—of Abbey's courage and forthrightness if they are going to hold their own and argue their cause successfully in the New America of diversity and multiculturalism that is surely coming if the government in Washington does not catch up in a hurry with the opinion of a public that is already resentful—and has been for years—of the huddled masses arriving daily in this country. Does anyone believe for one minute that a United States in which European-Americans are a minority and Third World peoples a plurality will leave in place, let alone add to, the rather vast body of statutory law relating to environmental protection? The most polluted region of the United States lies along the 2,700-mile border it shares with Mexico. And Mexico itself, where everything from tamale-wrappers to heavy industrial equipment, when finished with, is dispensed directly, immediately, and thoughtlessly into "the environment" so beloved of American preservationists, is incomparably worse. (The train lines and highways I have traveled in Mexico are *cordona pas-sanitaries* of garbage, detritus, and junk.)

Another form of environmental degradation produced by soaring population growth is likely to be a precipitous decline in traditional, accepted, and even cherished standards of social and political life in America. It is astounding that the same "conservatives" who are always yapping about the need for deregulation, freedom of enterprise and of action, "personal freedom," "property rights," the tyranny of laws, "over-regulation," and so on and so forth, have failed to make a connection between the tendencies they deplore and the increasing density and size of the U.S. population. The state of Wyoming, of which I am a proud and thankful resident, although comprising 97,203 square miles, is home to only about 450,000 people, which makes it the least populous of all the fifty states. It has, even by Western standards, generous laws and provisions regarding the taking of game animals of all sizes and of fish, cheap licenses, ready access to those enormous tracts of federally owned land that "conservatives" are always griping about, and so much *space* that, even at this late date, you can hunt all day without coming across another hunter. Of course, Wyoming's small population and the liberality of the laws—*all* of its laws!—are not coincidentally related. Take by comparison California, the most populous state in the nation, whose 28 million residents are cobwebbed with regulations stipulating such matters as what kind of car they may drive and what type of engine propels it, how much water they may put on their lawns, and whether they may burn a steak over charcoal in their back-yards. In the modern age, big populations mean big regulation, and big regulation means big government, increasingly centralized to the exclusion of subsidiary powers and authorities and the jurisdiction of community government. In addition to which, you have to drive at twelve miles an hour, bumper to bumper, in eight-lane traffic for four hours a day, spend your lunch hour in line at the bank, put up with snippy, arrogant, and often illiterate bureaucrats, and write account numbers the length of a Ford serial number at the bottom of your checks. O Brave New World—O New World Order!

I will not write that the threat to the environment posed by massive immigration from predominantly Third World countries pales by comparison to the threat to historical American culture, since the two strike me as being about equal in importance. Here again, the obviating oracles of optimism point to what they describe as a long "tradition" of "assimilation" in America by which people-from-many-lands have been acculturated to the wisdom, habits, and tastes of Jefferson, Emerson, Lincoln, and Madonna. This is a heartwarming reading of American history, but like so many heartwarming things it is essentially a false one. Until after the Civil War, the United States was a country composed chiefly of North European peoples having a great deal more in common than they had differences between them. It is only in the latter part of our history that "multiculturalism" has either been important or has been seen to be important, and now positively beneficial, to the point of making a fetish of it. Assimiliation, it should pain me to say, is *not* our tradition; rather homogeneity is, dissension having sprung along regional and geographic lines of demarcation.

If European-Americans were presently a strong and healthy culture, willing to tolerate a liberal immigration policy and to welcome people of non-European stocks and cultures in a spirit of confident generosity and manly self-esteem, there would be something genuinely heroic (though still wrongheaded) in its determination to do so. In fact, we are no longer a young, powerful, restless, and inexhaustibly optimistic society capable of surmounting great difficulties and eager to accept all challenges, in particular idealistic ones. Today we are a very different country from what we were in the nineteenth and twentieth centuries: middle-aged at least, perhaps prematurely old. We are no longer restless, we are bored and tentative; we are not optimistic but increasingly (and with good reason) the opposite; we have lost confidence in our heritage, our traditions, and above all perhaps our faith. This does not mean that we will necessarily adopt other traditions and other faiths; it does mean that we will have less and less of ourselves to offer peoples whom we would assimilate to the remnant of an indigenous culture. We know this. And so do the people who have recently appeared among us.

The stranger is within the gates and he smells blood. I do not mean he is bloodthirsty; he simply senses our weakness and is ready to exploit it as far as he can. He is taking advantage of us, and we cannot claim that we have not left ourselves open to, and even encouraged, him. "Multiculturalism" is a sign, maybe a proof, of this. As Lawrence Auster has written in a recently published book (*The Path to National Suicide: An Essay on Immigration and Multiculturalism*), the multiculturalist standard is the direct result of the Immigration Reform Act of 1965 which, by removing the national quotas provision of earlier immigration legislation, cleared the way of great numbers of immigrants from Asia, Africa, Latin America, and other non-European regions of the world. It is also notice served—by those immigrants and by others on their behalf—that "assimilation" is henceforth an outmoded concept, ethnocentric at best and racist at worse, and that this and future generations of newcomers will have no part in it, or of that Western civilization that is also under attack. And who, after all, is going to tell them differently? As the new immigrants arrive in their numbers in America, they will not only prove in plain fact unassimilable, they will be able, by the exercise of the suffrage, to alter American society to the extent that they will not need to assimilate to it; perhaps there will be nothing left of the original to assimilate to. Already this is seen to be the strategy of the leading Hispanic "rights" organizations, while there has been talk in the Mexican-American community for at least two decades of using their numbers and the vote to effect the secession of several of the southwestern states, which would either be incorporated by Mexico or form the new Nation of Aztlan. We have already experienced one episode of secession in our history; stranger things have occurred than that it should happen again. Just look at Canada.

There are further dangers inherent in multiculturalism beyond the foreseeable submergence of European-American culture and governance in the United States. The situation that is likely to evolve is not so simple a one as Us versus Them, White versus Brown, European versus Non-European. Jesse Jackson to the contrary, there will be no Rainbow Coalition—or if there is, it will be of very limited duration. Underlying the cant, the yes-saying, the cultural politics, and the silly celebrations of unity, profound resentments and antagonisms exist in multiethnic America that will surely grow stronger and deeper with time—and with continuing immigration from every part of the world. Nearly forty years after desegregation and a quarter-century after the civil rights legislation of the 1960s, relations between whites and blacks in this country are arguably worse than they have been at any time in our history. It is an open secret that blacks (collectively) despise Hispanics (again collectively) and vice versa, and that both groups are resentful and suspicious of Asians, who seem happy to return the compliment. Georgie Anne Geyer, the newspaper columnist, invites her readers to witness the disintegration of the Soviet Union and learn from it: the day of what she euphemistically terms the "socially complicated state" is over, she warns, or at least the writing is on the wall. Events throughout the world today have one great thing to tell us: namely, that everywhere blood is thicker than water. Modern nations that not only refuse to recognize this truth but deliberately fly in the face of it will do so at their peril.

In the light of America's immigration problem, James Burnham's "suicide of the West" takes on a newer meaning. From the time when the Puritans landed in Massachusetts, Americans have tended to think of themselves as members of a church whose reality has a secular dimension beyond the religious one. As the religious sensibility has waned in American society, the assurance of a quasi-religious mission has increased to the point where the United States at the end of the twentieth century seems to regard itself as a collective Christ figure, redeeming the world by example and by purity of intention. But if we do succeed in crucifying ourselves, after our crucifixion we shall not rise again, and there will be no inheritors and apostles of our peculiar faith. The third world—its cultures, its peoples—will remain emphatically in place, but we ourselves will have perished forever, having accomplished by our suicide no good for anyone save a relative handful of the world's refugees—and even those only in the short run.

Because we will have killed the goose that laid the golden eggs. The third world *is* its people, not its sinister, corrupt, greedy, and incompetent governments: where the people are, there the third world is, and will be. We have no magic alchemical atmosphere capable of imbuing third world peoples with the ability to maintain the first world culture that created and continues to create the economic and technical fruits for which they hunger. In the collapse of European-America, nobody will be a winner except for the chronically and pathologically resentful (from our own ranks as well as from those of our supplanters), and even theirs will be a Pyrrhic victory. Then America will correspond, at last and in reality, with the description falsely applied to it in the 1960s by Professor John Kenneth Galbraith of Harvard University, when he wrote that the United States was a land of private affluence surrounded by public squalor. It will, in other words, truly have become another third world country.

7

The Anti-History of Free Trade Ideology

William R. Hawkins

We ask, would not every sane person consider a government to be insane which, in consideration of the benefits and the reasonableness of a state of universal and perpetual peace, proposed to disband its armies, destroy its fleet, and demolish its fortresses? But such a government would be doing nothing different in principle from what the popular school requires from governments when, because of the advantages which would be derivable from general free trade, it urges that they should abandon the advantages derivable from protection.

This statement by Friedrich List in his 1844 book *The National System of Political Economy* sets out the basic difference in assumption about the way the world works held by free traders and nationalists. While free traders such as the French economist Jean-Baptiste Say, author of the classical paradigm "Say's Law of Markets," believed that "All nations are friends in the nature of things," their opponents on the Right considered economics a vital foundation of national strength in a world where international competition decided not just the fate of business enterprises but that of entire societies.

The nineteenth century saw an intense debate between these points of view in Europe; a debate that generated most of the theories and lines of arguments used, consciously or unconsciously, by those engaged in debate over American trade policy in the late twentieth-century. Free trade was then rooted in the then new school of classical liberalism of England and France. Nationalist thought drew on the ancient practices of mercantilism enlivened by insights from contemporary American and German thinkers, though all nations had adherents of both doctrines.

Friedrich List is the best-known "nationalist" writer. Forced into exile from his native Wurtemburg because of his advocacy of industrialization and a commercial union of the many states that then comprised Germany, List came to the United States at the suggestion of General Lafayette who introduced him to Andrew Jackson, Henry Clay, James Madison, and other national leaders. List found in the previous works of Alexander Hamilton a line of reasoning similar to his own. His pen was soon employed supporting the U.S. policy of protective tariffs against protests from British manufacturers who then dominated world markets. He saw in the United States the best model for economic progress and joined several groups promoting science and industry. Returning to Europe as an American diplomat, he promoted railway projects in Germany and joined the battle over trade policy with a barrage of articles and pamphlets culminating in *The National System of Political Economy,* a massive work that pitted history and *realpolitik* against the abstract theories and idealism of the classical liberals.

The New World Order: Old News

The basic flaw in the liberal theory according to List was that it "has assumed as being actually in existence a state of things which has yet to come into existence. It assumes the existence of a universal union and a state of perpetual peace." This is an overstatement, but it still speaks to the main point in dispute. The liberals did not so much assume that the world had turned peaceful, as they *expected* the world to turn peaceful as a result of the interdependence fostered by free trade. The British radical Richard Cobden, for example, claimed that commerce was "the grand panacea" and that under its influence "the motive for large and mighty empires, for gigantic armies and great fleets would die away." The French economist Frederic Bastiat argued that "Free trade means harmony of interests and peace between nations," and went on to state that "we place this indirect and social effect a thousand times above the direct or purely economic effect." It was not a global economy that the liberals were advocating. Trade on a world scale had been conducted for several centuries by the time the liberals came on the scene. It was a new world order that the liberals desired. Free trade was merely a means to that end.

Trade between Europe and Asia predates the discovery of America. However, most historians mark the start of a truly worldwide economic system at the end of the fifteenth century when maritime explorers discovered both the New World and the sea-route around the horn of Africa into the Indian Ocean. Both of these discoveries were largely motivated by a desire to control trade and markets. The advance of the Ottoman Turks in the Eastern Mediterranean, particularly the capture of Constantinople in 1453, forced the Genoese merchants out of the lucrative trade in silks and spices brought westward by caravans from Asia. Genoese sailors and capitalists needed a way to circumvent not only the Turks but also their Venetian rivals by finding a new route to Asia. They found it working through Portugal and Spain. The personification of this strategy was Christopher Columbus, a Genoese captain sailing for the Spanish crown in an attempt to find an Atlantic route to Asia to compete against the Portuguese route around Africa.

This age was dominated by a school of political economy known as mercantilism. Under this philosophy, governments encouraged trade and manufacture in order to create both a prosperous national economy and a powerful nation-state. Precise measures and objectives varied with time and circumstance. Policy needed to be flexible, but the strategic goal was consistent; if the nation's merchants and industrialists were productive and able to dominate large markets, then the governments had a strong material base to support their position by diplomacy and, if need be, by war.

The opening of the new trade routes to the East and of entire new continents in the West brought great prosperity to Europe and America while introducing substantial progress to Asia, but it did not bring peace. Wars both military and commercial were fought for control of the new wealth and resources with the winners able to expand the size and scope of their operations.

After each series of global wars, there arises for a time what can be called a liberal school of thought that argues that the time is ripe for a new world order that will put the age-old conflicts for wealth and power behind it. These movements are always strongest in the victorious countries whose enemies have, for the moment, vanished. Success leads some to believe that peace and prosperity can be maintained without further effort. The time has come, they claim, to enjoy the fruits of victory rather than make continued sacrifices for the future; the morally repugnant methods of national advancement can now be safely abandoned in pursuit of more enlightened goals.

The colonial wars of the eighteenth century, which were offshoots of the dynastic struggles and the balance of power in Europe, brought complaints from progressive thinkers. In England David Hume claimed that nations were mere "accidents of battles, negotiations and marriages." He denounced mercantilist trade practices for strengthening the state at the expense of individuals, for promoting wars, and for seeking to cripple the economic advancement of rival nations. Like other intellectuals, he considered himself a cosmopolitan. His love for French culture led him to oppose his own country's efforts in the Seven Years War (the war that pushed France out of North America) and to claim that there was "nothing ever equal in absurdity and wickedness as our present patriotism."

Across the channel, Voltaire complained of policies that enabled nations to "destroy each other at the extremities of Asia and America." Such activities make us "enemies of the human race" he cried. Both Hume and Voltaire became free traders to promote world peace. Hume constructed a simple model of price adjustments based on the flow of precious metals that would automatically bring trade into balance without the need for government controls. However, like later theories that offer devaluation as a cure for trade deficits, Hume did not adequately consider that trade could be conducted in terms of property and productive assets and not just in goods and services. Those who profit from a trade surplus generate capital that can be used not only to build up their own economies but also to dominate the finances of other states.

This was an old practice even when Hume wrote, and one that still worries practical statesmen. Indeed, in Hume's model a trade surplus is actually harmful in that it promotes both price inflation and low interest rates that drive out capital. Yet the recent history of Hume's day proved him wrong. Those who had run trade surpluses with Spain had prospered, while Spain had declined despite the output of its gold and silver mines in America. Hume was less than half right. He saw the price revolution as Spanish treasure moved through the European economy. But he missed the energizing effect this movement had on Spain's trading partners; an effect the surplus nations wanted to maintain, and their rivals wished to emulate. British merchants were always complaining that the influx of capital to Holland from its trade surplus allowed Dutch merchants to borrow at half the interest rate charged in London.

Misperception and Decline: Spain and Holland

In the short-run, Spain could consume but it could not produce which, in the long-run, proved fatal to its standing as a great power and as an advanced society. That Spanish leaders were deluded by a sense of false prosperity is betrayed in this boast of Alfonso Nunez de Castro in 1675:

Let London manufacture those fine fabrics of hers to her heart's content; let Holland her chambrays; Florence her cloth; the Indies their beaver and vicuna; Milan her brocade; Italy and Flanders their linens....so long as our capital can enjoy them, the only thing it proves is that all nations train their journeymen for Madrid, and that Madrid is the queen of Parliaments, for all the world serves her and she serves nobody.

Yet by 1675 Spanish per capita income had been falling in absolute terms for perhaps half a century. And though absolute decline probably bottomed out in the 1680s, relative decline continued as other nations grew faster than sluggish Spain. Today it is often forgotten that Spain was once the most wealthy and powerful state in Europe and America.

Spanish imports were double its exports and the precious metals became scarce within weeks of the arrival of the treasure fleets, as the money flowed to Spain's creditors. What industry there was, along with banking and shipping, was in the hands of foreign owners. As a modern historian Jaime Vicens Vives has concluded, "this was one of the fundamental causes of the Spanish economy's profound decline in the seventeenth century, maritime trade had fallen into the hands of foreigners." He concluded that the "opening of the internal market to foreign goods" produced a "fatal result." Spain's exports were at the same time under heavy pressure by competitors in third country markets. A nation that cannot control its domestic market will seldom be able to sustain itself in foreign markets which are inherently more vulnerable and unstable.

The Dutch played a major role in undermining Spanish power, but would soon fall prey to the mercantilist policies of England and France. The role of great power enjoyed by the United Provinces in the seventeenth century did not last into the next. Simon Schama's recent study of the Dutch at the height of their power is entitled *The Embarrassment of Riches,* but by the mid-1700s a different image was being conveyed by visitors to major Dutch ports. James Boswell wrote from Utrecht in 1764, "Most of their principal towns are sadly decayed, and instead of finding every mortal employed, you meet with multitudes of poor creatures who are starving in idleness. Utrecht is remarkably ruined."

Once again it was shown that those who rely on trade rather than on the strength of their own productive capacities have built their castles on sand. C.R. Boxer, the premier modern historian of the Dutch commercial empire, has described the process of its decline:

When the protectionist measures adopted by neighboring countries from the time of Colbert onwards effectively stimulated the consumption of their own manufactured goods at the expense of Dutch exports, the Dutch industrialists could not fall back on an increased internal demand, nor was it possible to greatly increase their sales in the tropical dependencies. Moreover, the Dutch industries had originally been primarily finishing industries for the products of other countries....but in course of time these countries made sufficient technical progress to undertake these finishing processes themselves.

The Dutch also lost control of the fisheries to foreign competition and saw their ship-building industry decline as the yards of other nations expanded with the aid of government subsidies and navigation acts that restricted foreign carriers. As the Dutch economy stagnated, tax rates were increased to cover expenses—a short-run expedient that further slowed economic activity. As historian Charles Wilson has noted, "The growing competition of rising economies like England and France and the increasing burden of taxes and costs was reflected in the absolute decline in former great centres of industry."

At the end of the seventeenth century, the United Provinces could send 100 warships to sea manned with 24,000 sailors and marines. The Dutch Stadtholder, William of Orange, could become the king of England in 1688. A century later, the Dutch could send to sea only seventeen warships with 3,000 men and the country had become a mere pawn in the struggle between the new world powers of England and France.

Ricardo & Co.: Classic Liberals

To the classical liberals, the rise and fall of nations and the profound impact of such changes on the lives of ordinary people are of little interest. As David Ricardo (whose theory of comparative advantage is still a mainstay of the free trade argument) stated in 1813, "parliaments have something more to do than furnish ministers with the means of preserving the greatness and glory of the country." England was at war with Napoleon and Ricardo, a member of the British House of Commons, was arguing against financing the war with debt as proposed by the Chancellor of the Exchequer. Ricardo favored the "pain" of a direct tax rather than a sinking fund to finance military operations because "when the pressure of the war is felt at once, without mitigation, we shall be less disposed to engage in an expensive contest." He felt it his duty to see that "the resources of the country are not misapplied by the arrogant and ambitious conduct of our government or used for purposes of ambition, rapine and desolation." He was quite the dove, which put him in the mainstream of liberal opinion.

Ricardo believed the gain from trade to be so great that nations would continue to trade with one another even in time of war. Thus England did not have to worry about being dependent on foreign imports of food and raw materials, since these flows would not be interrupted. This was an odd argument given that Napoleon had attempted to isolate England from European trade by invoking the Continental System. The Royal Navy had, of course, long blockaded France. The desire to destroy trade was so great in both Paris and London that in 1812 Napoleon invaded Russia to force compliance with the Continental System, and the U.S. declared war on England in part because of British depredations on American shipping. In this commercial warfare Napoleon failed because his armies were not as successful in dominating Europe's ports as the Royal Navy was in dominating the seas.

Nor did the future confirm Ricardo's optimism. The strategy of striking at the foundations of an opponent's economy, using everything from U-boats and strategic bombing to guerrilla raids and economic sanctions, became increasingly popular as the importance of production to the balance of power increased.

The conflicts of the French Revolution and Napoleon lasted a quarter-century, and in their wake came calls for a new world order. The principles for this order were laid out by Immanuel Kant in his tract *Perpetual Peace,* written in 1795 while the wars were still in their early stages. "There is only one rational way in which states coexisting with other states can emerge from the lawless condition of pure warfare." Argued Kant:

> Just like individual men, they must renounce their savage and lawless freedom, adapt themselves to public coercive laws and thus form an *international state (civitas gentium),* which would necessarily continue to grow until it embraced all the peoples of the earth.

Kant acknowledged that the time was not ripe for such a radical transformation, but he did believe that a "gradually expanding *federation* likely to prevent war" was possible. It would be necessary to prevent states from engaging in acts of imperialism, intervening in the internal affairs of others, maintaining standing armies, employing spies, or using public debt to finance war. And, of course, "free trade" was to be promoted to bind people together as individuals practicing peaceful exchange. These have been basic tenets of both classical (libertarian) and modern (welfare) liberalism ever since.

The nineteenth-century liberals drew on Adam Smith, depicting *The Wealth of Nations* (1776) as a work of doctrinaire free trade thinking. They were only partially correct. Smith did, in standard liberal fashion, denounce the "capricious ambitions of kings and ministers" and the "mean rapacity, the monopolizing spirit of merchants and manufacturers" who had prospered under mercantilism. Yet he did not take the final leap into cosmopolitan-pacifist ideology common to those further to the left. He thought "the art of war is certainly the noblest of all arts," and that England must be prepared for war because "a wealthy nation is of all nations the most likely to be attacked." In a famous passage, Smith wrote that "defense, however, is of much more importance than opulence," a statement which any mercantilist would agree.

Adam Smith's Mercantile Instincts

On the topic of the Navigation Acts, the centerpiece of British policy, Smith wrote that the "defense of Great Britain depends very much upon the number of its sailors and shipping. The act of navigation, therefore, very properly endeavors to give the sailors and shipping of Great Britain the monopoly of the trade of their own country." Smith also approved of paying bounties on the fisheries because they increased the supply of sailors and ships. He likewise approved of paying bounties for the production of naval stores in the American colonies and prohibiting the export of naval stores from the colonies to anywhere outside the British Empire. Such regulations made the empire less dependent on the importation of strategic goods from foreign sources.

Smith also felt that England was justified in using tariffs and other restrictions in retaliation for policies used by others to block British exports. Only if confronted by trade wars could foreign states be persuaded to negotiate reciprocal agreements to liberalize trade, Smith contended.

British historian Corelli Barnett, in his book *The Collapse of British Power,* criticizes Smith because "he could not foresee that national defense would come to depend not just on seaman and naval stores, but on total industrial and economic capabilities." This complaint is not entirely justified, inasmuch as Smith left the door open for an expanded application of mercantilist doctrine when he wrote:

> It may be advantageous to lay some burden upon foreign imports for the encouragement of domestic industry, when some particular industry is necessary for the defense of the country.... It is of importance that the kingdom depend as little as possible upon its neighbors for the manufactures necessary for its defense.

The dynamics of the Industrial Revolution, which was just getting started in Smith's day, quickly expanded the horizons of security planning. More than inventions and factories were involved; a system evolved that depended on the integration of a wide range of economic activity. This industrial depended on raw materials and power supplies; on one sector's manufacturing the inputs for other sectors; on greatly improved transportation, and on an organized effort of education and research aimed at maintaining the flow of new technologies. A mass market was needed to support mass production. Also needed was a government that could maintain order, since the disruption of one vital sector could cripple the entire economy. Thus an advantage would occur to any system that could be unified under a single national or imperial authority. The continent-spanning United States is a perfect example of a society with such an advantage, for it has never had to rely on external trade to any great extent.

Wealth Consumption vs. Creation

Each new wave of the Industrial Revolution has accelerated this trend, not only in the defense industry but in the economy as a whole. The 1991 Persian Gulf War proved again the importance of technological superiority on the battle field. American security depends on American industry maintaining its lead in a broad range of fields and production processes. Federal spending for weaponry does not provide a level of demand wide enough or deep enough to support technological pre-eminence for the economy as a whole. Commercial demand must do this both to keep domestic living standards and employment up during peacetime, and to provide an industrial base that can be mobilized in time of large-scale war. As economists Stephen S. Cohen and John Zysman argued in their 1987 book *Manufacturing Matters:*

> America must control the production of those high-tech products it invents and designs—and it must do so in a direct and hands-on way....First, production is where the lion's share of the value added is realized...this is where the returns needed to finance the next round of research and development are generated. Second and most important unless R&D is tightly tied to the manufacturing of the product....R&D will fall behind the cutting edge of incremental innovation.... High tech gravitates to the state-of-the-art producers.

That this is true has been documented by professors Richard Florida (Carnegie Mellon) and Martin Kenny (University of California-Davis) in their recent book *The Break-Through Illusion.* U.S. leadership in basic science and start-up technologies is not translated into mass production as readily as in Japan because of the nonintegrated nature of

American business. The isolation of basic R&D in small shops in the Silicon Valley or other high-tech corridors also allows foreign firms the same shot at acquiring American breakthroughs as U.S. companies in an open market auction. In recent years hundreds of small, high-tech concerns have been bought out by foreign firms.

With over a century and a half of modern industrial experience, it is odd that so many commentators have yet to grasp the extent of integration, or the long-run, dynamic nature of technological progress. Free trade advocates continue to cling to the largely static models derived at the very dawn of the Industrial Revolution, when the idea of rapid progress on today's scale was unknown. This explains the continued popularity of Ricardo's comparative advantage concept where a slight price difference at a given point in time is considered adequate cause to abandon an entire field of production *and its future development* in favor of imports.

List rejected this notion asking "Who would be consoled for the loss of an arm by the knowledge that he had nevertheless been able to buy his shirts forty percent cheaper?" He thus drew the vital distinction between consumption and production; between the use of wealth and the creation of wealth. In the long run, *"The Power of producing wealth* is infinitely more important than wealth itself," he argued.

American businessmen have been roundly criticized for short-term thinking; for being more concerned with making the annual report look good than considering where the firm will be ten years from now; for being more concerned with current profits than long-term market share as is the practice with many of America's overseas rivals. This can in part be blamed on the kind of thinking, espoused by Ricardo and the other classical economists, which permeates business schools and business publications. Businessmen may also feel financial pressure to behave in this manner, but those in government have no such excuse. National leaders have a duty to think strategically. They have been entrusted to make policy for a country whose existence is presumed to be perpetual. By its actions, government should work to counter the pressures that foster short-sighted thinking in the private sector, as is the case in those foreign states renowned for their success in the world market.

Hatred of Government or Sovereignty?

At the core of classical liberalism is hatred for government. It is this anti-statist bias that attracts so many modern conservatives to its creed.

It should be noted, however, that in the nineteenth century the bloated and intrusive welfare state which conservatives deplore had not been instituted. National security was the main activity of kings and cabinets. It was military preparedness, great power diplomacy, and empire-building that liberalism attacked in language that would warm the heart of any New Leftist. In classical liberal circles, according to historian Bernard Semmel, "Strategy, any plan for exerting or projecting military or naval power, was ipso facto wrong."

Those modern conservatives who adopt classical liberal doctrine in the belief that they have discovered a legacy left by a school of allies should ponder the actual priorities of these nineteenth-century activists. As Semmel observes, by the end of the century the Radicals were abandoning laissez-faire to embrace new social programs in an effort to win votes away from the conservatives who were promoting a program of national renewal:

> They acted to block labor support for a neo-mercantilist Tory policy by promising such reforms as old-age pensions and sickness and unemployment benefits...to enlist the interest of the trade unions against the alternative use of available tax revenues for armaments.

The same pacifist motives were at work among French liberals. Jean-Baptiste Say felt that in regard to national security "far from protecting it, a great military apparatus is what most jeopardizes it." He held to the fashionable view that fleets and armies invited wars rather than deterred them. Back in England, James Mill thought that war is where "the ruling few always profit at the expense of the subject many," but he believed the days of strife were over. Writing in 1821, Mill claimed:

> There is, in the present advanced state of the civilized world, in any country having a good government and a considerable population, so little chance of civil war or foreign invasion, that, in contriving the means of national felicity, but little allowance can be rationally required of it.

Any problems remaining, Mill would refer to an international court of arbitration. Like nearly all liberals, Mill believed that while a nation could have economic connections anywhere in the world, it had no legitimate political or security concerns outside its own borders.

Economics was to be separated from politics, wealth from power. Free trade meant non-political trade; a commerce of peoples replacing the rivalry of nations. Jeremy Bentham, for example, wanted to replace "offensive and defensive treaties of alliance" with "treaties of commerce and amity." Thomas Paine, finding that "war is the system of Government on the old construction.... Man is not the enemy of Man," listed among his revolutionary proposals that all warships be converted into merchant vessels. J.B. Say called for an end to the diplomatic corps, arguing that "it is not necessary to have ambassadors. This is one of the ancient stupidities which time will do away with." They should be replaced by consuls whose function would be to promote free trade.

These changes were advanced as part of the process of liberating individuals from external constraints on their actions. Liberals viewed people as equal individuals, not as members of particular national states. Civil society's only valid activity was the protection of individual rights; the nation-state had no independent status or mystical nature to which individuals owed any allegiance or duty that entailed any sacrifice of narrow self-interest. There would be no *national* interests, indeed no *international* relations—only "citizens of the world" going about their private affairs. Yet for the general population it was certainly a delusion to believe that as individuals they could still triumph if the nation they inhabited failed. An expanding society provides far more opportunities for individual advancement whether in business, science, the arts, or public service than does a society in decay. History is filled with stories of the decline and fall of nations, empires, and even entire civilizations. These have not been considered liberating experiences to be recommended to others.

Many liberals believed their ideal world could be brought into existence merely by an act of will. Frederic Bastiat, who is Ronald Reagan's favorite economist and whose works are still popular with modern libertarians, argued in 1849 that France should be a model for the world by both adopting free trade and by disarming unilaterally. "I shall not hesitate to vote for disarmament," he proclaimed, "because I do not believe in invasions." Bastiat continued:

> If the emperor Nicholas should venture to send 200,000 Muscovites, I sincerely believe that the best thing we could do would be to receive them well, to give them a taste of the sweetness of our wines, to show them our stores, our museums, the happiness of our people, the mildness and equality of our penal laws, after which we should say to them: Return as quickly as possible to your steppes and tell your brothers what you have seen.

Bastiat did not bother to mention how he would get the Russians to return to their steppes if they did not wish to go. Nor was this an academic question given France's problems over the next century with "visiting" Germans.

Cobden and the Setting of the British Sun

Bastiat was influenced by Richard Cobden, the leading champion of free trade in England and a tireless worker in the anti-imperialist and anti-war movements. Indeed, in 1842 he stated, "It would be well to engraft our free trade agitation upon the peace movement. They are one and the same cause." A "Little Englander," he hoped that free trade would destroy the British Empire as each colony and dominion formed stronger economic ties outside the empire than within it. "The Colonial System," he argued in 1835, "can never be gotten rid of except by the indirect process of free trade which will gradually loosen the bonds which unite our colonies to us by a mistaken notion of self-interest." Under free trade, Cobden opined, the colonies:

> ...will be at liberty to buy wherever they can buy cheapest, and to sell in the dearest market. They must be placed in the same predicament as if they were not part of His Majesty's dominions. When, then, will be the semblance of a plea for putting ourselves to the expense of governing and defending such countries?

By the end of the century, this liberal argument had come full circle with writers such as Norman Angell arguing that the empire should be liquidated because it no longer paid for itself, as other nations enjoyed an ever larger share of its trade.

As an economic determinist, Cobden would not have understood the ties of heritage and culture that rallied people in Canada, Australia, New Zealand, India, South Africa and the United States to England's side in the world wars. Yet free trade took its toll on the strength of the British and imperial economy; for under its sway, even though "the sun never set" on the world's largest empire, London never integrated its holdings into a balanced and secure base for economic expansion. By the dawn of the twentieth century, only one-fourth of the imports into the British Isles came from the overseas empire. Meanwhile, the United States supplied more steel to the empire than did England (an important statistic given that 60 percent of British investment in the empire was in railroad construction, a major user of steel). Indeed, prior to World War I, both the United States and—more significantly from a political standpoint—Germany surpassed England as industrial powers, by developing large and protected domestic markets augmented by advantageous trade agreements. Despite the rhetoric of liberals, the record shows that no nation reached the first rank of industrial power, or managed to stay there by adopting free trade.

The industries that formed the core of the British economy in the nineteenth century, textiles and steel, were developed during the period 1750–1840—before England abandoned mercantilism. Britain's lead in these fields held for roughly two decades after adopting free trade but eroded as other nations caught up. Britain then fell behind as new industries, using more advanced technology, emerged after 1870. These new industries were fostered by states that still practiced mercantilism, including protectionism. In the late 1800s, Britain ran large and consistent deficits in merchandise trade. It came to rely on revenues from shipping, insurance, and banking, and on income from overseas investments rather than industrial exports to keep the current accounts in the black.

By the 1880s, even some liberals were worried; prominent commercial lawyer and judge, Lord Penzance, asked: "Will the lion always possess his share? Does that not depend on how he conducts himself?" He went on to warn:

> The advance of other nations into those regions of manufacture in which we used to stand either alone or supreme, should make us alive to the possible future. Where we used to find customers, we now find rivals....Prudence is not alarm, and prudence demands a dispassionate inquiry into the course we are pursuing, in place of a blind adhesion to a discredited theory.

Hamiltonomics

Across the Atlantic, American statesmen had a different agenda than the classical liberals. Their goal was not to fragment an empire but to build one; to unite thirteen former colonies into a nation that could expand across a continent and develop its abundant resources. One of the seminal documents of American history is the "Report on Manufactures" written in 1791 by Alexander Hamilton, Secretary of the Treasury in President George Washington's administration. In it, Hamilton laid out the economic foundation of the new republic: balanced growth between the industrializing north and the agricultural south. Each section would be the best customer of the other. "Ideas of contrariety of interests between the Northern and Southern regions of the Union are as unfounded as they are mischievous" he declared. "Mutual wants constitute one of the strongest links of political connection."

The Constitution embodies this thinking. Article 1, section 10 removes the power to regulate interstate commerce from the states, thus creating a large internal market free of local barriers. This had been the dream of the seventeenth-century mercantilist Jean-Baptiste Colbert for France, but he had been unable to overcome the resistance of provincial interests. It was the dream of Friedrich List for Germany. And it is the dream of those who have put together the Europe 1992 economic union. Yet creating a large market is not an end in itself; it is to serve as a base for economic growth by the nation's business community and workforce. The Founders knew what Swiss historian Gabriel Ardant has generalized for all Western nation-states:

> We must not conceal the fact that the awareness of belonging to a nation depends to a degree upon the satisfaction that individuals derive or hope to derive from community life. In this respect, in contemporary industrial societies, we must attribute a very great importance to economic growth.

In pursuit of economic growth, Article 1, section 8 gives Congress the Power to regulate commerce with foreign nations, including the enactment of tariffs on imports. Section 9, however, prohibits the levying of taxes on exports. The clear purpose of treating imports and exports differently is that the former are to be controlled, the latter encouraged. James Madison, speaking at the constitutional convention, defended tariffs as necessary for "revenue, domestic industry and to procure equitable regulations from other countries." All three of these functions have been obscured in recent years.

Hamilton's report advocated a protective tariff, fearing that without import controls the southern states would turn to England and France for industrial goods rather than to the northern states. The lure of foreign trade with Europe could pull the Union apart. This nearly happened in the Civil War when the Confederacy turned to its overseas trading partners for aid. There was a wide-spread belief that "King Cotton" was so vital to the British textile industry that London would intervene on Richmond's behalf. Britain did provide aid to the Confederates that brought them to the brink of war until Union victories persuaded them that the rebellion was a lost cause. Interestingly, Cobden and his fellow liberals opposed British aid to the Confederacy on moral grounds, lecturing unemployed textile workers about how the abolition of slavery in the Southern states was worth the disruption of their jobs by the Union blockade on cotton shipments.

It was only after the war that the Hamiltonian strategy of a protected domestic market was fully implemented and the south was integrated into the national economy.

That foreign trade is still a divisive element is demonstrated by the fact that today a majority of American state governments maintain "economic development" offices in Tokyo where deals are negotiated on the basis of supposed state or local advantages even though such agreements may undermine the future of the U.S. national economy as a whole. In the absence of a comprehensive national policy, Tokyo has been able to play states and local communities against each other, winning huge concessions in taxation, financing and public services—gaining American subsidies for Japanese expansion.

Hamilton had read Adam Smith, but he did not believe free trade served the needs of the United States. Even before the revolution was over, he had written his famous "Continentalist" essays in which he stated, "There are some who maintain that trade will regulate itself [but] this is one of those speculative paradoxes...rejected by every man acquainted with commercial history." Richard B. Morris in his biography of Hamilton observed that his "brand of conservatism meant holding to the tried and proven values of the past, but not standing still....He could scarcely allow government to stand inert while the economy stagnated or was stifled by foreign competition."

Another of Hamilton's biographers, Forrest McDonald has argued that:

> While rejecting laissez-faire, however, Hamilton was emphatic in his commitment to private enterprise and the market economy. Primarily this commitment was moral, not economic. Hamilton believed that the greatest benefit of a system of government-encouraged private enterprise was spiritual—the enlargement of the scope of human freedom and the enrichment of the opportunities for human endeavor.

Hamilton's plan was to create an environment within which Americans could attain the highest levels of success; not merely sit on the sidelines as foreign entrepreneurs made the key decisions affecting the future of the nation's economy.

Thomas Jefferson initially opposed Hamilton's trade and industrial policies. As an agrarian, Jefferson was quite content to let the factory system, which he envisioned in terms of dirty smokestacks and urban slums, stay in Europe. Writing in 1785, Jefferson said, "Were I to indulge in my own theory, I should wish (our states) to practice neither commerce nor navigation but to stand, with respect to Europe, precisely on the footing of China. We should avoid wars and all our citizens would be husbandmen." Not a wise choice of comparison given that China would soon be carved into foreign spheres of influence by the industrial powers. Jefferson as President had attempted to implement several of the fashionable liberal notions about foreign affairs. He laid up most of the Navy, replacing what had been the best built and most heavily armed frigates in the world with tiny coastal gunboats which he thought were less provocative. He reduced the diplomatic corps. When British warships impressed American seamen he resorted to economic sanctions in the belief that the benefits of trade were so great, denying them to an enemy would force concessions. But following the sobering experience of the War of 1812, Jefferson changed his views. Writing to J.B. Say in 1815, Jefferson argued for a new industrial policy including tariffs:

> The prohibiting duties we lay on all articles of foreign manufacture which prudence requires us to establish at home, with the patriotic determination to use no foreign articles which can be made within ourselves without regard to difference in price, secure us against a relapse into foreign dependency.

The Hamiltonian program became the party line of the Whigs before the Civil War and the Republican Party afterwards. "By the election of 1880 protectionism virtually equaled Republicanism," states historian Tom E. Terrill in his book *The Tariff, Politics and American Foreign Policy 1874–1901*:

> The GOP, which included champions of industrialization and the spiritual heirs of Hamilton and Clay among its factions, naturally took up protection....The Grand Old Party could respond more positively to the needs of industry.

At the beginning of the twentieth century, as the United States became the world's leading industrial power, Theodore Roosevelt exclaimed, "Thank God I'm not a Free Trader." And Henry Cabot Lodge wrote an approving biography of Hamilton claiming that Hamilton's case for a protective system in support of "industrial independence and the establishment and diversification of history" had never been overthrown.

In contrast, the Democratic Party has been the home of a succession of groups hostile to industry: populists, socialists, environmentalists. In the nineteenth century, the Democrats tried to sell free trade on the grounds that imports would lower prices for the working man. However, the GOP held the votes of industrial labor because workers knew that they had to earn their pay before they could worry about how to spend it. Woodrow Wilson raised the peace issue when he made free trade the third of his "Fourteen Points" proposed to create a new world order after World War I. However, his efforts were not persuasive either at home or abroad.

As the first true "war of production," World War I served to confirm the validity of mercantilism for most practical statesmen. Even in England, the home of the free trade ideology, a serious rethinking of policy was triggered by the war. In 1917, the Imperial War Cabinet adopted a resolution calling for a system of trade preference within the British Empire, arguing that:

> The time was arrived when all possible encouragement should be given to the development of imperial resources, and especially to making the Empire independent of other countries in respect of food supplies, raw materials and essential industries. With these objects in view the Conference expresses itself in favour of:
>
> > (1) a system by which each part of the Empire....will give specially favourable treatment and facilities to the produce and manufactures of other parts of the Empire.

However, after seventy years of free trade, England's decline had progressed too far to be reversed, though some improvement was possible. In 1913, 80 percent of the imports to the British Isles came from outside the Empire. By 1938 this foreign share had been reduced to 61 percent. And non-Empire imports had been cut from 22 percent of England's GNP in 1913 down to 10 percent by 1938. Yet England still found its industrial base inadequate in the face of the revived threat from Germany under Hitler. Without the support of American finance and industry, England would have found itself bankrupt in 1942.

Today's New Mercantilism

This discussion of the historical roots of today's free trade philosophy is relevant on practical as well as intellectual grounds. As the British economic historian Charles Wilson has noted, the move towards a new mercantilism has accelerated in most of the world, the result being the "tendency of international trade to revert to conditions which in some ways resemble those of the seventeenth century rather than those of the nineteenth." The oil shocks of the 1970s started this trend, but it has been reinforced by the aggressive commercial policies of Japan and the East Asian "mini-dragons," and has been further advanced by the formation of the giant, united European economic bloc. The collapse of communism in Eastern Europe has opened a new world of intense competition between American, West European and Asian firms which cannot be isolated from their political-diplomatic ramifications.

The object is not to suspend trade, but to manage it in ways that support the advancement of the national economy. Just as arms control agreements do not automatically produce peace and security; trade agreements do not automatically produce jobs and profits. It is all in the details.

The wise policymaker knows that the game of international economics is competitive in the fullest meaning of the term. While there can be mutual gains from particular transactions, trade overall can be very asymmetrical in its effects, producing losers as well as winners. In a whole host of strategic economic sectors, the expansion of one nation's market share comes at the expense of the share held by its rivals. Since no people can live beyond their ability to produce, the battle is for control of the most productive industries and for a position from which future technological advances can be made. The United States, with the world's largest domestic market, a skilled work-force, and an established techno-industrial base, has every inherent advantage in this global contest. It only needs leaders in government who understand that the game is being played for very high stakes.

Of most concern to the United States has been the rise of Japan as a high-tech industrial rival that has also converted its trade surpluses into a substantial financial position in world capital markets and in banking. The policies of Japan's giant trading companies are reminiscent of those formed during the mercantilist era when statesmen like the French minister Jean-Baptiste Colbert compared his *Grandes Compagnies* to "armies" attacking the economic foundations of rival nations. Colbert believed that, "commerce is a perpetual and peaceable war of wit and energy among the nations." His use of the word "peaceable" is somewhat misleading; Colbert's mercantilism served a very militant policy of expansion under Louis XIV.

The penetration of the American market by Japanese products once again demonstrates the success of mercantilist practice against free trade theory. Charles F. Doran, an international relations professor at John Hopkins University, has noted that, "Japanese trading success is dependent upon access to markets more open than its own."

> Japan's giant trading companies concentrated the bulk of their operations at home; the jobs they created were Japanese jobs; the income they generated were taxed by the Japanese government....Part of the miracle of post-war Japanese economic growth was attributable to the capacity of the Japanese trading company to transfer, through trade, profits and jobs from abroad to the home economy.

Having established this firm domestic base, Japanese businessmen were then able to expand into other overseas operations.

The main factor that explains the success of this strategy is the free trade policy followed by the U.S. in the 1980s. Over the 1981–87 period, Japan's overall current account balance moved from a deficit of $11 billion to a surplus of $87 billion. Of that $98 billion swing, over half is attributed to the expansion of the U.S.-Japanese merchandise trade deficit from $10 billion to $60 billion. The U.S. has the most open market in the world and Tokyo has rushed to exploit it. As a 1990 Brookings Institution report on *Japan's Unequal Trade* concluded, "Evidence from a variety of measures identifies Japan as a nation with a peculiar trading pattern....Japan simply does not import manufactured goods." In 1988 Japan's trade surplus in manufactured goods was $178 billion. The report's author, Edward P. Lincoln dismisses the "creative attempt" by Japan's apologists to attribute the pattern to comparative advantage, finding that:

> The examples of barriers—both formal and informal—and the incidence of negotiating problems with Japan are so widespread that a conclusion of normality is difficult to sustain.

Unfortunately, Lincoln's suggested remedy is for Washington to persuade Japan to surrender its advantages by adopting free trade! Such is the liberal mindset. Yet would it not make more sense for the U.S. to adopt a successful strategy than to expect Japan to knowingly adopt a failed one?

This is what separates the Brookings analysis from that of Professor Doran. Doran's primary concern is not trade but the larger process of the rise and fall of nations. It is not so much the dollar value of the U.S. trade deficit, but the concentration of imports in strategic and high-tech fields such as computers, machine tools, and vehicles. Like most students of this process, he has concluded from history that "Economic considerations have to a large extent determined both the periodicity and the amplitude of the power curves of states."

The collapse of nations and civilizations is usually thought of in terms of cataclysmic events such as defeat in war. Yet such dramatics are only the climax of a much longer process; the result of decades of gradual economic decline often accompanied by domestic turmoil or political paralysis. The formal shifts in territory and institutional dominance are merely the surface phenomenon that ratify the underlying balance of power. The more decisive changes take the form of indirect control of external resources and industry, land and people through trade and investment—the factors that create the balance of power.

The term "commercial empire" is far from obsolete. In the 1980s, Japanese government circles began to talk about creating a "Comprehensive Security System" to control the sources of raw materials, food and fuel that Japan imports. Yoko Kitazawa, writing for a 1990 United Nations University project on Pacific Basin development, concluded that the plan "aims at achieving its objective by integrating the overseas investment structure of Japanese enterprises into a totally Japanese-centered system." The plan involves moving basic processing industries to Third World states, mainly in Asia, to take advantage of cheap labor, local resources and lax pollution standards. World demand has slowed for these industries since the 1970s, so Japan's strategy is to cut costs to maintain a competitive edge in America and Europe. Final product processing, where the real profit is made, will remain in Japan. The steel industry will also stay in Japan as it is tightly integrated with the automobile, shipbuilding, and electric power industries. Also remaining in Japan will be the new high technology export industries which the government will actively support and protect.

Another key element of this plan is to break Japan's dependence on American food imports by shifting to Japanese-owned farms in Brazil, Indonesia, and other third world countries, thus removing a source of U.S. economic leverage. This is a plan based very much on the age-old precepts of mercantilism: an industrial structure and international division of labor set not by the "invisible hand" of the free market, but by strategic planning in Tokyo to insure that the largest gains will go to Japanese firms and that these gains will be secure from outside interference. Kitazawa has termed this a "counter-revolutionary new international economic order."

There is no comparable American consensus on the nation's future economic strategy, let alone a plan of action. Leaders in government, business and the media cannot seem to get beyond the desire for a "level playing field." Yet this term trivializes the issue. This is not some schoolyard game where it doesn't matter who wins or loses. It is a struggle to control the world's wealth and resources, markets and territory; to provide for future generations and for the security of the nation. By defining the issue as one of fairness rather than outcome, the free traders have already steered thought into a dead-end channel.

The objective is not to either stifle or promote trade. Trade is a means, not an end in itself. Every great nation has engaged in trade; but those that have benefitted have used trade to enhance the strength of their own economy. They have not surrendered their sovereignty to the traders; they have managed trade so as to advance their own interests in the face of rivals who are trying to do the same. The composition and direction of trade is thus more important than its volume.

This is how the balance of power turns. New powers arise which eventually convert their economic gains into political and military power. The older power then suddenly finds that it no longer has the strength to prevail against overt challenges. Such a change in the balance of power is seldom due to the energetic actions of the challenger alone. More often than not the challenger's victory was only made possible by the failure of the older power to respond while it was still in a dominant position. The leaders of the older power were either blind to the developing threat, preoccupied with internal affairs (or simply apathetic to external events); or so overly optimistic in their assessment of the margin of safety available that they failed to act until it was too late. Leaders are seldom so irresponsible as to simply not care about the outcome of such contests, though that is the reckless advice being pushed today by the free trade lobby.

The Conservatives' Puzzle

Free traders never learn from history because they intend to transcend the past. Their doctrine is based on ideology, not analysis or experience. It is a leap of faith predicated on the notion that the world has or is about to assume a new order. A "world without borders" will replace "nationalistic fetishes" to use two frequent liberal phrases. Yet a review of the last five centuries reveals that those making this prediction have been proven wrong time after time. Free trade is a true sophistry; an idea that sounds plausible in theory but which proves fallacious in practice. It has been consistently associated with the decline of nations at the hands of their more cunning rivals. Yet its appeal continues because its advocates, like the ancient Sophists, couch their rhetoric in terms of unlimited progress and a basic revolution in human affairs. But wise and practical statesmen should know the difference between dreams and reality.

Unfortunately, the Bush administration is pushing hard for free trade as part of yet another "New World Order" that will supposedly break with the past constraints. This policy, minus the slogan, was actually implemented almost a decade ago under the Reagan administration with results which have so far been ominous. It was pushed by Secretary of State George Shultz and Treasury Secretary James Baker, both of whose backgrounds are rooted in a transnational corporate culture. They were backed by the many libertarian academics who flocked to Washington in the 1980s. Shultz often explained that "trade liberalization ....has sharply reduced the importance of national borders in economic affairs." Shultz, Baker and other spokesmen filled their speeches and state papers with references to "the global economy" as if the world were already unified as a single harmonious system.

That such naive statements could usher forth from an administration that had shown such a profound understanding of the ideological and military aspects of the Cold War aptly demonstrates the fallacy of treating economics as an autonomous variable in the world system. The disturbing question is why so many conservatives, who otherwise consider themselves nationalists and realists, accept such statements if couched in economic terminology when they would reject them out of hand in any other context—recognizing their roots instantly as utopian and dangerous.

It remains a fool's gamble to bet that this time the free traders have finally got it right. A sober look at the world reveals a globe divided into competing nation-states showing considerable political, cultural and ideological diversity. Nationalism, often supported by militant religious feelings, continues to be a powerful factor. The Persian Gulf War showed not only the continuing clash of national interests and the utility of armed force, but also that wars are still fought for economic objectives, in this case the control of oil. Economics cannot differ fundamentally from the broader political environment which defines how the world is organized. There is no *global* economy, only an *international* economy as has been the case for centuries. For U.S. policy to continue along free trade lines in a world that scorns its assumptions is to risk more than the country can afford to lose.

8

From Cottage to Work Station....
And Back Again: The Family
and Home Education

Allan Carlson

In a recent essay, Kentucky farmer and poet Wendell Berry describes the now dominant relationship of schooling to family:

> According to the new norm, the child's destiny is not to succeed the parents, but to outmode them. The schools are no longer oriented to a cultural inheritance that it is their duty to pass on unimpaired, but to the career, which is to say the future of the child. [H]e or she is educated to leave home. School systems innovate as compulsively and as eagerly as factories. It is no wonder that, under these circumstances, educators tend to look upon parents as bad influences and wish to take the children away from home as early as possible. And many parents, in truth, are now finding their children an encumbrance at home, where there is no useful work for them to do, and are glad enough to turn them over to the state for the use of the future. The local schools no longer serve the local community; they serve the government's economy and the economy's government.[1]

These observations by Mr. Berry are generally true, yet we are in the midst—or is it the cusp?—of a revolution in which hundreds of thousands of American parents are choosing not to educate their children to leave home, but to educate them *at* home. In 1970, the practice of home education could be found, of course, but mostly among scattered eccentrics, often tied to the counterculture, or among special cases such as American families living overseas. In 1995, over one million children in the U.S. studied primarily at home, and the number has grown rapidly in recent years.

For an historian, the obvious question becomes: Why now? To gain a full answer, we much reach back 150 years into the American past.[2]

Before 1840, the vast majority of Americans—over 90 percent—lived on farms or in small villages: the life of the cottage. While many adults had a specialized trade, most households aimed at—and commonly achieved—self-sufficiency in food, clothing, and other essentials. Families commonly preserved their own meat and vegetables and prepared their own meals. They spun and wove their own cloth; they sewed their own clothing. They made the chairs they sat in, the candles that gave them light, and they either walked or rode their own horses and drove their own wagons. Even many so-called "urban" families of the day kept a cow, a few pigs, chickens, and a kitchen garden.

As one historian has phrased it, these Americans raised and educated their children to succeed them, not just to succeed. By age five, children were active participants in the work of the household, as were elderly or unmarried kin. Husbands and wives were bound together in a partnership of home-centered work; they specialized in tasks, to be sure, but each needed the other to create the self-sufficient home, which they believed to be essential to their dignity and liberty. Divorce was out of the question. Children were everywhere, with the average family counting seven. Family loyalties rested not only on love and emotional companionship, but also on need: wife and husband, child and parent were functionally intertwined. These household economies operated on the principle of sharing: from each according to his or her ability, to each according to his or her need.

Charlotte's Web

This American world began to change, about 1840, as industrialists harnessed the logic of the vision of labor to the steam engine and to finance capital. The results included a considerable increase in productive efficiency; an accelerated output of goods such as wheels, shoes, and clothing; and a sharp lowering of their costs relative to the work of cobblers, tailors, smiths, and other displaced craftsmen. Decentralized, small, family-held enterprises gave way to large, joint-stocked, limited-liability firms. What economist Joseph Schumpeter has called "the creative destruction" of modern capitalism was creating material prosperity and destroying the household economy.

Although families could now purchase an array of cheaper consumer goods, the price this new freedom exacted was the surrender of productive family functions such as candlemaking, food processing, and weaving to the industrial sphere. It also meant moving the family production of goods, normally uncounted, into a cash nexus, here it would be counted and transformed into profit (and, later, into taxes as well).

The employer in the factory had no obvious economic reason to consider family ties in labor questions. Some, then as now, felt a moral obligation to pay heads of households a "family wage," sufficient to support a normal family at home. But the immediate interest of employers lay in keeping wages low and the pool of potential workers large. Wives, husbands, and children competed against each other in the sale of their labor, driving wages downward, to the level of individual subsistence.

In this new order, the home became separated from the factory and the office, a revolutionary shift in human living patterns. People now worked in one place—what we would someday call their "work station"—and slept in another. With mothers and fathers pulled out of the "cottage," the care of children became a social question; again, something altogether new in human affairs. Time for tending the cottage garden or the family cow disappeared, and families were forced to enter the market to buy all of their food. In general terms, the ownership of productive property such as land and tools gave way to a reliance on cash wages and factory-produced goods. Economic loyalties were no longer rooted in family relationships, but increasingly owed to the employing firm, which was, after all, the source of the cash needed for subsistence.

In 1898, the feminist economist Charlotte Perkins Gilman concluded, with glee, that home production had already been reduced in most urban families to but three functions: cleaning, cooking, and early child care. There was reason to believe, she added hopefully, that this trio would also be industrialized in the new twentieth century, and she envisioned an antiseptically commodified future of fast-food restaurants, commercialized day-care centers, and professional cleaning services that is disturbingly familiar.[3] We have been snared in Charlotte's web.

"In Which the Father Has No Competence"

During this fateful (if not fatal) century, 1840 to 1940, the modern social-welfare state took form as it, too, claimed nurturing functions that had throughout human history belonged to the family. The first and most important of these was education. Beginning in the 1840s, in the same time and place as early industrialization, the common school movement, backed by compulsory education laws, took children out of the home for moral and practical training. Established in Massachusetts under the tutelage of Horace Mann, the movement in its early years aimed at the indoctrination of immigrant Catholic children into the liberal Unitarianism of the Boston elite. After the Civil War, the New England system would be imposed on the defeated South, as a tool of political reconstruction. By 1900, the movement adopted the sentimental, atheistic socialism of John Dewey and his colleagues at the Columbia Teachers' College.

The consistent goal was state control of children. As one turn-of-the-century school inspector in South Carolina explained, "The schools exist primarily for the benefit of the state rather than for the benefit of the individual. The state seeks to make every citizen intelligent and serviceable."[4] More recently, Princeton University sociologist Norman Ryder has described (appropriately enough, in the *United Nations Bulletin on Population*) the basic challenge posed by state schools to the family: "[State] education of the junior generation is a subversive influence....The reinforcement of the [family] control structure is undermined when the young are trained outside the family for specialized roles in which the father has no competence....Political organizations, like economic organizations, demand loyalty and attempt to neutralize family particularism. There is a struggle between the family and the state for the minds of the young." In this conflict, Ryder continues, the state school serves as "the chief instrument for teaching citizenship, in a direct appeal to the children over the heads of their parents." The public school also is the medium for communicating a "state morality" and a state mythology to replace those of family and religious faith.[5]

This aggressive social-welfare state captured other family functions as well. For example, the years near 1840 also marked the advent of the American legal concept of *parens patriae,* or "the parenthood of the state." Twisting ancient English chancery law to new purpose, a Pennsylvania court used the term to justify the seizure and incarceration of children, over the protests of families, when the natural parents were deemed "unequal to the task of education or unworthy of it."[6] Reform schools, the "child saving" movement, the juvenile-justice system, and the vast child abuse and neglect apparatus all grew, ruderally, out of the *parens patriae,* representing as it did the family's surrender of its protective functions to the state.

Child labor laws, despite their benign appearance, further expanded the modern state's socialization of children's time. Parents' control over the training and future of their children, advocates said, must be subordinated to the higher interests and superior wisdom of the government bureau. Again, the family retreated.

The creation of state-level pension programs, and ultimately of the national Social Security system, erased other basic features of the family economy: security between the generations and care of the ill and infirm. Until modern times, grown children and other relatives provided security and support to elderly persons, particularly the indigent and the invalid. Adults bore an obligation, moral as well as social and legal, to care for their own; they also knew that their security might depend someday on the children they had reared and on the example they had set in giving care to their own parents. New systems of state pensions and health insurance shattered these security bonds between the generations of a family. Indeed, since the state now funded pensions and nursing care through general payroll taxes, the incentives toward childbearing actually reversed. A person would be ahead if he avoided children altogether: "let others raise the children who will support me in my old age" became the new and ruthlessly correct logic.

So the modern state and the industrial sector grew side by side, strange allies in constructing a new way of life on the wreckage of a family-centered world. The supposed opposition between industry and government, a theme underlying much of our standard political mythology, was—so far as the family is concerned—mere illusion. Applying a rough metaphor, the state and the factory might better be viewed as two jackals quarreling over the carrion of the natural family and the gobbets of its shattered economy.

From Fertility to Sterility

During those one hundred years 1840 to 1940, we can also chart a steady decline in the quality of American family life. Divorce—virtually unknown at the beginning of this period—showed a distressing increase. The average age of first marriage, for both men and women, climbed as well, as the practical logic for entering a marital union weakened. Most dramatically, the birth rate steadily declined, from an average of seven children per family to about two by the early 1930s.

There is direct evidence here of cause and effect. For example, demographic historians have shown that the spread of state schooling was a principle cause of family shrinkage. Data from 1871 to 1900 reveal a remarkably strong negative relationship between the fertility of American white women and an index of public school expansion, a bond evident even in rural streets, where children were still worth something, economically speaking. Indeed, for each additional month that rural children spent in a state school, the average size of affected families declined by twenty-three children.[7] This is the most direct evidence that I have seen of how state education literally consumes children.

The crisis of the family, did not go noticed or unlamented. A family advocate named Ralph Borsodi described the situation in his 1929 book, *This Ugly Civilization:*

> The large family is [now] an economically handicapped family. Every additional child is merely an additional handicap. In the family of today the children, the aged, and the home-staying women are on the liability side of the family balance sheet; only the actual moneymakers are on the asset side. Hence the family of today tends to restrict the number of its children; to shift the responsibility for caring for its aged relatives to public institutions; to drive even the wife and mother out of the home into moneymaking and to place its infirm and crippled members in hospitals of various kinds.[8]

With a keen eye, Borsodi also saw how the modern position of children as "economic catastrophes" for families must lead to ever more contraception, abortion, and sterilization. Family renewal, he said, could come only if families became functional again, with the home rebuilt as an "economically creative institution." He even understood that education would be the key to restoring "normal family living" in productive households. But at this critical point in his argument, Borsodi's confidence in the family failed, and he called instead for "superior men" to impose family values by gaining control of existing government schools.[9] Another careful diagnostician who wrote careless prescriptions.

Such voices, however wise, did not carry. More characteristic were writers such as Arthur Calhoun, who concluded in his influential *Social History of the American Family,* first published in 1917: "American history, consummates the disappearance of the wider familism and the substitution of the parentalism of society....[Children now pass] into the custody of community experts who are qualified to perform the complexer functions of parenthood ....which the [natural] parents have neither the time nor knowledge to perform."[10]

"Organization Man" and "Household Engineer"

Startlingly, family renewal of a sort actually did come in the middle decades of the twentieth century, roughly from 1940 to 1965. In light of the accelerating family decline of the prior century, the statistics from the 1940s and 1950s are truly astonishing: the average age of first marriage fell to historic lows (twenty for women; twenty-two for men) while the proportion of adults who were married soared; the divorce rate after World War II declined by 50 percent; and the birth rate surged ahead 60 percent, with average completed family size shooting from 2.3 children in 1940 to nearly four children in 1957. It is imperative that we understand what happened in this remarkable period, both the original sources of renewal and the causes of ultimate failure.

The first source of family renewal was, I believe, a strengthened "family age" culture. Since the 1840s, eccentric business leaders, labor unions, reformers, and religious theorists had struggled to blunt the pressures of industrialism on the home through creation of a "family wage," delivering an industrial income to male heads of households adequate to sustain a family. Their proudest achievement was the liberation of many married women from toil in the factory, so that they might care for the home and children and so prevent the full industrialization of human life. To be sure, such a system did rest on intentional job and wage discrimination against women: the widely accepted argument was that women workers deserved only an "individual" wage, since they usually had no dependents or worked only to supplement a husband's income.

Wartime regulations in 1942 ended direct wage discrimination against women: equal pay for equal work was basically achieved by 1945. But for another twenty years, "job segregation by gender" more than compensated for this. Women workers crowded into so-called "women's jobs"—such as clerk typist or nurse—that invariably paid less than "men's jobs," and the "wage gap" between males and females actually grew. As Nobel Prize-winning economist Gary Becker has shown, this sort of change should be associated with more marriages and more births, which is just what occurred.[11]

Public policy contributed to family renewal. Tax reforms in 1944 and 1948 created a strongly pro-family U.S. tax code. While marginal tax rates were high, the personal exemption was set at $600 per person, roughly 18 percent of median household income. In effect, the progressivity of the federal income tax was offset by family size. Congress also introduced "income splitting" in 1948, giving a strong incentive to marriage and placing a real financial penalty on divorce. Through these reforms, legal marriage and children became a citizen's most valuable tax shelters. Meanwhile, federal housing subsidies for families grew dramatically. Tax benefits included the exemption of both imputed rent and mortgage interest from income taxation. Subsidized VA and FHA loans were restricted by custom and regulation almost exclusively to young, married-couple families.

A third factor was the revival of family-centered religion. The fertility increase in the late 1940s was largely the consequence of new marriages and a "catching up" on babies deferred during World War II. But something else occurred in the period after 1950: a deliberate return of large families of four or more children. This was particularly true among American Catholics. In 1953, only 10 percent of Catholic adults under age forty reported having four or more children, virtually identical to the 9 percent for U.S. Protestants. By 1958, the Protestant figure was still 9 percent, but the Catholic figure had more than doubled, to 22 percent. Amazingly, these new large families defied a law of sociology: they were concentrated among the better educated, with the greatest increase among Catholic women with college degrees. The fertility increase among Catholics also was positively associated with weekly attendance at Mass. In short, it could be fair to label this real U.S. "baby boom" largely a "Catholic thing."

Fourth, the militarization of society played an indirect role in family renewal. Instead of demobilization after victory in World War II, as had happened after all other U.S. wars, Americans entered a Cold War and sustained a large peacetime standing military throughout the 1950s and early 1960s. For a majority of American males, military service became a common experience, and the conformity and obedience learned there seems to have translated into conformity in the civilian domain, as so-called "organization men" settled into family life.

And fifth, *intellectuals* lent their support as well. Harvard University's Talcott Parsons, the era's most influential sociologist, celebrated the "upgraded" family system of the 1950s, which he called the "compassionate family," focused on the "personality adjustment" of adults in the suburbs.[12] In the field of psychology, John Bowlby set the tone by stressing the importance of a full-time mother for children, particularly infants.[13] And the discipline of home economics reached the peak of its influence, as it sought to give content to the title 'household engineer."

This reorganized U.S. family of the 1950s—whether in the sociologists' image of "an organization man" married to "a household engineer" in a "compassionate marriage" focused on "personality adjustment" in the suburbs or in the alternate image of fecund well-educated Catholics—was a unique and partially successful effort to restore family living in a modern, industrialized environment. But it passed quickly. Statistics from the 1965–80 period—the "baby bust"—tell the tale:

The marriage rate for women, ages twenty to twenty-four, fell a stunning 55 percent; the divorce rate soared by 125 percent; the birth rate tumbled 46 percent.

What caused this rapid collapse of the "traditional family" of the 1950s? (Or, viewed another way, this return with a vengeance of the long-term trends?)

The obvious cause was the reversal or collapse of the social forces that had nourished family renewal a quarter century earlier. To begin with, the conformist America, born in a patriotic militarizing of society, was a casualty on the rice paddies of Vietnam.

More importantly, Christianity failed in its family-sustaining tasks. Sermons on "chastity" and "fidelity" disappeared from many Protestant pulpits. So-called "mainline" Protestant leadership actually went on the attack, with a National Council of Churches panel in 1961 labeling marriage an "idolatry" and embracing the "sexual modernist" agenda of opposition to population growth, support for readily available abortion, and the promotion of contraception.[14]

The Roman Catholic laity, meanwhile, grew disoriented in the wake of the Vatican II conference of the mid-1960s, opening divisions on family and sexual issues that have only widened. Given the widely publicized disputes among Catholic theologians over sexual issues, it appears that the Catholic laity threw in with the modernists. Even the large family ideal vanished. In 1967, 28 percent of "devout" Catholics still planned to have five or more children; by 1971, less than seven percent did.

For a time, American Mormons—Latter-Day Saints—carried the philoprogenitive banner. While fertility tumbled elsewhere in the U.S. during the "baby bust" of 1965–80, the birthrate rose in Mormon-dominated Utah, as did average completed family size. Doctrinal constancy was the key; the church remained committed to the desirability of large families. After 1980, however, Mormon fertility fell, apparently due to the flow of wives and mothers into the paid labor force. Large families could no longer be easily sustained on one income, while the two-career family could scarcely accommodate many offspring. The Catholic and Mormon examples suggest that religious enthusiasm, by itself, can defy modern economic incentives for only a generation or so, before being vanquished by material pressures.

Government action further eroded the "fifties family." The addition, as an afterthought, of the word "sex" to Title VII of the Civil Rights Act of 1964 became, by 1970, the chief tool used by the state to eliminate job segregation by gender. This brought to an end the nation's informal "family wage" system and increased the pressures and incentives in favor of the outside employment of married women. From the Tax Reform Act of 1963 through the Tax Reform Act of 1986, Congress and the Presidency dismantled the pro-family/pro-marriage tax code created in the late 1940s, sharply increasing the relative tax burden of married-couple families with children. Government welfare programs transferred still more income from families based on marriage to families created through "out-of-wedlock births." Payroll taxes rose dramatically, their full regressive weight falling on younger families. Meanwhile, regulatory changes stripped federal housing subsidies of their pro-marriage/pro-family biases in favor of "non-discrimination." By the early 1980's, the evidence even suggested that these subsidies were encouraging divorce and discouraging procreation.[15]

A legal revolution commenced in the courts, where the rights of individuals triumphed almost completely over duties toward family and community. The old liberties were out, replaced by "no-fault divorce," "children's rights," "the right to privacy," and "abortion on demand."

During the 1960s, leading intellectuals turned on the recently praised suburban "companionate" family, excoriating it as "distorted," "sexist," even "fascist." As fear of global overpopulation increased, U.S. political leaders mobilized support for restrictions on fertility. In fact, the 1972 Presidential Commission on Population Growth and the American Future declared an open policy war on the American "three child family system."[16]

But there were deeper sources of failure as well, suggesting that the restored family of the 1940–65 era—what most call "the traditional family"—was in fact a fragile creation, a jury-rigged structure lacking a real foundation.

One subterranean force was the mounting sexual revolution. The mobilization of 28 million young men and women for war and factory work in World War II shook traditional restraints on courting and sexual behavior, changes ably summarized in John Costello's *Virtue Under Fire*.[17] Alfred Kinsey's infamous volume, *Sexual Behavior in the Human Male*, appeared in 1948, raising pornography to the level of popular science.[18] The first issue of *Playboy* arrived on the newsstands in 1953. American film makers quickly moved from the light portrayal of seduction in *The Moon is Blue* (1953) to the extramarital entertainment of *The Apartment* (1960). While most statistical measures of family life suggested a new wholesomeness, rates of illegitimacy and venereal disease climbed at a startling pace in those supposed "happy days."

More important, though, was the failure of this family renewal to return functions or tasks to the household in any meaningful way. The field of "home economics," rather than focusing on the restoration of productive tasks in the home, tended instead to emphasize the informed consumption of factory-made goods (as in "whiter than white toilet bowls"). Except among Roman Catholics, public education enjoyed nearly complete triumph in the America of the 1950s, with somewhat healthy local variations progressively snuffed out through school consolidation and bureaucratic controls. Driving the new medium of television, advertising whetted ever more appetites for consumer goods, and by its very nature discouraged all forms of family self-sufficiency. The "small farm" sector of American agriculture in the South and Midwest, still alive even if deeply troubled as late as 1940, collapsed in these years, pouring a last great stream of economic refugees into the cities and factories.

Unleashed sexuality and expanded consumerism: these, rather than the authentic family and the household economy, were the true winners of the 1950s. When fresh ideological challenges to the family arose in the following decade—from feminists, militant atheists, neo-Malthusians, and members of the New Left—the "traditional family" cobbled together in the 1950s simply vanished, as smoke in a gust of wind.

G.K. Chesterton had diagnosed the deeper linkage of perverse sexuality and consumerism back in 1934, for the brilliant, short-lived (why must those adjectives so often meet?) journal, *The American Review.* He wrote: "Now the notion of narrowing [household] property to merely enjoying money is exactly like the notion of narrowing love to merely enjoying sex. In both cases an incidental, isolated, servile, and even secretive pleasure is substituted for participation in a great creative process; even in the everlasting Creation of the World."

Real Hope

Yet the story does not end there. Despite the corruptions of greed and lust, the death that is the wages of sin, the desire to create and live in families cannot ever be extinguished. To be "familial" is part of the nature of human beings. The urge is planted in our genetic inheritance, in our hormonal systems, and in our souls. Humans can try to deny this aspect of their nature, but the desire still returns, in some way, to each generation, opening again the possibility for renewal.

And so, in the 1970s, specific events—federal efforts to regulate public and parochial education, Supreme Court decisions blessing the sexual revolution, the breakdown of discipline and standards in local schools, the appearance of books by John Holt and Raymond Moore encouraging a radical break with existing patterns of learning[19]—inspired a critical mass of pioneers to bring their children home. They soon discovered that, indeed, there's no place like home for the education of their children. These pioneer families also found that the nature of their relationships changed, almost overnight. No longer mere consumers sharing the same roof and television set, they had become members of a learning enterprise who needed each other and who profited— morally and practically—from each other.

A key production function lost to the family over a century ago— education—had come home, and the results were at once remarkable and predictable. Most of these families began to find ways to bring our functions home as well—gardening, food preservations, or a family business—and they tasted the satisfactions of an independence unknown to several American generations. Home educators created a demand for appropriate books, curricula, and software; and new, family-held, "cottage businesses" blossomed. Families shared with friends and neighbors the fruits of their newfound independence. "Home schooling" communities emerged locally, regionally and nationally.

What once was lost has now been found. Viewed from the historic angle, homeschooling is the most promising effort at family institutional reconstruction undertaken in America during the last 150 years. The family, born to and naturally residing in the symbolic "cottage," then uprooted and ravaged by factory and state, has found a path back to its true home.

But take warning: in shaking free from standardization, statism, and consumerism, and in seeking true liberty and autonomy, homeschooling families pose a basic threat to the existing regime. Bringing the children home endangers both the government's economy and the economy's government, to use Wendell Berry's phrases. When you bring your children home, not only do school districts lose money; the gross national product also goes down, as schooling passes back into the uncounted realm of home production. This joint threat explains the legal obstacles and denunciations that home education faces in every state, and now from the federal leviathan as well. As the number of homeschooled children climbs beyond the "insignificant" category—and it probably now has—the dangers will only grow. These realities explain the vital need for organizations such as the Home School Legal Defense Association and the National Center for Home Education, which provide the legal, political, and intellectual shelters under which home education might survive during this critical phase of growth.

A second, and more subtle, danger ties in what my colleague Thomas Fleming calls the American genius for spoiling something fine and true by transforming it into a standardized, marketable lifestyle. Home educators must resist that temptation. While maintaining high standards, they must encourage the eccentrics and experimenters. They need to patronize the cottage businesses, even if the short-term price advantage appears to lie with the mega-store. They must defend the creative anarchy of home education from all efforts at centralization: whether from state, industry, or homeschoolers themselves.

Residing again in the family cottage, we can relearn certain philosophical truths. Two hundred years ago, Adam Smith, the philosopher of liberty, wrote: "Domestic [or home] education is the institution of nature—public education is the contrivance of man. It is surely unnecessary to say which is likely to be the wisest."[20] Closer to our time, the leading American sociologist Robert Nisbet, wrote:

> We can use the family as an almost infallible touchstone of the material and cultural prosperity of a people. When it is strong, closely linked with private property, treated as the essential context of education in society, and its sanctity recognized by law and custom, the probability is extremely high that we shall find the rest of the social order characterized by that subtle but [powerful] fusion of stability and individual mobility which is the hallmark of great ages.[21]

And so a cultural revolution has begun, with home education at its heart, aimed at recovering learning standards, family integrity, and sustainable community. The next five to ten years will be crucial in determining this revolution's success or failure. Will it be the catalyst for rebuilding family-centered communities, or merely another passing social oddity, brilliant and—tragically—brief?

Notes

1. Wendell Berry, *What Are People For?* (San Francisco: North Point Press, 1990), pp. 162–164.
2. The discussion in the following paragraphs receives fuller treatment in my *From Cottage to Work Station: The Family's Search For Social Harmony in the Industrial Age* (San Francisco: Ignatius, 1993).

3. Charlotte Perkins Gilman, *Women and Economics: A Study of the Economic Relations Between Men and Women as a Factor in Social Evolution*, ed. Carl N. Degler (New York: Harper & Row, 1966 [1898]), pp. 235–317.

4. W.H. Hand, "The Need For Compulsory Education in the South," *Child Labor Bulletin* 1 (June 1912): 79.

5. Norman Ryder, "Fertility and Family Structure," *Population Bulletin of the United Nations* 15 (1983): 18–32.

6. *Ex Parte Crouse*, 4 Wharton, Pa. 9 (1838).

7. Avery M. Guest and Stewart E. Tonay, "Children's Roles and Fertility: Late Nineteenth Century United States," *Social Science History* 7 (1983): 355–80.

8. Ralph Borsodi, *This Ugly Civilization* (New York: Simon and Schuster, 1929), p. 351.

9. Ibid, p. 432.

10. Arthur W. Calhoun, *A Social History of the American Family: From Colonial Times to the Present*, Vol. III (New York: Barnes and Noble, 1945 [1917]), pp. 165–75.

11. Gary S. Becker, *A Treatise on the Family* (Cambridge, Mass.: Harvard University Press, 1981), chapter 5.

12. Talcott Parsons, "The Normal American Family," in *Man and Civilization: The Family's Search for Survival*, ed. Seymour M. Farber (New York: McGraw Hill, 1965), pp. 31–49.

13. John Bowlby, *Maternal Care and Mental Health* (New York: Schocken Books, 1950).

14. Elizabeth Stell Genne and William Henry Genne, eds., *Foundations for Christian Family Policy: The Proceedings of the North American Conference on Church and Family*, April 30–May 5, 1961 (New York: National Council of Churches, 1961).

15. See George Sternlieb and James W. Hughes, *America's Housing: Prospects and Problems* (New Brunswick, N.J.: Center for Urban Policy Research-Rutgers University, 1980), pp. 58–66.

16. *Population Growth and the American Future: The Report of the Commission on Population Growth and the American Future* (Washington, D.C.: U.S. Government Printing Office, 1972), pp. 12–15, 98, 103–04.

17. John Costello, *Virtue Under Fire: How World War II Changed Our Social and Sexual Attitudes* (Boston: Little, Brown, 1985), p. 9

18. Alfred C. Kinsley, Wardell B. Pomeray, and Clyde E. Martin, *Sexual Behavior in the Human Male* (Philadelphia: W.B. Saunders Co., 1948).

19. John Holt, *Teach Your Own: A Hopeful Path For Education* (New York: Delacorte, 1981); and Raymond Moore, *School Can Wait* (Provo, Utah: Brigham Young University Press, 1975).

20. Adam Smith, *The Theory of Moral Sentiments* (New Rochelle, N.Y.: Arlington House, 1969 [1759]), p. 326.

21. Robert Nisbet, *Twilight of Authority* (London: Heinemann, 1976).

9

Is the American Experience Conservative?

M. E. Bradford

Having recently urged upon my fellow conservatives the necessity for attaching a priority to distinctions and definitions, having in the *Intercollegiate Review* insisted that such exercises are properly antecedent to all questions of policy, I was obliged to attempt a reflection on this theme when Mr. Hart proposed it to me. Moreover, this place, this institution, devoted as it is to the immediate prudential questions which confront a government, session by session, day by day, is an appropriate setting for my remarks on the American experience read large. For there is no useful prescription to be drawn from that record if it cannot be translated for the here and now—brought forward for application to the ongoing business of the Republic. Therefore I am gratified by both the assignment and the context, and will try to bring the two together according to the canons of rhetoric given to me by my Southern preceptors, men who honored no deracinated truth and tolerated no speech indifferent to the audience for which it was prepared.

A great part of the answer to the question posed by my title can be drawn from the beginnings of the American experience in the first 150 years after the coming of Europeans to the shores of North America. Furthermore, the reason that my response is (with certain qualifications) in the affirmative is because we had such a good start and drew so much momentum from the pattern established here with the creation and development of the various colonial regimes which were antecedent to our composite independence as a nation. Recognition of this pattern as continuing to operate among us to this day is a predicate to my conviction that the original American experience was on the whole conservative in both its essential and its accidental properties.

It is fundamental to my understanding of the American heritage that our earliest forefathers, those who settled the country, came here to acquire land and the status of freeholder—distinctions of the first order of importance in the European societies which they left behind them. They sought what the law still calls "real property," recognizing the connection between personal self-respect and such ownership—the impossibility of achieving the status of freeman or citizen without "locating the blood." Professor Bernard Bailyn's recent work in *The Peopling of British North America: An Introduction* and *Voyages to the West* has begun to document much of this process, to tell us of the motives of the colonists who came this way in great expectation. In a word, they were, once Americans, determined to be from somewhere—an objective not adequately described by speaking of the commercial spirit of America or a commitment to economic liberty. I so maintain even though Americans did generally prefer free enterprise—once they had their land grants and a political structure which allowed them to protect such holdings. It is to my point that the Swiss, though not at that time rich, had their own domain. This fact was not separable from their status as a nation of freeholders, or from the respect which they enjoyed among the nations.

Another feature of colonial American life which planted among us the proper inertia toward liberty and order, under God and in law, is the failure of a series of English kings to set up among us a peerage, a viceregal court, and a fully established church—an episcopacy. These omissions, combined with the remoteness of final authority and the disposition of the Crown to leave British America to govern itself in all things local (everything apart from imperial economic and foreign policy) had guaranteed that we would not have here the kind of revolution against unearned privilege and violations of conscience that tore European society apart in the seventeenth and eighteenth centuries. We were republican long before we were a Republic. In British North America life meant self-defense (the citizen soldier) and work. It subsumed a connection between worth and effort. The gentleman, as we know the social norm and archetype from colonial times, was here no merely decorative creature; instead, he was an honored figure whose lofty status was matched by his function and large responsibility, encouraging the kind of deference which gives to excellence its social utility. Louis B. Wright describes persuasively the respect for energy and application exhibited by the original Virginia aristocracy in his *The First Gentlemen of Virginia* (1940). And what he says about the Old

Dominion before 1800 will apply just as well in Connecticut, South Carolina, or Massachusetts.

The moral and emotional bases for Jacobin *ressentiment* are not present in such societies—especially when they embody so much in the way of opportunity. Captain Smith told the lazy courtiers at Jamestown that they had a choice of useful labor—or death. In Massachusetts, a Dionysian and promiscuous mixture of Christians, Indians, and bears, the borderland culture of the trading post and the uncivilized fringe, was replaced by the authority of Captain Endicott and the General Court—with the Maypole cut down and (in Hawthorne's story of the event) those capable of reformation brought back to a situation within the bonds of society, where they could join in the adult business of marching "heavenward." Medieval life may have been properly summarized in the image of a dance. But life in early America was better represented by less festive symbols—such as hunting, planting, and harvest, militia muster, and group prayer.

Finally, because the American colonials grew to embody their own version of a civil order, rooted in an adumbrated version of the English past but without regimentation according to some plan for their political development, it is natural that they have left among their descendants a hostility to the idea of teleocratic government: the kind of government defined by large purposes, not by its way of operating. Managed development (as opposed to "benign neglect") is the idea that helped bring on the American Revolution. After 1763 and the conclusion of the Seven Years War, it was a decision of the Grenville administration that the North American colonies be governed according to a policy, so that they might sustain some of the costs of defending their borders: that they might serve the interests if Great Britain while serving their own. It was from the first recognized as an innovation, a change in management style and in constitutional arrangements. Patriots saw in it not a legitimate exercise of authority but a first step in a design to repeal most of their inherited freedoms—their "way of life" (see Professor Bailyn's *The Ideological Origins of the American Revolution*)— binding them "in all cases whatsoever."

The most English feature of this established order (until 1776) was its legalism, its devotion to Constitution and common law, and its dependence on lawyers—men of law, who grew to be numerous and important in the colonies as soon as they were well organized and began to make money. Nothing could be more natural than that, once we lost one Constitution and Bill of Rights through revolution (an act based on elaborate constitutional arguments), we established another Constitution and another Bill of Rights—or rather, several of both—as soon as possible. There is no way of understanding the origins of our fundamental law apart from eighteenth-century English constitutionalism, than which there is no doctrine more conservative.

Add to all of this wholesome patrimony a religious inheritance and my explanation of the conservative influence of our colonial origins is rounded out. We have been a troublesome and unruly people from the beginning, with little respect for legitimate authority and little appreciation for the keeping of right order or public service. We have exhibited a blind faith in technology or commercial ingenuity and in the value of mere mobility, with an indifference to what is providentially given in the human condition which no Christian can contemplate without uneasiness and regret. Too often Americans have said in their hearts, *"Sicut eritis dei"* ("You shall be as gods"). And as a people we have deceived ourselves in this way from the first, have been too inclined to believe that we can always have what we want. Also, outside of New England, our Fathers were a religious people without much in the way of a clergy or many churches. On the frontier and in the backwater, settlers were prone to forget the Apostles' Creed and, like their descendants, were religious without the necessary minimum of doctrine.

Professors Robert Bellah, Martin Marty, and Cushing Strout, however, are mistaken about the prevalence of a merely civil theology among early Americans and about the importance of Enlightenment apostasy— a favorite myth of the scholars—in the generation which put its special mark on the future destiny of the nation: in our character as an independent people. Irreligion is spawned in comfort, not in the struggle to survive the frontier. What exploded in the Great Awakening had been there among the people long before, an undercurrent of fierce devotion, a hunger for personal grace dispensed in large draughts and for the communion of saints. For in the great empty spaces they had walked the lonesome valley, been there by themselves, and needed to testify as to their good fortune. Christian faith discouraged in the Fathers the modern tendency to seek salvation in politics, protected a private sphere, and discouraged men from divinizing the state. Moreover that faith has minimized among us for 360 years the influence of the besetting virus of modern politics, the power of envy to make amity almost impossible— has done this by making the most of our lack of a "privileged" class.

Perhaps its generically American influence on the composite self of the Republic has been in sustaining our national disposition to be sanguine. I have been slow to recognize that there was anything conservative about belonging to the party of hope. One of the lessons of the Reagan years is that avoiding the sin of despair with an optimistic conviction that hope and life go together is not the same thing as hard millenarianism and is, furthermore, definitely American—not being so burdened by history that we cannot climb up to the shining city. If we remember what makes despair a sin and an insult to our Creator, we will better understand why American conservatism is often cheerful—and is that way for religious reasons.

Though we conserve its results, the American Revolution was not, strictly speaking, a conservative event. We made war against the common blood and we rationalized our decision outrageously. But we came out of the experience committed to distrust remote, arbitrary, and indifferent authority—authority which imposes its agenda on our local affairs. And we also came out with our assorted civil myths intact—the myth of the New Jerusalem so dear to New England, the myth of the New Eden over the hill, the myth of transplantation, of a new Troy in the West—which the South continued to cherish, despite its complicity in putting much of our colonial history (and England with it) behind us. And finally, the myth of the middle states, of the man who can invent himself, which I connect with Philadelphia and *The Autobiography of Benjamin Franklin.* All of these myths helped us to preserve more or less intact the momentum which we drew from the colonial experience, and to carry it westward to fill up the land. The West, *per se,* as opposed to the idea of getting there, had no corporate myth; and therefore, as our literature tells us, the presocial, state-of-nature men and women found there they brought to an end as swiftly as they could, in their civilizing labors calling to mind the quip of Gouverneur Morris of New York, the son of the patroon, that if men really wished to enjoy full equality, they should "live alone"....in the forest, "where natural rights are admitted." Or rather, live there, outside the protections of society, until the wolves arrive.

Our version of self-realization has been (unless we get too abstract about it, which is uncharacteristic) what Richard Weaver calls a "social bond individualism"—a freedom which has as its precondition the survival of an anterior social identity. Whatever we have said of the Declaration of Independence, we begin to think socially by assuming that specific rights are determined by an individual's place in the social reality, are measured by that reality and are inseparable from it. Even in Pennsylvania, a community (in colonial times) proud of its chartered independence of Crown influence, when the Proprietor during the Seven Years War refused to pay his share of taxes to defend the lives of people on the frontier, Pennsylvanians were shocked and turned away from their devotion to the family of William Penn, calling for a royal governor. All of our social myths presupposed some version of the corporate life—that man is a social being, fulfilled only in the natural associations built upon common experience, upon the ties of blood and friendship, common enterprises, resistance to common enemies, and a common faith. Since, unlike the European nations, our identity is not part of the order of large causes, we are obliged to grow, to develop by stages with the social bond, working upwards, out of local things, communities, neighborhoods, and private associations such as clubs and church congregations; and as the colonial and early national eras provided us with that material, out of history and through law, which in the Constitution we have made into a sovereign.

What I have said thus far explains why I believe that our original American heritage was fundamentally conservative—up through about 1819. Our subsequent departures from that original heritage have been more or less the measure of what is not conservative about American society in our day. Yet the example of our cultural beginnings has continued to retain authority among us, even as we have failed to follow after it, resulting in a dialectic of several alternative Americas with which we are quite familiar.

I cannot on this occasion comment upon how that long and dramatic story may be organized by the question put to us today. We might speak here of our disposition to periodic fits of simplistic moralism, of our national passions for bigness, change, and mobility, or about the earlier dispersal and present decline of the family as an institution—none of it evidence of conservatism, but part of the inheritance of young Americans growing up today. There is nothing conservative about the throwaway society, about social restlessness and frenetic land speculation, or about the kind of individualism which loses track of its grounding in the belief that each person has an immortal soul. By giving the subject matter a reading slightly more Southern (and more Protestant) I could spin out an alternative construction of the evidence organized in Russell Kirk's *The Roots Of American Order* and Daniel Boorstin's *The Americans: The Colonial Experience, The Americans: The National Experience,* and *The Genius of American Politics*—books for which my admiration is a matter of record. It is not a task even for outlining in the compass of a brief address. I reserve it for another time.

But I will speak of one development within the American experience which, at this point in our national history, threatens to subvert our particular version of the conservative heritage. From my reaction to alterations in the meaning and authority of equality as a term of honor among us, you will easily infer my reaction to many other changes in the American value system which have occurred within my lifetime.

Equality is the right of any people (the "we" speaking in the Declaration) to expect their government to provide them the protection of law—security for person and property and hope of a future: a notion which has been with us from settlement times. Also there is the equality which results when the law is the same for every citizen who comes before it—at least within the limited sphere of its operation—and the kind of equality which results from having no privileged class of people who are to some degree above the law. The latter condition had resulted in the kind of *ex officio* equality of which Charles Pinckney spoke in the Great Convention—an equality coincident upon the general availability of free land and the shortage of labor, to say nothing of the institutional arrangements established here by the mother country. This equality is full of opportunity but is not "equal opportunity." The influence on these shores of various European ideologies introduced here since 1789, coupled with the development among us of a distinctive (and alienated) intellectual class, a class which owes its exalted status to being protectors of its vision of equality, has brought us away from being a nation of citizens *de facto,* coincidentally, "almost" equals before the law, toward the kind of systematic equality of condition which is the necessary precondition of equality of opportunity. (On this process, see my old friend, the late John East, senator from North Carolina.) Even among conservatives this axiomatic passion for equality and equal rights, based on a misunderstanding of our heritage from the Declaration of Independence and from the Christian promise that grace is available to all, threatens to swallow up our reverence for law, responsible character, moral principle, and inherited prescription.

All of us know that it is "disreputable" and explosive, even in a Washington governed by Ronald Reagan, to complain of egalitarianism, except for the strictly economic variety, which we manage to resist. However, if we continue to commit ourselves to this confusion, not one component of that rich patrimony of which I have spoken can survive. For equality of condition *qua* equality of opportunity will fill in all the valleys and pull down the hills—create a power which in the name of all good purposes will be enabled in all cases whatsoever to do with us as it will. Those who wish to follow that broad road to Zion (or perdition) may do so. There is a safety and an accommodation with the powers in such choices. You will not be called "insensitive" or "racist" or "cruel." Your position will be respectable (as the enemy defines respectability), but not conservative, as any of our Fathers would have understood the word. For we can only do as the Left does if we begin all of our deliberations concerning practice and policy with its fundamental premise in the place of our own.

10

Trollopes in the Stacks

Thomas Fleming

Nineteen ninety-two, if not quite an *annus mirabilis*, was a year "crowded with incident," as Lady Bracknell would say. The reprecussions of Gorbachev's fall, the hot war in Bosnia that took the self-congratulatory edge out of the end of the Cold War, and the rise to power of Flem Snopes's grandson illuminated American television sets during the dinner news hour.

For most of us, these incidents touched our lives, if at all, for only a few moments a day. They took place somewhere in the fairyland of images where heroes and antediluvian monsters still do battle for the principle of one man/one vote. Most Americans seemed more interested in the goings-on of the white-trash British royalty that get paid handsomely for misbehaving. In America, where we used to be, according to Fisher Ames, "too poor and too proud to acknowledge a king," our own version of royalty was making even better money, posing for naughty pictures. People who had never been to a bookstore before were standing in line to buy their own copy of Madonna's *Sex*. Some could not wait to get out of the store with their treasure and began tearing off the plastic wrap that sealed the contents against dampness, dirt, and free riders who wanted to look without buying.

America may be taking its time about coming out of a recession, but we still have more money than sense. Some felt cheated of the fifty dollars they paid. Pornography connoisseurs expressed disappointment with the all-too-predictable permutations of body parts, accessories, and animal acts. It is hard to shock us any more, and *Sex* represented a breakthrough only in the sense that the Clarence Thomas hearings were a breakthrough. The filth that used to be confined to the wrong side of town or the Playboy Channel can now appear on CNN and on the *CBS Evening News,* in Waldenbooks and in libraries started with grants from Andrew Carnegie.

Even Christian Americans are jaded, and the sale of a book portraying group sex and bestiality stirred little controversy. Libraries, however, are civic institutions that are generally thought to reflect the values of the community. I do not now how many public libraries decided to purchase *Sex.* Here in Rockford, the director of the public library stirred up predictable controversy by making the predictable decision to buy the book. The library received about twenty requests, offset by 400 letters in opposition. By the rules of American democracy, the ayes have it, even when they are outvoted twenty to one, so long as the ayes represent fashionable opinion.

There was a public hearing at which various people pointed out that the book was pornographic, offended local standards, and possessed no redeeming social value. No one, in fact, defended the book on its merits, but the head of the library (and his supporters) insisted it was a free speech/free press issue, even though what was at stake was not the right to publish or distribute or look at (somehow "read" is not the right verb) the book. The only significant question concerned the proper use of taxpayers' funds. Some sort of compromise was reached—they bought the book but promised to restrict access—but the controversy illustrates certain features of the cultural battle that is being waged at the end of the millennium.

Put aside any consideration of the First Amendment, which was never meant to apply to local matters, and bracket, for the moment, the question of the book's merits or demerits, because the same tired arguments are used everywhere in the battle of the books that is being waged in libraries across the country as concerned citizens debate the appropriateness of teenage sex manuals or the use of the word "nigger" in *Huckleberry Finn.* Both sides in these debates see the library as a powerful instrument that can be used for public enlightenment or abused for moral corruption. The outcome of these battles, so it is believed, determines which side will stamp its image on the community. Will this nation be a Christian America, whose reading is limited to *Heidi, Pollyanna,* and the confessions of Pat Boone, or will it be the open society that reads *Justine, Tropic of Cancer,* and *Last Exit to Brooklyn?* That public libraries were established as educational institutions meant to elevate public taste above both Henry Miller and Pat Boone is almost never mentioned.

I had several discussions with Christians who did not want *Sex* in the library. (It is hard not to repeat Tiny Tim's retort to Johnny Carson, that he wanted to get sex out of the movies and put it back where it belonged—in the home.) When I asked each of them about their other attempts to influence library policy, they told me of previous controversies over questionable books. Had any of them actually asked the library to buy a book? Did their churches request books? Rockford is a heavily Lutheran and Catholic town. Were the works of Luther and Melanchthon available in German (and Latin) or even in translation? What about standard editions of the Church Fathers? St. Thomas? Did the library own a complete set of the Loeb classics (bilingual editions of Greek and Latin authors) or Trollope's novels or the recently published complete edition of Robinson Jeffers? Could one find standard editions of Hume and Locke? Could a freshman at a decent college do a credible term paper on any topic by using the library's resources?

The answer to all of the above is no. American Christians in this age of the world do not care for such things, neither the laity nor the preachers. They are too busy with stewardship, financial planning, and bingo. So long as the library does not positively offend them, they are content to let their taxes be squandered on best-selling novels and books, on rose gardening or travel. Libraries have long since ceased to fulfill their original function of providing good books. They are now media resource centers that are used to facilitate lifestyles. One day a librarian caught my ten-year-old daughter reading a book. The kind lady took her by the arm, led her over to a computer terminal, and taught her to play a video game.

I do not begrudge anyone her rose garden or erotic fantasies. What I do not understand is why libraries should receive tax funds to assist people with their foibles and hobbies. We do not subsidize movie theaters, bowling allies, or exotic dancers. If one were to make a moral distinction between the modern library and "Girls! Girls! Girls!" it would be in favor of the strip joint, where vice is not packaged as culture or civic duty but as a commodity bought on the open market. If people want to read Danielle Steel, they can buy her "books" for a few bucks at the checkout line in the supermarket, and if they have enough money to fly to Paris, they can spend fifteen or twenty dollars on a guidebook.

I agree with the limited objectives of the book-burning fundamentalists who want to purge the libraries of selected filth, but these campaigns are based on the false assumption that there really is a "moral majority" in the United States. There is not. On the contrary, we have only minorities as defined by race, sex, religion, and lifestyle, and each of these minorities has a claim on our cultural institutions. Books in the library, the school curriculum, music on the radio are viewed as so many weapons in a civil war, and in the fighting, whatever sense of common culture we once had is torn to tatters by leftists, racists, decency activists, and civil libertarians. Shakespeare and Sophocles? Both racists, sexists, and classists. Hemingway and Fitzgerald? Anti-Semitic pagan pornographers. Faulkner is a bigot, but James Baldwin is homosexual. Who is left, in the end: Phyllis Wheatley? She is black, female, Christian, and moral. Too bad my ten-year-old daughter writes better.

No good can come of a political struggle over who can read what and where. If each church congregation in Rockford were to request the library to order great literary classics, two things would be accomplished: a large selection of important books would be available for the first time in the city's history, and the library would be unable to waste the people's money on the trivia and filth that are purchased automatically from wholesalers who make decisions for the illiterate acquisition librarians who order but do not read books. If the library refused 100 requests for Goethe or Bishop Berkeley, then it would be time to accuse the library of censorship. But the churches will not do anything like this, because they are not part of any culture that binds them either to the past or to the other minority groups within this society. Instead of working to improve the common culture, they are content to rail against the immorality of the "secular humanists." After decades of efforts to ban nasty books, rate movies, and put warning labels on records, the Tipper Gores of America have contributed nothing, literally nothing positive to our culture. If only we could take all the money wasted on "decency" (including the money sent to TV evangelists) and spend it on good books by living authors. We could dominate the bestseller lists and enable decent writers to earn an honest living outside universities. We would have the beginnings of a cultural counterrevolution that could bypass the corrupt political process and go straight to the hearts and minds of the American natives.

On the left, it was Antonio Gramsci and, to a lesser extent, Trotsky who understood the importance of culture and won the undying affection of New York intellectuals who think that writing book reviews constitutes a serious political act. In the case of Trotsky, at least, concern with culture was on a plane only slightly higher than for the vulgar Marxists (e.g., Mike Gold) who judged literature and art according to simple ideological rules. Fiction, according to this interpretation, was propaganda with a story line. The so-called conservatives who have taken to railing against the culture have followed the Trotskyist line, cannot conceive of a good film directed by a communist, and page rapidly through popular novels, looking for the "family values" that are conspicuously absent in their lives.

This word "culture," as potent a talisman as it is in politics, derives some of its power from the multiple senses in which it is used. We speak of the "Hopi culture," of people who have or have not got culture, and even of bacteria culture. Is there a thread that runs through all these usages or is culture simply one of those words with several unrelated meanings, like "gimlet" (a cobbler's tool, a drink with gin and lime) or "leaves"(departs, more than one leaf)?

The first thing an English speaker thinks of when he hears the word culture is the sense in which Matthew Arnold used the word to mean something like the liberal arts, "the acquainting ourselves with the best that has been known and said in the world." In popular usage, Goethe and Bellini represent culture or, at least, "high culture" as sometimes distinguished from "pop culture."

Anthropologists, however, have appropriated the term to nothing less than the object of their inquiry. If sociology could be defined as the study of "society," then anthropologists, in marking the boundaries of their discipline, devised culture by way of analogy. There are dozens of anthropological definitions, beginning with that of E. B. Tylor, who introduced the word from German. Reaching not quite at random, one might use Paul Bohannan's lucid and elegant formula to illustrate this usage. Bohannan calls culture "a summary of behavioral phenomena" and later elaborates on this theme: "Culture, as it is acquired with the growth of the personality, becomes the *medium* of that personality. You cannot swim without water, and water is the medium of swimming; you cannot paint a picture without paint, and paint becomes the medium for expressing the message of the picture. The difference between culture and personality is the same as the difference between the medium and content of a picture."

There is a wide gap between culture as medium and culture as art, but fundamentally Tylor and Arnold were attempting to describe, if not the same set, then at least overlapping sets of phenomena. Both were influenced by German usage, and in German *Kultur* is seen in its educational aspect. To understand the root sense, however, one has to know Latin (as both Arnold and Tylor did) as well as German.

Latin *cultura* derives from the verb *colere*, which means to till or take care of a field or garden plot. *Cultura* is, therefore, tillage, and in an extended sense it can refer to the care and nurture of various things: fields (agriculture), grapes (viticulture), and bees (apiculture). In English we still speak of culturing pearls or bacteria, but the more relevant and lively derivative word is "cultivate." One can cultivate a field or a taste for good wine and good music.

If the root meaning of culture means something like the fostering or nurturing of growth, what is it that is being grown in the medium of culture, either in the high art sense or in the anthropological sense? Bohannan supplies the answer:

> Into every culture and every civilization, year after year, hordes of uncultured "barbarians" descend in the form of newborn babies. In every society a major—indeed, an overwhelming—amount of social energy, must be spent in making cultured creatures out of this human plasm.... The habits that are acquired by youngsters are part of the culture in accordance with which they are brought up. In one sense, the habits *are* the culture: if all the habits of all the people were changed, the culture would have changed.

The object of culture, its product, are human beings who have acquired the habits that are necessary for life in their society. More specifically, it is their character or (to use a more technical-sounding word) their personality that is formed by the culture.

Some aspects of human culture are, more or less, universal. However, family, law, religion, and art are abstract and generic categories, and the reality of human life is in the gritty details: the bickering among a man's two wives, the judge's wig and the archaic language of the common law, the life-and-death struggles over communion in two kinds or whether one crosses oneself from left to right or right to left. In the case of character, too, there are quasi-universals: the intemperance that leads to murder, theft, and incest, variously defined, is frowned upon, while bravery in war and care for children are generally esteemed. But a brave man of Bohemia or Bali might be regarded as a coward in Montenegro or Texas, and a faithful Irish father who spends most evenings in the pub might not receive high marks among English Methodists or American Lutherans.

Of the catalogue of virtues that occupies so much of Aristotle's *Ethica Nicomachea,* some of them have a familiar ring in English. Courage, truthfulness, and justice can fairly represent what the Greek philosopher was trying to discuss, but it is harder in the case of *megalopsychia,* often translated as "pride" but without any of the negative connotations. This virtue is a greatness of soul, whose opposites are humility and undue vanity. A modern Christian or post-Christian can conceive of a kind of pride that steers a course between Poo Bah and Uriah Heep, but it is hard even to grapple with the classic Greek virtue, *sophrosyne* (temperance, self-control), for which we lack not only the specific word but even the general language and context for a discussion.

Culture, in general, produces character, in general, as well as those universal traits of human nature, but it is specific cultures that form the habits (whose plural is character) of men and women in real societies and give rise to concrete and historically bound conceptions of right and wrong. Change the habits, says the anthropologist, and you have changed the culture; but, says the political reformer, change the culture and you change the habits and character of the people.

Of the various institutions of culture, none is more powerful than religion. By its rituals and according to its rules, the primary stages of life are marked: birth, coming of age, marriage, and death. It is through religion that human beings are joined with their ancestors and their unborn descendants in a communion that is the largest community, and it is through the rites and practices of religion that the dreadful powers of the universe can be pleased, appeased, propitiated. To the pious, sentence of excommunication or a religious curse, because it reaches beyond the grave, holds terrors more fearful than death. The law can take away property and liberty, even life, but churches (or the priests or the gods themselves) have the power of binding and loosing souls.

Christian churches still play an important role in forming the character not just of "Christian America" but also of pagan Europe, where a great many practicing nonbelievers grow up hearing the stories and taking part in the major festivals. De-Christianized Europe is still a province, although much dilapidated, of Christendom. The French film *Cousin, Cousine* pays a cynical, backhanded compliment to the power of Catholic culture by portraying a Parisian family that spends Christmas Eve watching midnight Mass on television, while the cousins are betraying their spouses in the back bedroom.

I do not wish to minimize the importance of formal indocrination, but catechism classes provide nothing more than a shorthand summary of what the child is imbibing from other sources: from sermons, from conversations with parents and other church members, and from learning and internalizing the magic words of creed and prayer. In most Christian societies, the arts of painting, music, and poetry were enlisted into the service of the church. Frescoes and stained glass windows tell the great stories for those who do not read, and sacred hymns use verse and music to convey a message more powerfully than any sermon or list of questions. The history of the church can be traced in the hymns of Venantius Fortunatus, Martin Luther, and the Wesleys, and the first serious music written in what became the United States were the hymns composed by Moravian musicians for their religious communities.

But the most powerful tool of Christian indoctrination, from the very beginning, has been the collection of texts we still call, in English, the Bible. One of the earliest Christian conversion stories is the account of the Ethiopian eunuch who had gone to Jerusalem to worship. On his way back, the Ethiopian, reading the prophecies of Isaiah, was overheard by the apostle Philip, who explained that "He was led as a sheep to the slaughter" was a reference to Jesus.

The Christian character is formed by reading, hearing, and interpreting stories. Jesus himself couched his messages in the form of scriptural quotations and striking parables. Some Christians, from the very beginning, have wanted to purify their faith of the taint of Jewish history, traditions, and "superstition," and one of the most important early heretics, Marcion, based his sect exclusively on Luke and Paul. A Christian purified of Jewish stories and superstitions was the desire of Thomas Jefferson and many other Enlightenment *philosophes*, who regarded the moral teachings of Jesus as statements of universal benevolence and justice.

The Christian ideal, divorced from Jewish tribalism, was Locke and Kant in the form of beatitudes and parables, and that is, more or less, the Christianity of the mainline churches in Europe and the United States. "Great God I'd rather be a pagan suckled on a creed outworn." Half of the worst damage done to the peoples of the world in recent centuries has been inflicted under the banner of a Christian sentimentalism that rips Christ's provocative and paradoxical pronouncements out of context and treats them like a guidebook for everyday life.

It is necessary, always, to keep in mind that Jesus was addressing himself to an ancient tribal people, as parochial, narrow-minded, and bigoted as a Greek polis or a Calabrian village. But, quite apart from the context it provides, the Old Testament gives us a portrait of a "primitive" society, rooted in worship of God and organized according to principles of kinship and clan.

It really should not matter much to a Christian whether the portrait of social life contained in the early books of the Old Testament is historically accurate or a later idealized conception. By accepting these stories as Holy Scripture and in committing them to memory, we are slowly molded according to a patriarchal pattern of life that emphasizes familial integrity.

The "higher" morality of Christianity turns to poison when it is ripped from its solid roots in kinship and nationality. "He that loveth father or mother better than me is not worthy of me" makes sense only in a family-centered culture. Repeated out of context, it is an invitation to break the commandment "honor thy father and thy mother."

The Gospel's injunctions on forgiveness and compassion, uprooted from the solid earth of Judaic law, become an ethic of suicidal defeatism. While it is possible to construct a pacifist/nonviolent ethic out of selected passages of the New Testament, the Old Testament throws a bucket of cold water on such fantasies: Rabbi Jacob Neusner observed last December in *Chronicles* that in the Torah "justice overrides sentimentality" and added that this justice allows room for execution, war, and self-defense.

The real culture of Christendom is international, in preaching "the unity of faith and the bonds of love," but also national, tribal, and clannish in its stories of warring Jewish kindreds who were only unified in their hatred of the Gentiles. A Christian who is not metaphorically a Jew is only a reciter of creeds whose heart and mind have not been nourished on the living record of one nation's love-hate relationship with its God.

Christians, Jews, and Muslims alike, we are all people of the book, and not only because we trace our spiritual ancestry from the Old Testament. To a great extent, our culture is the books we read, mere secular works of history, philosophy, and literature as much as the sacred Scriptures we hear read on holy days. Ultimately, the censorship controversies in America form a skirmish line that marks the boundaries between warring ethical visions. For Christians and Jews, it must be a losing battle, because it is always fought according to the enemy's rules: openness, majority rule, impartiality, notions that are poison to any vital religious tradition claiming to represent the truth.

Unfortunately—and this is cause for more dismal reflections—few Christians today are part of Christendom, that civilization of knives and forks, Dante and Bach. At best, they read C. S. Lewis or Francis Schaeffer. My son once won a gift certificate to a Logos bookstore, and try as we might, we could not find one real book, apart from the Bible, in the whole place.

If Christians want to do something about the moral state of the nation, they might begin by setting their own houses in order. If they feel they really must deal with public institutions, then let them swamp the libraries with so many orders for good books that there will be no time or money for Madonna. But on the whole, they ought to concentrate on setting up their own libraries and filling them with the classics of Christendom. They might proceed to straighten out their wretched seminaries, which, at best, are turning out well-intentioned illiterates. Instead of throwing their money away on expensive video series for teenagers (who uniformly make fun of them), let them establish solid Bible study classes in which the learning of scriptural languages (Hebrew and Greek) is encouraged.

Ultimately, as the existentialists used to insist, each human being, by behaving as he does, is setting an example to the world. If decent and moral human beings care about the culture of the United States, they had better start spending their money on the good books that are being written by living authors who are forced to spend most of their time teaching, instead of writing, in order to feed and clothe their families.

Brighten the Corner Where You Are is the title of a recent book by Fred Chappell. It is good advice, and the best thing my readers could do is to go out and buy ole Fred's books, as well as the books of fiction, verse, history, and philosophy written by our other contributors. If a serious novel sells 5,000 copies, it is a triumph, and a book of verse is a sensation if it sells more than 500. The crazies not only control most of the grant money in America, they also buy most of the serious books. So long as "conservatives" who profess their faith in the free market are content to get their culture from *Masterpiece Theatre* and public libraries, the future will not belong to us.

11

Reconfiguring the Political Landscape

Paul Gottfried

In 1927 Carl Schmitt published *The Concept of the Political*, wherein he set out to explain political life. According to Schmitt, political activity, whether pursued within a system of nation states, Greek *poleis*, or imperial administration, is about the organization people as friends and enemies. More precisely, it is about the organization of those who become allies when confronting shared enemies.

According to Schmitt, political groups are essentially life-and-death associations. What distinguishes political relations from other kinds is the intensity of the bonding involved, in the face of the adversary. Unlike economic or aesthetic enterprises, political constructs create peril for the individual, who stands or falls with his group. They are agnostic and often violent, and were it not for the European state system, by which central governments could monopolize and curb religious conflicts, culture, commerce, and what Hobbes called commodious living would not have been possible.

Nonetheless, Schmitt believed that the weakening of sovereign states had initiated an age of intensified strife and administrative dislocation. This would continue until the Western world could produce acceptable alternatives to the old European order of geopolitically and legally fixed states disposing over their subjects or citizens. Significantly, a number of Schmitt's disciples have advocated regional and populist solutions to the erosion of nation-states. In the European case, the Schmittians' argument for regionalism is that regions are already cohesive and can therefore provide a cultural base for a reconstructed political order. As Gianfranco Miglio has pointed out, historical regions can easily rule themselves democratically because of their residual cultural homogeneity. For Miglio and other European Schmittians, the citizens' self-identity is basic to their capacity for self-rule.[1] Where populations do not share culture and history, so this argument goes, they are less likely to be able to live together as a community and to agree on the collective good.

It is a commonplace that the U.S. is different from European nation-states and their odious ethnic baggage. Unlike Europeans, Americans are praised for letting everyone in and then promoting unity in diversity—although lately programs have had to be developed to "sensitize" people to the presence of diversity. According to a *Wall Street Journal* editorial, the U.S. is based not on a fixed culture or on a "longshared history but on something better, the idea of freedom."[2] Several weeks earlier the same paper had proclaimed this "better idea" to be democracy, broadly understood as openness to new populations. Moreover, Harry Jaffa insists that America was founded on a proposition that all men were created equal and that the acceptance of this proposition should be the basis of American citizenship.[3] Curiously, the American Founding Fathers had different thoughts about this matter. Hamilton, Jefferson, Madison, Jay, and Franklin all spoke out against liberal immigration and warned against admitting into the new republic those who had come from cultures markedly different from the one they were entering.[4]

Another view expressed most forcefully by the followers of Leo Strauss is that the U.S. is a modern democratic republic—one distinct in almost every respect from ancient popular regimes. Ancient republics were indentitarian and organic, anchoring citizenship in heredity and "long-shared history." By contrast, modern republics are meant to protect individual material interests and are indeterminately elastic with regard to size and composition. Anyone could or should be able to become a citizen of a modern democracy which recognizes a common humanity, while also reducing it to a material common denominator. Unlike ancient or premodern republics, liberal democracy is portrayed as an open vessel receptive to ever-changing social and cultural contents.

To anyone familiar with the writings of Thomas Prangle, Allan Bloom, Walter Berns, and other Straussians, these ideas will not seem strange. They are also the lynchpin of Paul Rahe's 1,200-page discussion of ancient and modern republics.[5] The underlying distinction, however, goes back to Numa Dénis Fustel de Coulanges, who dealt with the kind of collective solidarity demanded of Greek and Roman citizens.[6] The sense of civic obligation extended to all things in the ancient city, including the duty to take sides in a fractional war. Greeks who refused to become partisans in civil strife—those who remained *astasiastoi* when their fellow citizens had become fractious (*stasiastikoi*)

—were viewed not as responsible but as unpatriotic, as Fustel points out in a graphic illustration of the duties of ancient citizenship. But modern liberal and democratic theorists have also not been pure atomists—at least not to the extent that contemporary globalists suggest. Contrary to the view of a long popular political philosophy textbook, neither John Locke nor Jean-Jacques Rousseau believed that citizenship in a well-ordered society should be open to everyone. For Locke and Rousseau self-government requires the vigilant setting of limits on who should or should not become a citizen.[7]

Thus, in the *Second Treatise of Government*, Locke is careful to state that once individuals compact to form society, they act "as one body" and through a majority "express a single will."[8] As Peter Schuck and Roger Smith show, even in this most atomistic of social philosophers there is still an awareness of the corporate personality of the body politic.[9] Locke assumes that when individual property holders come together to build society, they create something that can exercise a unified will. But that single will animated by the resolution of individuals is supposed to act in a way consistent with the concerns that bring it into being. It cannot be turned arbitrarily against the lives and property of its founding members or be changed by adding to the political community those not acceptable to the contractees. If such were allowed to occur, then the authors of the social contract would no longer be expressing *their* single will. The society in which they lived would no longer enjoy *their* consent, and it might be necessary for them to make "an appeal to Heaven" (which is Locke's euphemism for revolution) in order to reestablish an accountable society.[10]

For Rousseau, a restrictive concept of citizenship is even more axiomatic, given his coupling of civic life and civic virtue. Rousseau admired ancient Sparta, the Roman Republic and Geneva for teaching selfless devotion to the public good. He identified social corruption with individual greed and cosmopolitan taste. In *The Social Contract* he tried to depict a polity without these flaws. Such a project demands adherence to a civil religion and such overpowering cultural homogeneity that each authorized member of the community knows instinctively what is right for all. In one particularly evocative image, Rousseau shows free peasant-holders gathered under a sprawling oak to deliberate.[11] In this model democracy they are so much alike that for them the common good has become, for the most part, second nature. Laws are unnecessary, and those proposed win immediate acceptance among transparently identical citizens.

Immigration advocates, public administrators and democratic globalists are wrong when they claim to represent America's liberal and democratic roots. Whatever they represent, it is not the eighteenth-century wisdom embodied in the current talk about the U.S. as a universal nation. Nor is there a long tradition of equating democracy with something done by public administrators: with democracy as a managerial activity and not as an exercise in self-government. Much of the recent discussion about immigration underscores this difference in perception. Until the Progressive Era in the U.S. and the implementation of national social democratic policies in European industrial nations, democracy designated the political practice of self-governing communities. This was particularly true of American democracy, which until the twentieth century was only minimally affected by the European Jacobin tradition. By now the change from the older American democratic thinking and practice has been so sweeping that basic questions about the identity of democratic people are no longer permissible. Democracy, after all, is supposed to be about paying taxes, observing sensitivity rules (however they may be defined on a given day) and voting for the office-seekers of two national parties who, unlike bureaucrats and judges, do not really govern. In a *reductio ad absurdum* of this current concept of democracy, Leon Wieseltier chided the poet Stephen Spender for wondering whether self-government requires cultural cohesion of some kind: "Democracy is a discipline to be learned that goes against our common nature."[12] Until recently democracy did mean what Spender was accused of believing it to be—the act of self-government by a people united by culture and history.

On a similar note, Christopher Lasch attacks the wayward American elite that has neither a sense of place nor loyalty to anything beyond career ambition.[13] He attributes the present fragility of the American state to the overthrow of the traditional Western bourgeoisie by New Class social planner. He insists that the term "bourgeois" has been robbed of any historical specificity by being linked to the interests of test-taking yuppies or the economic situation of middle-income earners. What Lasch sees as the historical bourgeoisie were not only the architects of capitalism and urban civilization, and the righteous Calvinists of the seventeenth century, but also the class which brought down the feudal order in alliance with kings and other national sovereigns.[14]

Lasch believes that only blue-collar Americans have not been touched by the treasonous elites, because of their relative isolation from the yuppie gravediggers of traditional culture and morality. Along with other populists, Lasch appeals to Middle American virtue against the entrenched elites. What is not clear is how this will play itself out politically: whether a populist strategy will have any effect other than to relegitimate the present political class as the "spokespersons" for Middle America, the yuppies, the multinationals, and the underclass. There will be cooptation unless populism is joined to a program of political reconstruction—a reconstruction committed to the restoration of effective self-government. This may be possible if done regionally—an organizational idea that seems to appeal to a remarkably diverse group including Gore Vidal, George Kennan, and, most recently, the League of the South. Lasch is correct in claiming that New Class power is linked to globalist projects which demand the blurring of, among other things, regional distinctions. It may therefore be useful to strengthen such distinctions as a counterweight to New Class power. Within politically viable regions there should be controls concerning the franchise, eligibility for welfare assistance and immigration. All this will inevitably enrage the national media and activist judges, and will certainly require substantial constitutional amendment. While the U.S. Constitution presupposes a federalism shared by the federal and state governments, it does not take into account other political units.

In any case, there is a genuine call for a politically decentralized America, refounded on self-government, which is not the same as sensitivity-training, multiculturalism, or having one's life managed by public administrators. The populist revolt Lasch calls for cannot succeed within a friend-enemy grouping established and dominated by the New Class. The federal managerial regime and its largely derivative state organizations will swallow any decentralizing movement which seeks to work with them. Thus, public aid to private schools is not likely to preserve the private character of the institutions being aided. More likely, it will bring them under federal and federally managed state control through anti-discrimination and affirmative action guidelines, both tools of New Class domination.

Both Lasch and Sam Francis have suggested that populists should steer clear of the twin shoals of New Class ruination: a globalized society and a balkanized U.S. They have also identified a sound populist movement with American nationalism, and both believe in a revived American nation state as a populist goal. The question today is whether it is still feasible to uncouple the American nation state from its administrative apparatus and New Class character. Along with Paul Piccone and others, I doubt this can be done. Almost a century of managerial consolidation has taken place in national political life. From the modern welfare state begun in the first decade of the century there has been a steady move toward administrative-therapeutic regime that seeks to interfere with every aspect of life, while becoming inaccessible to popular recall. A rich but depressing literature already exists on America's transition from a bureaucratic state providing social services and engaging in income redistribution to a government primarily concerned with raising and lowering self-esteem and rewarding or punishing citizens as victims or victimizers.[15]

Such a development has set a pattern which may now be impossible to reverse. Unlike Mediterranean parliamentary regimes, the U.S. government is relatively uncorrupt but, alas, remarkably intrusive, and does not have to worry much about traditional liberal or democratic restraints. It enjoys massive media support whenever it expands to deal with insensitivity and social injustice; and if it does not like what the people decide through referenda, it can and does use the courts to quash the popular will. There is, in short, a family resemblance between this managerial government and the Nominalist Deity, who does what He wills save for when He chooses to restrain His will for His own mysterious reasons. The only way the managerial Deity will be deflated is by fashioning a new politics, one that pits the kind of constituency Lasch describes against the current New Class and its allies. This new politics must call for a reorganization of government, one that will allow for the replacement of rule by public administrators and judges with something more closely resembling self-government. This can only happen if the locus of power is shifted toward governing units that have not already been co-opted from above.

Economic and cultural wars may rage, but how they turn out hinges on political questions that are definitely not of secondary importance. The American managerial state has been essential to cultural and social change. Indeed, the entire struggle over expanding rights by proliferating victim groups goes on within the jurisdiction of judges and public administrators who have the power to legitimate or delegitimate claims. Without the government's enforcement of affirmative action and anti-discrimination programs, American universities and the texture of American social and economic life would be significantly different. The cultural wars, to a large extent, result from a critical political development: the replacement of a bourgeois political class, with a restrictive sense of constitutional legality, by the New Class, disguised as experts and policy wonks. It is this new political class which interprets laws and foundational documents and designates the collective enemy: an unreconstructed humanity. It is this Old Adam, identified with sexism, racism, fiscal frugality, the Religious Right, and undemocratic regimes, against which it is necessary to mobilize. According to Robert Nisbet, since World War I and increasingly the 1960s, the American administrative state has prepared its subjects to engage in wars or in the moral equivalent thereof.[16] In mandated crusades against prejudice and insensitivity, the fist of judicial as well as administrative governance has been felt. In Kansas City, Missouri, Rockford, Illinois, and other municipalities, federal or state courts have reorganized school districts, rearranged school classes, and raised taxes to finance these programs. Judges have done these things, without democratic authorization or a declared revolution, because they have decided to inflict their own notions of racial balance on public institutions. Like public administrators, they have come to exercise the prerogatives which among the Athenians defined hegemony: the levying of taxes (*tachsis phoron*) and the universal designation of friends and enemies. Such impositions were considered proper by the Athenians in dealing with subject peoples, though for themselves they decided these matters through public deliberation.

While the liberal Left has cheered *guided* democracy, the "respectable" Right has done little to resist it. This "moderate" Right has benefited from the growing public sector, by taking funds from the CIA and by working in Education, USIA, NEH and other federal departments. It has also called for the further empowerment of Washington bureaucrats, to impress upon the nation's youth "Judeo-Christian," "democratic," and/or "family" values. William Bennett, Michael Novak, and R.J. Neuhaus have added to these accomplishments an even more noteworthy one, plotting the spiritual descent of Martin Luther King from Aristotle and St. Augustine.[17] Other "conservatives" have made comparable archeological discoveries, such as finding the roots of deconstructionism in William of Ockham, by way of Hegel, Lenin, and Hitler. This particular kind of linkage crops up with some regularity in one predominantly Catholic and Anglo-Catholic conservative journal.[18] Traditional disciples of Eric Voegelin make vigorous use of the term "gnostic," while the neocons reach for "anti-Semitic" and "racist," to anathematize those who ask embarrassing questions.[19]

In any case, conventional political conservatives have as little to contribute to significant political change as their New Class liberal competitors for government patronage. Their talk about values in public policy is either cynical or pointless. Public adminstrators are not milkshake machines out of which different colored liquids will come, depending on which ice cream flavor is put in. New Class managers have their own values, and these are often implicit, as Max Weber long ago explained, in the work of rationalizing and homogenizing social relations.[20] Public administrators will not be turned from Joycelyn Elders into Girolamo Savonarola because some ephemeral politico makes a speech on family values. Given their tenure and entrenched power, administrators and judges can and do survive electoral whims and alternating parties.

For all of these reasons, it is necessary to forge alliances among those who are not likely to be invited to join *The Capital Gang*, but who do recognize at least one inescapable fact: that the restoration of genuine self-government requires structural decentralization and, above all, the derailing of the present political class. Without that, it is unlikely that there will be any accountability from insulated public administrators, rotating collectors of patronage, or judicial social engineers.

From much of the available literature, it may seem that populism is an exclusively proletarian and lower middle-class reaction directed against social and economic modernization. Richard Hofstadter popularized this view in the 1960s.[21] According to Hofstadter, populism expresses the anger and fears of socially marginalized groups. On this view, this populists' anti-elitism signifies hostility toward those identified with unwelcome social and cultural change. Populist leadership is equated with the manipulation of popular passions, particulary resentment, and not surprisingly populism is made to illustrate the "paranoid, anti-intellectual style" which Hofstadter claimed to find in American politics. In a recent analysis of French and Latin American populist movements, Pierre-André Taguieff incorporates these interpretations in describing the "liberal-elitist vision of populism." Liberal-elitists "pay special attention to this manipulative dimenision, so that populism can never be anything but a synonym for demagogy, indeed for mass democracy involving rhetoric intervention by a savior."[22] Such an interpretation seems simplistic, particulary when applied to long-standing government. Taguieff notes that critics of the Brazilian leader Getulio Vargas persist in presenting him as a rabble-rouser, implied in the characterization of Vargas as a "Brazilian populist." Such a description ignores the fact that Vargas's rule lasted almost twenty-five years and resulted in the creation of a modern centralized state.

Even more egregious errors abound in the received opinions about populism in the U.S. The holders of these opinions fail to acknowledge two limits on their hasty generalizations. First of all, leading American populists, from William Jennings Bryan onward have not fitted the demonology their predominantly Northeastern academic critics have attached to them. Thus, Senator William E. Borah grew up in populist Kansas in the 1880s and opposed American internationalism, first, as a populist and, later, as a Western Progressive. Along with the Nebraskan Bryan, Borah condemned American imperialism, favored the independence of the Philippines and for many years fought for women's suffrage. He nonetheless drew fire from American anti-Nazis when he tried to block the repeal of the Neutrality Act in 1939. But as Justus Doenecke points out, this had nothing to do with anti-Semitism or xenophobia.[23] Borah was a firm opponent of American military involvement, who believed that privileged business interests and Eastern politicians had deceitfully pulled the U.S. into World War I. He decried the American mobilization of the late 1930s as a repetition of earlier follies. Whether or not Borah was right is beside the point. His populism did not proceed from the pathologies contemporary anti-populists attribute to the objects of their criticism.

Secondly, the appeal to populism is necessarily selective. It is not an attempt to replicate the politics of a past age or of a different culture. Rather, it raises issues earlier populists set out to address, without being mere imitations of them. Accountability in government and the understanding of democracy as meaningful self-rule are both foundations of the present populist renewal. This quest to reinvigorate democracy does not exclude particularity. It does not require the reconfiguration of a decomposed liberalism which characterizes the projects of such self-styled critics of intolerance as Jürgen Habermas and Amy Guttman. Both these "left liberals" call for the establishment of participatory democracy informed by "democratic discourse" in a situation of enforced cultural fluidity. Through *their* behavioral norms and an imposed form of tolerance, Habermas and Guttman seek to make others accept a way of life set up by them and likeminded types. By contrast, true federal populism, can only benefit from cultural unity. It welcomes regional differences that can make possible a nonengineered basis for democratic consensus.

There is no reason that the call for popular referenda, strong local government, and release from remote but intrusive bureaucracies must come out of the social depths. A populist movement can certainly be regionally based, which was true in the American plains of the 1890s as it is in Europe today. The American populists were nationalists in their resistance to foreign military entanglements, but they were also advocates of local and state control of economic and political affairs. Whether this involves the extensive economic regulation favored by Kansas and Nebraska populists or the market economy desired by the *Lega Nord* is a matter of choice for the citizens of a particular region. Public accountability should be the only criterion of a populist economic policy.

In a long critical observation about the populist mentality, Taguieff notes that populists can be either anticapitalist or devoted to the free market, depending on the elite against which they have risen in protest. Thus while French populists of the Bernard Tapie-variety denounce the collusion of public administrators with corporate capitalism, middle-class populists contrast democratic self-expression to social democratic policy. For want of others, Taguieff comes up with two constant features of *bona fide* populist movements: they are antielitist protest forces and they all stress the solidarity and self-identity of an embattled people. Much of this populist protest, Taguieff explains, has now been directed against social democrats; the "antiliberalism" he and other critics associate with populism is shown to be in many cases a reaction to social engineering. Taguieff properly designates the surging populists waves in France, Italy, Austria and the U.S. as "phenomena of post socialism."[24]

One definitional problem with many investigations of populism is the growing irrelevance of liberalism as a polar opposite. In France, the National Front favors an internal free market, while opposing third world immigration and seeking to limit international free trade. In the U.S., paleolibertarians such as Lew Rockwell, Murray Rothbard, and Jeffrey Tucker advocate a total market economy but severe restrictions on immigration and a populist crusade against the "parasitic government bureaucracy." By contrast, recognizably social democratic publications such as the *New Republic*, the *New York Times* and the *Washington Post* support both free trade agreements and a generous immigration policy, even for those without job skills or legal right of residence. The *Wall Street Journal*, which also advocates the same positions, favors less government control of commerce, but is generally comfortable with the American managerial state, give or take a few agencies. In no way do its editorials approach the indignant call for bringing down the federal administrative apparatus, which is characteristic of the populist paleolibertarians.

It is idle to ask which of these sides represents most consistently the "spirit of liberalism." All appeal to a liberal heritage which harks back to an earlier century, yet none stands entirely within it. Some left-liberals, most notably Stephen Holmes and Justice William Brennan, equate the liberal legacy with universality and an expanding list of human rights, but herein lies a problem. Whereas it may be possible to defend the current left-liberalism with odds and ends from Locke or Jefferson, liberals in other ages took political stands that would simply not fit the left-liberal agenda. Indeed, most populist movements embody less what is antiliberal than what self-declared liberals have not wished to transfer from an older liberalism to their own. The combination of debureaucratization, regional autonomy and anti-immigrationism typical of such populist movements as the *Lega Nord* and the Austrian *Freiheitliche Partei* does not indicate "antiliberalism" as such. Rather, it points up positions that today's journalists and academics have carefully removed from their own sanitized liberalism.

Thus opponents of the *Lega Nord* complain that a federal reconstruction of the Italian First Republic will undermine the "anti-fascist educational process" begun with the postwar constitution. This may or may not be true, but has no bearing on what the *Lega Nord* is proposing. Its call for a semi-autonomous regional republic, one featuring free trade and a free market economy, recalls the language and mindset of Italian classical liberals. As Miglio points out, the *zoccolo borghese* on which the league stands is not a company of *lazzaroni*. It consists of those who would have rallied to the liberal monarchy which unified Italy in the 1860s. The *leghisti* are now abandoning, or so they plausibly argue, not a therapeutic experiment in anti-fascism but a "corrupt patron-client regime." It is one that Miglio condemns for betraying the fond patriotic hopes of his Milanese merchant forebears.

Even more pertinent to this discussion have been Habermas's fears that a German political culture not exclusively anchored in his rules of democratic living may return to the Nazi past. Habermas insists that Germans think of themselves as a new people—one created exclusively on the basis of "human rights" and postwar democratic norms. While such ideas may coincide with someone's reconceptualized liberal heritage, very different positions can be drawn from the liberalism of the past. Most continental liberals in the nineteenth century were nationalists and, incidentally, did not hold those generous views on free trade popularized by Richard Cobden and John Bright. In the U.S. the acceptance of tariffs and of severe limits on immigration was the prevalent view of the founders, and one that Jefferson also held and stated. Contemporary liberals would likely gag at this passage from John Jay's reflections on America's providential blessings found in Federalist No. 2:

> With equal pleasure I have as often taken notice that Providence has been pleased to give this one connected country to one united people—a people descended from the same ancestors, speaking the same language, professing the same religion, attached to the same principles of government, very similar in their manners and customs.[25]

Not exactly the idiosyncratic musing of an isolated bigot, these are in fact eighteenth-century commonplaces about the suitability of a people for republican institutions. They were also the sentiments that an esteemed author of the U.S. Constitution and later first chief justice of the U.S. Supreme Court was expressing to sympathetic readers. From Locke on, classical liberals drew a sharp distinction between natural rights to life and property and the rights and responsibilities attached to citizenship within a particular society. Locke and Jefferson perceived no contradiction between limiting citizenship in a body politic on the basis of cultural compatibility and the existence of universal "natural rights."

It may be helpful, then, to retire the changing standards of liberal orthodoxy in favor of a more applicable and less invidious political taxonomy. The rise of the new populism may offer the opportunity for this, inasmuch as it dramatizes the polemical nature of the charge of antiliberalism being raised by antipopulists. These critics wish to ignore whatever liberal heritage their opponents are invoking; and they think of democracy as a form of thought-control at the disposal of enlightened administrators and public educators. Taguieff finds it disconcerting that populists appeal to Aristotle's view of the ancient *polis* as a regime founded on the absolute identity between rulers and ruled.[26] Jefferson also believed this kind of identity was integral to self-government, and it may be one of the few beliefs he extracted from ancient republicanism. Such self-rule *avant la lettre* may not always be practicable for a heavily populated country demanding multiple social services, or at least so it is claimed. But it does tell much about "problems in American democracy" (as today's compulsory high school civics course are named), that journalists such as David Broder and Al Hunt mock those who "refuse to face the fact" that self-government is about public administration and public policy. Though this administrative regime may be about policymaking, it is only marginally about citizens governing themselves.

In place of the overworked contrast between "liberals" and inhabitants of outer darkness, it may be useful to substitute a new conceptual polarity—one between political and economic globalists and their populist opponents. One of the main targets of current populist formations is rule by a transnational managerial class. This rule is seen as more or less the same, whether associated with corporate capitalism, "human rights" experts, or social democratic administrators. It is massive impersonal control parading as progress, which fans populist hostility. In the face of this tide of enmity, certain strategies have been brought to bear. As soon as debate begins, the political class, or its academic cheering gallery, reach for their dog-eared copies of *The Authoritarian Personality* or *The Rise and Fall of The Third Reich*, whereupon, after stern admonition, they hold forth on the need for "democratic education." Members of what Francis calls the "archaic Right" can also be counted on to fall into line, and they do this by repetitiously reciting a civics lesson, i.e., that the Constitution set up a representative republic, not a direct democracy.[27] All this, of course, is self-evident but also historically irrelevant. The framers did not have to deal with widespread criminal violence in their streets, the nationalization of the franchise, invasion by illegal immigrants, rule by unelected "civil servants" and legislating judges, and much else that has occurred in the twentieth century. They also had no reason to assume that most politics would not continue, as it did in their time, to go on at the local level.

In dealing with the populist temptation of the Left, Ellen Willis exemplifies the possibility of conducting a political discussion without anachronistic name-calling.[28] An avowed internationalist and an advocate of women's and gay liberation, Willis warns leftists against embracing populism as "a nonstatist, decentralized model of democracy." Populism, she insists, "does not aim to abolish class distinctions." It "defines membership in a community through the exclusion of others and defends the received values of that community against outsiders." She cites the "dark side of populism," seen to "function as the protective guardian of local community and autonomous social institutions against the meddling of the Left and its social engineering." Unlike the custodians of liberal terminology, Willis pursues *her* debate with the populist Right in terms of the issues of the day. As a supporter of a left-liberal administration calling for cultural revolution, naturally she has no desire to preserve traditional communities in the name of decentralized democracy. Nor does she fall back dishonestly on communitarian language when her intent is to reconstruct social relations. One may differ with her politics, but Willis does not misrepresent what she favors. She labels her opponents as reactionary, but not as deviationists from some imaginary eternal liberal verity.

Anti-populists should learn from this clean form of debate. Further talk about the "politics of illiberalism" will not silence the growing opposition. Such talk is invariably tendentious. Those engaged in it pretend to belong to a liberal faith that has come down from some primitive church, more or less inviolate. But this kind of ecclesiology has become hard to sustain now that the liberal faith lies scattered across the political spectrum. New frames of reference are necessary to comprehend the political landscape in this age of postmodernity and post-liberalism.

Notes

1. Gianfranco Miglio, "La Prospettiva Teorica del Nuovo Federalismo," in *Federalismo e Societa*, vol. 1, no. 2 (1994), pp, 27-28; and "Cultural Roots of Federalism," in *Telos 97* (Fall 1993), pp. 33–39.
2. *Wall Street Journal* (November 14, 1994).
3. Harry V. Jaffa, "Equality as a Conservative Principle," in *Loyola of Los Angeles Law Review* no. 8 (June 1975), p. 475.
4. A revealing anthology because of quotations from the American founding fathers designed to embarrass the intelligentsia is Madison Grant and C.S. Davieson, eds., *Founders of the Republic on Immigration and Aliens*, (New York: Scribner's and Son, 1928).
5. Paul Rahe, *Republics Ancient and Modern: Classical Republicanism and the American Revolution* (Chapel Hill: University of North Carolina Press, 1992). See also my review of Rahe's book in *Modern Age,* vol. 37, no. 3 (Spring 1995) pp. 264–269.
6. N. D. Fustel de Coulanges, *La Cité Antique* (Paris: Hachette, 1866), pp. 226–241 and 338–397. It may be useful to look at the original text of this magisterial study for the Latin and Greek citations (mostly in footnotes) dealing with ancient restrictions on *jus connubii*. In Athens as late as the fifth century B.C., intermarriage with those from other Greek cities was forbidden, unless specifically permitted by agreement. The existing law stipulated that *"nothos ho ek zenes e appakidos...hos an me ex astes genetai nothon einai* [a bastard is one descended from a foreign woman or from a concubine. One who is not born of an authorized citizen is illegitimate.] Note that the restriction here was placed not on epigamia with barbarians but rather on union with other Greeks who were not Athenians. In Aristotle's *Constitution of Athens* (Osbord Classical Text), 26.4, 2.1, Pericles is shown appealing to the popular party by advocating the restriction of Athenian citizenship to descendants of pure-blooded citizens. This act was the political debut of Pericles as a spokesman for democratic change.
7. One of the most widely used textbooks in political theory, William and A.O. Ebesntein, *Great Political Thinkers* (Fort Worth, Tex: Holt, Rinehart, and Winston, 1990), on Locke's merits as an advocate of revolution for nondemocratic societies and on Rousseau's uses in building social democracy. Presumably Americans have already followed the prescriptions of both thinkers.

8. John Locke, *Two Treatises of Government* (New York: Hafner Publishing, 1947), p. 184. See also the attempt by Richard Ashcraft to reconcile Locke's majoritarianism with his defense of property in *Revolutionary Politics and Locke's Two Treatises* (Princeton, N.J.: Princeton University Press, 1987), especially pp. 570–583.

9. Peter H. Schuck and Roger Smith, *Citizenship Without Consent: Illegal Aliens in the American Polity* (New Haven, Conn.: Yale University Press, 1986).

10. *Two Treatises of Government, op. cit.*, pp. 224–227 and 245–247.

11. Jean-Jacques Rousseau, *Du Contrat Social* (Paris: Flammarion, 1966), pp. 76–78.

12. Leon Wieseltier, "Abracadabrant," *New Republic* (January 6, 1992). pp. 28–29.

13. See Christopher Lasch's remarks about the nature of bourgeois society in "Revolt of the Elites,"*Harper's* (November 1994), pp. 48–49; and Sam Francis's restatement of them in *Chronicles* (October 1995), pp. 8–9.

14. Interestingly enough, Miglio has defended the governing capacity of his northern Italians by citing their bourgeois history and Calvinist disposition. Unlike central and southern Italians, Miglio contends, Lombards favor not feudal patronage but hard work and civic responsibility. See the appended section to Miglio's *Io, Bossi e la Lega. Diario Segreto dei Miti dei miei Quattro Anni sul Carroccio* (Milan: Mondadori, 1994).

15. See Benjamin Ginsberg, *The Captive Public* (New York: Basic Books, 1988); Jack D. Douglas, *The Myth of the Welfare State* (New York: Norton, 1991); Willard Enteeman, *Managerialism: The Emergence of a New Ideology* (Madison: University of Wisconsin Press, 1993); and Allan Carlson, *Family Questions: Reflections on the American Social Crisis* (New Brunswick, N.J.: Transaction Publishers, 1988).

16. Robert Nisbet, *The Present Age: Progress and Anarachy in Modern America* (New York: Harper Collins, 1989): pp. 20–40.

17. Paul Gottfried, *The Conservative Movement*, revised edition (New York: Twayne-Macmillan, 1993): pp. 124–127.

18. While the specific reference is to *Modern Age*, this tendency on the Catholic and Anglo-Catholic Right goes well beyond any one journal. On this and related points, see my concluding chapter in *The Search for Historical Meaning* (DeKalb: Northern Illinois University Press, 1986), pp. 104–134.

19. See Ellis Sandoz, *The Voegelinian Revolution: A Biographic Introduction* (Baton Rouge: Louisiana State University Press, 1981); R.J. Neuhaus' review of a biography of Will Herberg in *National Review* (July 14, 1989), p. 52; William F. Buckley, "Unpleasant Business," in *National Review* (June 16, 1989); and Norman Podhoretz, "Anti-Semitism, Right and Left," in *Commentary*, no. 83, pp. 36–38.

20. Max Weber, *Polittk als Beruf*, eighth edition (Berlin: Duncker & Humbolt, 1987), pp. 36–38; and Wolfgang Mommsen, *The Age of Bureaucracy and Perspectives on the Political Sociology of Max Weber* (New York: Harper and Row, 1974.)

21. Richard Hofstadter, *The Paranoid Style in American Politics* (Chicago: University of Chicago Press, 1979); and *Anti-Intellectualism in American Life* (New York: Vintage, 1966).

22. Pierre-Andre Taguieff, "Political Science confronts Populism: From a Conceptual Mirage to a Real Problem," *Telos*, Spring, 1995.

23. Justus Deonecke, "American Dissidents," *Reason*, vol. 11, no. 8 (1979), pp. 45–49; and "The Anti-Interventionist Tradition: Leadership and Perceptions," in *Literature of Liberty*, vol. 4, no. 2 (1981), pp. 7–67.

24. Taguieff, op. cit., p.35.

25. *The Federalist Papers* (New York: The New American Library, 1961), p. 38.
26. Taguieff, op. cit., p. 35.
27. Samuel T. Francis, *Beautiful Losers: Essays on the Failure of American Conservatism* (Columbia: University of Missouri Press, 1993), especially pp. 222–231. Francis blames the antipopulist mentality of the Old Right for its strategic blunders and eventual marginalization. Though this Right criticized extensively the "postbourgeious managerial regime," it also sought an accommodation with its enemy and finally allowed itself to be captured by neoconservative New Class representatives.
28. Ellen Willis in the *Village Voice* (20 December 1994).

12

Restoring the Republic

Clyde Wilson

A history textbook used by thousands of college freshmen for the last twenty years tells fledgling citizens that democracy is the system of government which "trusts the average man to free himself from tradition, prejudice, habit, and by free discussion come to a rational conclusion." This tissue of sophistry encapsulates the derailment of republican self-government in our time. Most certainly democracy has something to do with the "average man," the common people, the many. But one of the numerous defects of the modern and artificial definition above is that it leaves out three-fourths of the moral and historical context that was taken for granted by the Framers and Founders of the American federal republic when they talked about a government of the people. The definition, in fact, subtly shifts democracy away from substance to procedure, from ethics to instrumentality. The pins have been kicked out from under democracy, leaving it balancing precariously on one leg.

The definition, to begin with, abandons virtue for reason. Our forefathers took it for granted that virtue was necessary in a ruler—whether it be the one, the few, or the many. And where in the definition do we find the ends and limitations of government? In other words, where is the Constitution? What tells us which things men in the collective are entitled to come to "rational conclusions" about, and what things are they to leave alone? What restrains the 51 percent from coming to a "rational conclusion" to expropriate, enslave, or exterminate the 49 percent? And why is it necessary for the common man to divorce himself from "tradition, prejudice, habit?" In fact, the average man at all times and places (and the wise man too) is fond of tradition, prejudice, and habit, and rightly so. If we believe in the rule of the many, are we not obliged to respect their traditions, prejudices, and habits as well as what we deem to be their rational conclusions? What, after all, are our liberties and democratic forms—freedom of the press and assembly, fair play, parliamentary procedure, due process of law—if not traditions, prejudices, and habits handed down by our forefathers over centuries, which owe their survival to inheritance as much as to abstract argument.

Most assuredly "free discussion" is indispensable to democracy. That is, free and candid, and tolerant deliberation among differing opinions and interests in the process of arriving at decisions—decisions on those things which the public is entitled to decide. But free discussion divorced from "tradition, prejudice, habit" rather leads us away from the common man. It describes a type of society loved by the few, not by the many. Who exactly is it that is "trusting" the "average man" to arrive at a "rational conclusion"? "Rational" according to what system of values? According to whose views and interests? Here is the most insidious part of this peculiar democracy—the rationale for a hidden elite. If the average man perversely refuses to come to a "rational conclusion," what happens?

What happens is a government of the few who decide, against the will of the many, that "free discussion" requires a foreign-born pornographer be subsidized to create obscenity; a government in which the few enforce "rational" social policies (such as busing, affirmative action, coddling of criminals) overwhelmingly considered unjust and oppressive by the many; a government in which schools, local authorities, and even the taxing power (immemorially reserved to the people) are taken over by unelected and untouchable judges. Democracy suddenly requires the people to submit to their betters, whether they will or not. This, of course, is not democracy at all, but oligarchy, as our Fathers would have immediately recognized.

Again and again, we have seen the self-government of the American people frustrated by the few, the oligarchy, in the name of "rational democracy." This is the problem of republicanism in our time— our chief dilemma in society and government—the consolidation of power in the hands of the few. It explains that, while sophisters (whenever they raise their snouts from the public trough long enough) shout hosannas to the triumph of democracy, the American people, everywhere, have ceased to believe that the government they elect is really theirs or that they will be allowed to make the institutions ostensibly theirs respond to their will. Everywhere an ideological construct mislabeled "democracy" has triumphed. And everywhere the people feel powerless.

For those who really value the rule of the people, as well as the special constitutional heritage of American federal republicanism, the task of the day is not to spread democracy about the world while we congratulate ourselves on our success. The task is to restore the federal republic at home. In order to carry out this task we will need the spirit of liberty that animated generations of our forefathers—not an obeisance to their forms, but an imitation of their spirit. For forms may survive when the soul is fled from them.

What we need is a return of power to the many. Not a concentration of power in the hands of the few for the alleged benefit of the many, abstractly conceived. That way lies Hitler and Stalin. Rather a dispersal and deconsolidation of power. Only power can check power. And self-government is in its nature local and individual. Only then is it real.

For our Fathers, liberty consisted in a negative upon government. It was not a boon bestowed by government, but something that must be asserted against government. It will not increase the power and liberty of American families in the least for the government to bestow upon them a voucher to spend on a limited choice of schools under stipulated requirements. It will rather further consolidate power and further intrude the government into as yet unregulated spheres of life. The only way to increase the power and liberty of the family is not to collect the taxes and not to lay down the regulations to begin with. Both our governing parties agree on the consolidation of power—they argue only over marginal aspects of administration.

Unlike us, the attitude of our Founders toward democracy was not ideological and not self-congratulatory. They believed in the right of those who were capable of governing themselves to do so. They were pleased that Americans had the fortunate opportunity to live under self-government at at time when, unlike today, most of the world was hostile to the very idea. They hoped they might set an example for oppressed mankind. They did not entertain a duty to spread democracy about the world by fire, sword, harangue, and money. They were the opposite of self-congratulatory and arrogant. Their demeanor was cautious, monitory, and self-demanding.

"Well, gentlemen," Dr. Franklin is supposed to have said at the Philadelphia Convention, "you have made a republic—if you can keep it." If republican self-government was to survive, if Americans were to go on governing themselves, then government must be watched. Republican liberty could always be subverted by lust for power on the part of the cunningly ambitious few and by the decay of those strenuous and demanding virtues among the many that made self-government possible. When our Fathers spoke of America as an experiment, they did not mean a glorious mission of revolution. They meant an experiment in the exercise and preservation of republican virtues.

"Power is always stealing from the many to the few," was the motto of a Washington democratic newspaper in the early days of the republic. It was a paraphrase of Mr. Jefferson's "the price of liberty is eternal vigilance." Mr. Jefferson also said that the tree of liberty must be watered from time to time by the blood of tyrants, and of patriots, that a little revolution now and then is a good thing.

Because Jefferson has been, since the mid-19th century, enveloped in a dense fabric of lies woven by Jacobin democrats and made the symbol of consolidated power in the name of equality, it is difficult for us to see what he meant. But what he meant was exactly what I have described above as the task of the day—the occasional need to restore the republic. He was not suggesting the overturn of society, a perpetual revolution for ever greater consolidation of power in the name of equality. Jefferson is nothing if not the enemy of consolidated power. It is not society that is to be overthrown—it is society, as in the American Revolution, that is to assert itself and overthrow those rulers who have usurped the power of society.

Jefferson's democracy ran thus. No one can be trusted with power. Government, though necessary, must be confined within narrow limits and dispersed. The average man, the many, is the least dangerous receptacle of power, lacking the opportunities for usurpation that afflict the few. But the essential point is the limitation of power. As he asked Adams: "If a man cannot be trusted to govern himself, how can he be trusted to govern others?" That was his answer to the Federalist convention that the weakness of human nature required popular government to be restrained by checks and balances and the deference of the "average man" to his betters. Jefferson put the finger immediately on the hidden elitist assumption, the hidden elitist agenda, that lurked in the convention—as it lurks in our guardian democracy today.

Trusting or not trusting the common man to arrive at a "rational conclusion" was the wrong way to put the problem. It was Jefferson's point that the "betters" are just as corruptible, probably more so, than the popular mass—that is, more likely to abuse the limits of power, which are the essential thing. Jefferson is here exactly in agreement with C.S. Lewis's Christian defense of democracy. That democracy makes sense exactly because of original sin—precisely because man (all men) cannot be trusted to govern himself, much less others. But the Federalist idea has prevailed since the War Between the States, and in this century, given the consolidating tendencies of the modern form of society, it has become overwhelming.

Jefferson's occasional revolution is not, then, revolution but reaction. Not a new utopia, but something radically conservative—a radical returning to the roots, to old viruses and old principles lost by the dilutions of time and the distortions of usurpation. In the American system this can only happen by the revival of states' rights, the only true force for limiting power. Which is exactly what Jefferson's own "Revolution of 1800" meant to him and his generation.

What we need is a reaction, a renewal, a true return to roots. We should approach our constitutional heritage and our governing establishment in exactly the spirit of our forefathers—with both deep respect and intelligent flexibility. To conserve is to save the essence, not the dead form, as true conservatives have always known. Our heritage is something to be understood and used by us to meet our present dangers. As Calhoun said, constitutions are human contrivances, and what man does and his reasons for it surely ought not to be beyond man's capacity to fully comprehend.

Let us contrast such an attitude with that of our current oligarchy. They want us to treat the Constitution with mystical awe and submission, but their Constitution is not the one handed down by our forefathers for our use. Rather, it is whatever the oligarchy mysteriously discovers it to be, by the alchemies of natural rights and evolution, which can justify any abuse of power on their part. On the other hand, they twist and distort the plain historical sense in the most petty and deceitful ways. Thus we get the worst possible combination of a phony tradition and constructive innovation.

Many of the constructive innovations are already known at the grassroots level, and others will emerge in the course of popular revolt. They seek to recover the spirit of the Constitution, to return power to the people. These would include term limits, for the federal judiciary as well as the Congress; a balanced budget amendment with inviolable restraints upon taxing and spending power; a line-item veto for the executive to check legislative irresponsibility, with balancing devices in the Congress to check executive warmongering; and the restoration of the Tenth Amendment to what Madison, the Father of the Constitution, said it should be, the cornerstone of our government. We have nothing to fear from a new constitutional convention, if necessary. Such a convention cannot destroy the handiwork of our Fathers. That has already been destroyed and must be restored. Whether we are able to accomplish this will be the measure of whether we have enough moral and social substance left to be a self-governing people.

We have not one problem to cure but two—the consolidation of power and the decay of virtue. But from the viewpoint of the classical republicanism of our Fathers these are but one and the same, two inseparable evils that feed upon each other. Consolidation of power breeds the decay of virtue in the people, and decay of virtue in the people breeds consolidation of power.

Our forefathers were neither economic determinists nor, like us, materialists. But they realized that, as Burke put it, the revenue is the state, that the power of taxation and expenditure is the master of all other powers. There is no clearer principle established in the American Revolution and the whole heritage of British liberty that preceded it. Put another way, the restoration of power to the people can only come with limitations on the taxing and spending power of the federal government, which has become autonomous and limitless. We despise our representatives and yet we reelect them at the greatest rate in history. This paradox is a key to our times. Our forefathers would have recognized this condition immediately as a symptom of decayed republican virtue. Our politicians buy us, with our own money. The habit of spoils is so deeply ingrained that only the most radical remedy will cure it.

The Cold War has ended, making possible a great decrease in the burden of expenditure carried by the American public for more than a generation. A responsible republican government would do two things in this situation—reduce taxes and retire debt. That is, the people would enjoy a great boon in the lifting of burdens, a peace dividend. It is a measure of our degradation that neither of our ruling parties has considered either alternative. Instead both parties and both branches of government have conspired to raise taxes. They have considered only the opportunity to broker funds in new ways and buy old allegiances. The peace dividend is not ours, but theirs. Like all economic questions, this is at bottom a moral question, which our leaders evade by seeming to see only a technical question. So accustomed are we to the evil system that we hardly notice the unreality of the debate.

The people must not only put limits on government. They must break their own dependence upon the corrupt system, give up the expectation that things will be done for them, and demand the return of our resources to ourselves, to dispose of in our own way. For liberty plain and simple is the ability to decide and dispose. This is even less easy than it sounds, because demands upon the Treasury always come disguised as public benefits; because we have as a people almost lost the ability to distinguish between public necessity and private subsidy; and because we have created an immense clamoring clientele that exists only on and for ever increasing patronage.

To restore the federal republic, we will have to begin to level up rather than level down, to substitute liberty for equality as our chief goal. Ideological equality is the enemy of republican citizenship. It is in its guise as the imposer of equality that the overweening state has taken most power to itself, even more so than in war, and become the arbiter of society. Government programs for preferential groups must be ended, and all citizens become equal under the law. In no way else can we restore morale and productivity, belief in fairness and opportunity. We must take away from the oligarchy the brokering of how differing groups of a pluralistic society live together. Also, in order to restore the value of republican citizenship, it will have to be restricted. That means that immigration has to be reduced to a small number determined specifically by the future and current interest of the American people, not by any philosophical or economic consideration. We must end the system by which any respiring creature who manages to sneak under the fence becomes immediately entitled to all the rights and privileges of citizenship. To say that everyone in the world who can manage to get here is an American citizen is to say that there is no such thing as an American citizen in any meaningful sense, to cheapen our citizenship beyond toleration. The restriction of immigration and citizenship rights will make American citizenship more valued and viable, not less so.

Democracy, as our forefathers clearly recognized, is not a group of people living under common procedures and economic exchanges. It is a social fabric of tradition, habit, and prejudice that makes self-government possible in a way that no proclaimed set of procedures or even carefully balanced interests can. A miscellaneous collection of people are not citizens of a republic but interchangeable ciphers of imperialism. The aspiration of a globalized citizenship is not the vision of republicanism but the dream of empire. In order for American society to begin to feel its power and reassert itself against government, it must have a period of stabilization. We must have time to absorb the great immigration we have received in the last three decades. Otherwise we will have a society increasingly fragmented rather than pluralistic, divided into hostile groups competing for advantage, a situation in which democracy cannot long survive, as the history of the world shows. Unlimited immigration serves the rich and the government, not the people.

Here we find the deep moral problem of modern society. Our unrestricted immigration, the celebration of constant and endless social transformation, does not result from allegiance to democracy or liberality of spirit. It results from the same state of mind as our economic irresponsibility—the inability to care about posterity and act for the future. A healthy society, like that of our forefathers, will automatically take account of the welfare of its posterity when it makes decisions. There can be no posterity in a society whose citizens are merely interchangeable parts of a politico-economic machine.

It is true that we live in a very different world from our Fathers and that our solutions cannot always be the same as theirs. But our problem is the same—the harnessing of power. They solved the problem for their time, and the problem is solvable in our time, given sufficient will and political genius. There is much in modern society that makes convenient the dispersal and devolution of power as well as its consolidation. The computer can serve decentralization as well centralization. There is no reason why we cannot have many small humane factories or schools rather than a few large ones. As Edward Abbey observed in one of the wisest insights of our time: "Growth is the enemy of progress." Consolidation of power is not so much inherent in our current state of society as it is the product of choices made and institutions constructed in the past that showed a bias in favor of gigantism over humane scale, centralized control over freedom, and elitism over democratic rule. In imitation of our Fathers we may solve the problem of consolidated power.

Allen Tate observed that our Founders "had a profound instinct for high style, a genius at dramaticizing themselves at their own particular moment of history. They were so situated economically and politically that they were able to form a definite conception of their human role; they were not ants in an economic anthill, nor were they investigating statistically the behavior of other ants. They knew what they wanted because they knew what they, themselves, were." It may be that this sense of self-determination of free men enjoyed by our Fathers is an impractical goal, not fully realizable in the modern world. But unless we recover it at least as an ideal and a point of reference toward which we direct our collective selves, the American experiment has failed.

The restoration of the federal republic will not in itself solve all our problems because the ends of human life do not rest in government and because modern society is in deep spiritual crisis, as every great thinker of our century has observed. But the restraint of power is a necessary first step for all progress—moral, economic, political, cultural. Leviathan has gotten loose from the harness our forefathers so skillfully fashioned for him. He has knocked over the fence, laid waste our gardens, and waxed fat on our substance. We must begin to look to our husbandry, but first we will have to chain the beast. In this task we have one great advantage—the preponderance of the American people are still republican at heart.

13

Nationalism, Old and New

Samuel Francis

In the course of American history, nationalism and republicanism have usually been enemies, not allies. From the days of Alexander Hamilton, nationalism has meant unification of the country under a centralized government, the supremacy of the executive over the legislative branch, the reduction of states' rights and local and sectional parochialism, governmental regulation of the economy and engineering of social institutions, and an activist foreign policy—expansionist, imperialist, or globalist—that costs money and requires at least occasional wars. Nationalism and its proponents have historically been Anglophiles, emulating the mercantilist dynastic state that flourished in Great Britain from the eighteenth century, and for all their claims of overcoming sectionalism and private interests, they have been identified with the Northeastern parts of the United States and its institutions—New England, New York City, the Ivy League, Big Banks and Big Business, Wall Street, and Washington. The national state the nationalists defended and constructed was born with the ratification of the U.S. Constitution, reached adolescence in the victory of the North in the Civil War, and grew to a corpulent adulthood in the twentieth-century managerial state of Woodrow Wilson, Herbert Hoover, Franklin Roosevelt, and Lyndon Johnson.

The principal opponents of nationalism in American history have been republicans, and it is one of the ironies of our history that the political party that claims the republican name has been the chief vehicle since the Civil War of antirepublican nationalism. The Antifederalists who opposed ratification of the Constitution were men immersed in the political theory of classical republicanism, a school of thought that originated in modern times with Machiavelli, found ex-

189

pression in the seventeenth-century British resistance to the powers of the monarchy, and in the eighteenth century influenced both radical Tories and radical Whigs. Deeply suspicious of centralized power of any kind and of the corruption it bred, the Antifederalists opposed ratification, demanded a Bill of Rights to limit federal power, insisted on a strict reading of the constitutional text as the basis of law, defended the states against the federal government and the Congress against the Presidency, and were generally content with the limitations on wealth and national power that a small, restricted state imposed, in preference to what they condemned as the "luxury" and "empire" that national consolidation and an interventionist foreign policy would encourage. "The anti-federalists," writes Professor Ralph Ketcham in his introduction to a popular edition of their writings:

> [Looked] to the Classical idealization of the small, pastoral republic where virtuous, self-reliant citizens managed their own affairs and shunned the power and glory of empire. To them, the victory in the American Revolution meant not so much the big chance to become a wealthy world power, but rather the opportunity to achieve a genuinely republican polity, far from the greed, lust for power, and tyranny that had generally characterized human society.

Though the Antifederalists lost, their ideas, far more than those of Edmund Burke and Adam Smith, have informed the long American tradition of resistance to the leviathan state of the nationalists, appearing in the thought and on the lips of John Randolph, John C. Calhoun, the leaders of the Confederacy, the Populists of the late nineteenth century and the Southern Agrarians of the early twentieth, and in the Old Right conservatism of the era between Charles Lindbergh and Jesse Helms.

In the eighteenth century, when the debate between these two sides of the American political coin still sparkled, it was possible for the American people and their leaders to choose republicanism and to institutionalize its ideals. Perhaps it was possible to do so as late as the early twentieth century, before the managerial state began to crystallize. Today it is no longer possible. The national state has long since triumphed, and with it, wedded to it like Siamese siblings, multinational corporations, giant labor unions, universities and foundations, and all the titanic labyrinth of modern bureaucratic organizations in both the "public" and the increasingly illusory "private" sectors have won as well. To establish republicanism in anything like its classical form would involve a massive rejection and dismantlement of the main features of the twentieth century—the physical and social technologies

by which modern, centralized, bureaucratically managed mass organizations operate—and while the continued existence and dominance of
such features are not inevitable in any Hegelian sense, no one save a
few romantic reactionaries seriously contemplates doing away with
them. Not only do technology and its organized applications entice us
with "luxury"—what we today complacently call a "high standard of
living"—but also they offer to those who understand how to manipulate them a degree of power unknown to the most imperious despots of
the past. The elites that manage modern mass organizations and master
the technical skills that allow these organizations to function cannot
permit the decentralization and autonomy that characterize republican
civic culture simply because their power would vanish, and these elites
are lodged not only in the state but also in the dominant organizations
of the economy and culture so that our incomes and our very thoughts,
values, tastes, and emotions are conditioned and manipulated by them
and their apologists. Short of a new Dark Age (or perhaps it would be a
Golden Age), in which knowledge of scientific and organizational technology is lost, there is no prospect of reversing the trend toward mass
organization and its absorption of local and decentralized institutions.

Moreover, as most students of classical republicanism understand,
the distinctive principle of its theory is its concept of "virtue," a quality
that consists less in moralistic purity than in personal and social independence. Owning and operating his own farm or shop, usually producing his own food and clothing, governing his own family and his
own community, and defending himself with his own arms in company
with his own relatives and neighbors, the citizen of the classical republic neither needed nor wanted a leviathan state to fight wars across the
globe in behalf of democracy nor to pretend to protect him and his
home. Nor did he need or want a job in someone else's company, or a
pension plan or health benefits or paid vacations or five-hour work-
days. He did not want to shop in vast shopping malls where nothing is
worth buying and nothing bought will last the year. It did not occur to
him to enroll himself or his children in therapy courses or in sensitivity
and human-relations clinics in order to find out how to get along with
his neighbors, and he sought no edification or instruction from the mass
media to entertain him continuously or indoctrinate him with the current cliches and slogans of public discussion or trick him into buying
even more junk for which he had no use and no desire. If the citizen
succumbed to such temptations, then he had become dependent on someone or something other than himself and his extension in family and

community. Men who become dependent on others cannot govern themselves, and if they cannot govern themselves, they cannot keep a republic.

Today, virtually everyone in the United States is habituated to a style of living that is wrapped up in dependency on mass organizations of one kind or another—supermarkets, hospitals, insurance companies, the bureaucratized police, local government, the mass media, the factories and office buildings where we work, the apartment complexes and suburban communities where we live, and the massive, remote, and mysterious national state that supervises almost every detail of our lives. Most Americans cannot even imagine life without such dependencies and would not want to live without them if they could imagine it. The classical republicans were right. Having become dependent on others for our livelihoods, our protection, our entertainment, and even our thoughts and tastes, we are corrupted. We neither want a republic nor could we keep it if we had one. We do not deserve to have one, and like the barbarians conquered and enslaved by the Greeks and Romans, we are suited only for servitude.

Classical republicanism, then, is defunct as a serious political alternative to the present regime, but this does not mean that Americans should either embrace the old, Hamilitonian nationalism or merely squat passively in their kennels waiting for the next whistle from their masters. Even though virtually no one today subscribes or adheres to the classical republican ideal of virtue and independence, even though most Americans are too "corrupt" (in republican terms) to support a republic, there remain a large number of Americans, perhaps a majority, whose material interests and most deeply held cultural codes are endangered by the national (and increasingly supranational) managerial regime. These "Middle Americans," largely white and middle class, derive their income from their dependence on the mass structures of the managerial economy, and, because many of them have long since lost their habits of self-reliance, they also are dependent on the services of the government (at least indirectly) and the dominant culture. Yet despite their dependency, the regime does little for them and much to them. They find that their jobs are insecure, their savings stripped of value, their neighborhoods and schools and homes unsafe, their elected leaders indifferent and often crooked, their moral beliefs and religious professions and social codes under perpetual attack even from their own government, their children taught to despise what they believe, their very identity and heritage as a people threatened, and their future—political, economic, cultural, racial, national, and personal—uncertain. They find that no matter which party or candidate they support, no matter what the candidates and parties promise, nothing substantially changes, except for the worse. Although they do the labor that sustains the managerial system, pay the taxes that support it, fight the wars its leaders devise, raise the families and try to pass on the beliefs and habits that enable the regime and the country to exist and survive, what they recieve from the regime is never commensurate with what they give it.

They are the Americans sneered at as the "Bubba vote," mocked as Archie Bunkers, and denounced as the racists, sexists, xenophobes, and hate criminals who haunt the dark corners of the land, the "Dark Side" of America, even as their own energy, sacrifice, and commitment make possible the regime and the elite that despise them, exploit them, and dispossess them. They are at once the real victims of the regime and the core or nucleus of American civilization, the Real America, the American Nation.

Throughout this century, Middle Americans have gradually acquired a collective consciousness, an awareness of who they are and what their position is in the regime that exploits them. In economically prosperous periods, the radicalism of that consciousness is largely dormant, but in the Depression, the inflationary crunch of the 1970s, and the recessions of the early 1980s and the early 1990s, material insecurity has served as a trigger for a heightened consciousness, a radicalization, a sharper self-perception of their plight. Neither liberalism and the ideologies of the left nor mainstream conservatism, an entrepreneurial version of classical republicanism, adequately expresses their plight or their interests and values or offers much of a solution.

The left offers nothing but economic redistribution predicated on egalitarian and universalist dogmas, and in practice this means that liberal-left politics reflect the interests of the nonwhite underclass and the intelligentsia that designs the formulas and policies of the left. Hence, the left is incapable of defending the specific interests and concrete cultural norms of Middle Americans. The right, though it defends (in theory) Middle-American cultural norms and institutions, offers a vision of decentralism, strict constitutionalism, economic individualism, and a minimal state that fails to speak to Middle-American material interests and the challenges that they typically encounter. What Middle Americans need is a political formula and a public myth that synthesize the attention to material-economic interests offered by the left with the defense of concrete cultural and national identity offered by the

right. The division of the American political spectrum into the categories of right and left makes the political expression of such a formula
virtually impossible.

The appropriate formula for the expression of Middle-American
material interests and cultural values is nationalism. The managerial
state and its linked economic and cultural structures have succeeded in
breaking down the regional variations, local and sectional autonomy,
and institutional stability and independence of Middle Americans, and
the regime now lurches happily toward a globalization that seeks to
integrate all Americans (and all other peoples as well) into a planetary
political, economic, demographic, and cultural order in which national
identity will eventually disappear entirely. The homogenization of
subnational social and regional differences through political centralization, urbanization and mobility, mass communications, and mass
consumption and production means that the older, decentralized identities of particular social classes, sections, communities, and religious
and ethnic groups no longer effectively mobilize Americans for political action. Identities as Southerners or Midwesterners, Catholics or
Protestant, Anglo-Saxon Old Stock or European ethnic, small business-
man or assembly-line worker, no longer seem to offer sufficient bonds
or common interests for serious political cooperation for any goal beyond immediate special interests. The emerging identity of Middle
America, however, appears to convey sufficient meaning to serve as
the foundation of a politically and socially important force, and a nationalism that is politically and culturally based on Middle Americans,
expresses their material interests, and affirms their cultural norms as
the dominant public myth of American civilization is today the only
possible vehicle for effective resistance to managerial globalism and
the national and cultural extinction it threatens.

Moreover, only nationalism seems capable of organizing offensively
on a collective scale. One reason for the failure of classical republicanism and similar decentralist movements was that they were capable of
only defensive maneuvering and were never able to overcome divisions of particular and divergent interests and identities sufficiently to
organize an effective offensive strategy aimed at dominance rather than
mere survival and liberty. The defensive strategy mounted by the
Confederacy during the Civil War was one of the main reasons for its
military defeat, and similar defensiveness has crippled conservative
tactics as well. Activated only by immediate threats to local or private
interests, conservative forces have organized mainly around striking

personalities and "single issues"—tax revolts, religious and social issues of largely sectarian concern, antibusing and educational movements, anticommunism, deregulations, term limits—and they tend to
disband or wither when their favorite personality is elected or the threats
to their immediate interests and pet causes seem to be pushed back.
Nationalism, through its historically proven capacity to mobilize passions of mass solidarity and sacrifice and its aggressive invocation of
collective identity, offers a practical instrument for overcoming the
burden of a purely defensive conservatism and aspiring to enduring
cultural and political power.

The old nationalism of the Hamilitonian tradition will not suffice for
this purpose, however. It was the explicit mission of Hamilitonian nationalism to obliterate what Hamilton's best and most recent biogra-
pher, Forrest McDonald, calls "the inertia of a social order whose per-
vasive attributes were provincalism and lassitude." The means by which
Hamilton determined to accomplish that "revolutionary change" was
money—wealth, economic growth—aided and supported by the national state. "To transform the established order," writes Professor
McDonald,

[To] make society fluid and open to merit, to make industry both rewarding and
necessary, all that needed to be done was to monetize the whole—to rig the rules
of the game so that money would become the universal measure of the value of
things. For money is oblivious to class, status, color, and inherited social position;
money is the ultimate, neutral, impersonal arbiter. Infused into an oligarchical,
agrarian social order, money would be the leaven, the fermenting yeast, that would
stimulate growth, change, prosperity, and national strength.

But by making money "the universal measure of the value of things,"
the defining principle of the national identity, and joining it to centralized power, Hamilton ultimately defeated his own purposes. In the first
place, because his nationalism set itself against existing social institutions and habits, it was necessarily alienated from and adversial toward
the norms by which most Americans lived, and its alienation has persisted for two centuries to inform the cultural style and attitudes of the
dominant elites of the managerial system toward the rest of the country. Secondly, because his nationalism was based on the abstraction of
money, it was unable to win the support of any but economically ambitious Americans and unable to express or sustain a genuinely national
or even any genuine social bond. Hence, Hamilton's nationalism—rational, calculative, pragmatic—degenerated into a mask for individual,
factional, and sectional acquisition. It was not and could not be an au-

thentic nationalism that controlled and disciplined the parts within the
whole but only a pseudo-nationalism that allowed the parts to seize
control of the whole and define the whole in terms of the parts and their
interests. As another of Hamilton's biographers, John C. Miller, writes,
the failure of Hamilton's nationalism probably "stemmed from the fact
that he associated the national government with no great moral issue
capable of capturing the popular imagination; he seemed to stand only
for 'the natural right of the great fishes to eat up the little ones whenever they can catch them.'"

American nationalism after Hamilton, especially through Abraham
Lincoln, sought to rectify this flaw by defining the ideal of national
unity in terms of (more accurately, masking it with) a "great moral
issue." Manifest Destiny was one such issue, and it quickly became a
mask for territorial expansion, surviving in Wilsonian internationalism, the messianic anticommunism of Cold War liberalism, and the
global democratism and "New World Order" of the post-Cold War
neoconservatives. Equality was another such issue, and it too served as
a mask for acquisitive individualism. Harry Jaffa is in a sense correct
that the "principle of Equality" as he perceives it in the Declaration of
Independence and in Lincoln's thought "is the ground for the recognition of those human differences which arise *naturally*, but in *civil society* when human industry and acquisitiveness are emancipated," though
he is wrong in claiming that equality is "far from enfranchising any
leveling action of government." This very process by which human
acquisitiveness is "emancipated" involves the obliteration by the state
of social barriers to acquisitiveness, and so it did in the attack on property and federalism that Lincoln unleashed in the Civil War. Hence,
M.E. Bradford is also (and more importantly) correct when he writes
that the depredations and corruptions of the Gilded Age, the "era of the
Great Barbecue," the original "vulture capitalism," "began either under [Lincoln's] direction or with his sponsorship" and that Lincoln's
administration laid "the cornerstone of this great alteration in the pos-
ture of the Federal government toward the sponsorship of business." It
was indeed the cornerstone of the modern corporate state on which the
twin towers of managerial capitalism and managerial government are
grounded. The "great moral issues" that the old nationalism eventually
selected, therefore, were little more than fantastic and easily penetrated
costumes in which even older human passions of greed and lust for
power sallied forth to their orgy.

Precisely because the old nationalism assumed an adversarial relationship toward the norms and institutions to which most Americans adhered, it could locate few forces in American society with which it could join, and it therefore came to rely almost entirely on a centralized state as the only "nationalizing" instrument available for its mission. Hence, the old nationalism was intimately bound up with abstraction, alienation, the serving of special rather than authentically national interests, and the consolidation of state power against its own society.

What a new, Middle-American nationalism must seek is a redefinition of nationalism away from the terms of the old. Since a Middle-American nationalism bases itself on the actual interest and norms of a concrete social group, it will not display the same adversarial alienation that affected the pseudo-nationalism it seeks to replace, nor will it need to rely on the power of the national state to the same degree or in the same way. Nevertheless, the mission of the new nationalism must be not merely the winning of formal political power through elections and roll-call votes but also the acquisition of substantive social power and the displacement of the incumbent managerial elite of the regime by its own elite drawn from and representing Middle-American social stratum. No social group becomes an elite unless it makes use of the instruments of force that are at the heart of the state, and hence, a Middle-American nationalism cannot expect to achieve its goals unless it employs the state to reward its own sociopolitical base and exclude its rivals from access to rewards. A Middle-American nationalism must expect to redefine legal rules, political procedures, fiscal and budgetary mechanisms, and national policy generally in the interests of Middle Americans, and it must do so with no illusions about rejecting, decentralizing, or dismantling the national state or the power it affords. Middle-American interests are dependent on the national state through various educational, fiscal, trade, and economic instruments, and a Middle-American nationalism ought to announce an explicit agenda of consolidating and enhancing these instruments. At the same time, a new nationalism must recognize that many of the organs of the national state exist only to serve the interests of the incumbent elite and its underclass allies—the arts and humanities endowments, and most or all of the Departments of Education, Labor, Commerce, Housing and Urban Development, and Health and Human Services, and the civil rights enforcement agencies in various departments—and it should seek their outright abolition, as well as that of those agencies and departments in the national security bureaucracy that serve globalist and antinationalist agendas.

But power based merely on the state is insufficient for the reconstitution of American society under Middle-American dominance. State power indeed, though a prerequisite for the emergence of a new elite, is by itself a weak support, and it must be supplemented by cultural dominance. Under the incumbent elite and its regime, characteristic Middle-American norms of sacrifice for and solidarity with family, community, ethnicity, nation, religion, and morals, and their rules of taste and propriety, are under continuous attack, subversion, and delegitimization by the cultural and intellectual vanguards of the elite. In place of such norms, the elite offers an ethic of hedonism, immediate gratification, and cosmopolitan or universalist dispersion of concrete identities and loyalties, an ethic that serves the interests of the incumbent elite by encouraging a passive and homogenized (though fragmented) culture of continuous consumption, distraction, entertainment, self-indulgence, surrender of social responsibilities to mass organizations, and the erosion of the concrete social identities and intermediary institutions that restrain the centralized manipulative power of both political and corporate structures.

By far the most strategically important effort of an emerging Middle-America counter-elite would be a long counter-march through the institutions of the dominant elite—universities, think tanks and foundations, schools, the arts, journalism, organized religion, the professions, labor organizations, and corporations—not only to assert the legitimacy of Middle-American cultural and ethnic identity, norms, and institutions but also to define American society in terms of them. Instead of an ethic of acquisitive individualism, immediate and perpetual gratification, distraction, and dispersion, the new nationalism should assert an ethic of solidarity and sacrifice able to discipline and direct national energy and reinforce national, social, and ethnic bonds of identity. The pseudo-nationalist ethic of the old nationalism that served only as a mask for the pursuit of special interests will be replaced by the social ethic of an authentic nationalism that can summon and harness the genius of a people certain of its identity and its destiny. The myth of the managerial regime that America is merely a philosophical proposition about the equality of all mankind (and therefore includes all mankind) must be replaced by a new myth of the nation as a historically and culturally unique order that commands loyalty, solidarity, and discipline and excludes those who do not or cannot assimilate to its norms and interests. This is the real meaning of "America First": America must be first not only among other nations but first also among the other (individuals or class or sectional) interests of its people. Unless a Middle-American nationalism (or any other sociopolitical movement) can achieve such cultural hegemony through the formulation of an accepted public myth, its political power and economic resources will remain dependent on the cultural power of its adversaries and eventually will succumb to their manipulation as it takes it cues on goals and tactics from its oppponents.

If a new Middle-American nationalism is in some respects a synthesis and a transcendence of the conventional poles of right and left, it is also in another sense a resolution of the popular conflict between the classical republicanism and the nationalism around which so much of American political history has swung. Like the nationalist tradition, it concerns itself with the pragmatic defense of national interests in foreign affairs, military security, and political economy, but unlike the old nationalism it perceives a national interest beyond this pragmatic dimension in the preservation of the distinctive cultural and ethnic foundations of nationality, recognizing that pragmatic, material, and economic considerations may and should defer to the more central norms without which pragmatism is merely a meaningless process. The affirmation of national and cultural identity as the core of the new nationalist ethic acquires special importance at a time when massive immigration, a totalitarian and antiwhite multiculturalist fanaticism, concerted economic warfare by foreign competitors, and the forces of antinational political globalism continue to jeopardize the cultural identity, demographic existence, economic autonomy, and national independence and sovereignty of the American nation.

Like the republican tradition, the new nationalism is essentially populist in tactics, locating the cultural and moral core of contemporary American society in a stratum that is the main victim of the regime that now prevails in the United States. Like republicanism also, it is less interested in the abstract pursuit of luxury and empire than in the defense of the characteristic norms and identity of the people it defines and represents, and like republicanism it calls that people to a duty higher than mere accumulation and aggrandizement, to a destiny of knowing who they are, where they came from, and what they can be. If they remain able to answer that call, they and their posterity may yet achieve both a virtue and a power that neither old republicans nor old nationalists were ever able to create.

Contributors

M.E. Bradford (1934–1993) was a professor of English at the University of Dallas and a leading disciple of the Vanderbilt Agrarians. His many books of political and literary criticism include *A Better Guide Than Reason* and *Remembering Who We Are: Reflections of a Southern Conservative*. At the time of his death in 1993, Dr. Bradford was editor of the Southern Classics Series (published by J.S. Sanders & Company) and at work on a biography of his friend and mentor, Donald Davidson.

James Burnham (1905–1987) followed an intellectual odyssey that included careers in academia, journalism and Cold War politics. For many years, he was a professor of philosophy at New York University and later a senior editor at *National Review*. During the Truman administration, he was also a consultant for the fledging Central Intelligence Agency. His most best-known books are *The Managerial Revolution, The Macheavilleans* and *Suicide of the West*.

Allan Carlson is president of the Howard Institute and editor of *The Family in America*.

Frank Chodorov (1887–1966) was one of the driving forces behind the libertarian revival of the late 1940s and 1950s. He was the founding editor of *Analysis* and a co-founder of the Intercollegiate Society of Individualists. His books include *One is a Crowd* and *The Income Tax: The Root of All Evil*.

Thomas Fleming is president of the Rockford Institute and editor of *Chronicles*, published in Rockford, Illinois. He was the founder of the the *Southern Partisan* and is co-founder of both the John Randolph Club and the League of the South.

Samuel Francis is a nationally syndicated columnist and a contributing editor for *Chronicles*. He previously served as a legislative aide to the late Senator John P. East of North Carolina and as an editorial page writer and columnist for the *Washington Times*.

Paul Gottfried is a professor of humanities at Elizabethtown College. He is a contributing editor to *Chronicles* and the editor of *This World*.

William R. Hawkins currently serves as a Senior Research Analyst on the staff of Rep. Duncan Hunter (Republican-California).

Russell Kirk (1920–1994) was the author of *The Conservative Mind*, widely regarded as the most important book of the post-World War II conservative intellectual movement. In all, he was the author of more than thirty books, including *The Roots of American Order, Eliot and His Age* and *Enemies of the Permanent Things*. Dr. Kirk was also the founding editor of both *Modern Age* and the *University Bookman*. He was the only American to hold a doctorate degree from St. Andrews University in Scotland. At the time of his death, he served as editor for Transaction's Library of Conservative Thought.

Murray Rothbard (1926–1994) was the author of, among numerous other books, *For a New Liberty*, a landmark document of modern libertarian thought. A prolific author, Dr. Rothbard was also a professor of economics at the University of Nevada, Las Vegas. His other well-known books are *Man, Economy and State* and *Conceived in Liberty,* a three-volume history of America's founding era.

Richard Weaver (1910–1963) was the author of *Ideas Have Consequences,* which along with *The Conservative Mind*, was one of the handful of books that inspired the creation of the traditionalist wing of modern conservatism. For many years, he served as a professor of English at the University of Chicago. Dr. Weaver's other works include *The Southern Tradition at Bay* and *Visions of Order*.

Chilton Williamson, Jr. is senior book editor for *Chronicles*. He served for a number of years in the same capacity at *National Review*.

Clyde Wilson is a professor of history at the University of South Carolina where he also serves as editor of the Papers of John C. Calhoun.

Bibliography

Bradford, M.E. *A Better Guide Than Reason: Federalists and Anti-Federalists*. LaSalle, Ill.: Sherwood Sudgen, 1979. Reissued by Transaction Publishers, New Brunswick, N.J., 1994.

————. *A Worthy Company: Brief Lives of the Framers of the Constitution*. Marlborough, N.H.: Plymouth Rock Foundation, 1982.

————. *Generations of the Faithful Heart: On the Literature of the South*. LaSalle, Ill.: Sherwood Sugden, 1983.

————. *Remembering Who We Are: Reflections of a Southern Conservative*. Athens: The University of Georgia Press, 1985.

————. *The Reactionary Imperative: Essays Literary and Political*. Peru, Ill.: Sherwood Sugden, 1990.

————. *Against the Barbarians: And Other Reflections on Familiar Themes*. Columbia: The University of Missouri Press, 1992.

————. *Original Intentions: On the Making and Ratification of the United States Constitutions*. Athens: The University of Georgia Press, 1993.

Burnham, James. *The Managerial Revolution*. Bloomington: Indiana University Press, 1940.

————. *The Machiavellians: Defenders of Freedom*. Chicago: Henry Regnery Company, 1943.

————. *The Struggle for the World*. New York: The John Day Company, 1947.

————. *The Case for DeGaulle: A Dialogue between André Malraux and James Burnham*. New York: Random House, 1948.

————. *The Coming Defeat of Communism*. New York: The John Day Company, 1950.

————. *Containment or Liberation? An Inquiry into the Aims of U.S. Foreign Policy*. New York: The John Day Company, 1953.

————. *Congress and the American Tradition*. Chicago: Henry Regnery Company, 1959.

————. *Suicide of the West: An Essay on the Meaning and Destiny of Liberalism*. New York: The John Day Company, 1964.

Carlson, Allan. *The Swedish Experiment in Family Politics: The Myrdals and the Interwar Population Crisis*. New Brunswick, N.J.: Transaction Publishers, 1990.

————. *The Family: Is it Just Another Lifestyle Choice?* London: FA Health and Welfare Unit, 1993.

————. *From Cottage to Work Station: The Family's Search for Social Harmony in the Industrial Age*. San Francisco, Cal.: Ignatius Press, 1993.

Chodorov, Frank. *The Income Tax: The Root of All Evil*. New York: Devin-Adair, 1954.

————. *The Rise and Fall of Society: An Essay on the Economic Forces that Underlie Social Institutions*. New York: Devin-Adair, 1959.

————. *Out of Step: The Autobiography of an Individualist*. New York: Devin-Adair, 1962.

Fleming, Thomas. *The Politics of Human Nature*. New Brunswick, N.J.: Transaction Publishers, 1988.

————. (with Paul Gottfried), *The Conservative Movement*. Boston: Twayne Publishers, 1988.

Francis, Samuel. *Power and History: The Political Thought of James Burnham*. Lanham, Md.: University Press of America, 1984.

————. *Beautiful Losers: Essays on the Failure of American Conservatism*. Columbia: The University of Missouri Press, 1993.

————. *Revolution from the Middle: Columns and Articles from Chronicles, 1989–1996*. Raleigh, N.C.: Middle American Press, 1997.

Gottfried, Paul. *Conservative Millenarians: The Romantic Experience in Bavaria*. New York: Fordham University Press, 1979.

————. *The Search for Historical Meaning: Hegel and the Postwar American Right*. DeKalb, Ill.: Northern University Press, 1986.

————. (with Thomas Fleming), *The Conservative Movement*. Boston: Twayne Publishers, 1988.

————. *Carl Schmitt: Politics and Theory*. New York: Greenwood Press, 1990.

————. *The Conservative Movement* (revised edition). New York: Twayne Publishers, 1993.

————. *After Liberalism: Mass Democracy in the Managerial State*. Princeton, N.J.: Princeton University Press, 1998.

Hawkins, William, R. *Importing Revolution*. Washington, D.C.: American Immigration Control Foundation/U.S. Business and Industrial Council Foundation, 1994.

Kirk, Russell. *Randolph of Roanoke: A Study in Conservative Thought*. Chicago: University of Chicago Press, 1951.

————. *The Conservative Mind: From Burke to Santayana*. Chicago: Henry Regnery Company, 1953. (This book has gone through seven editions, the latest titled *The Conservative Mind: From Burke to Eliot*, published also by Regnery in 1994.)

————. *Academic Freedom: An Essay in Definition*. Chicago: Henry Regnery Company, 1955.

————. *Beyond the Dreams of Avarice: Essays of a Social Critic*. Chicago: Henry Regnery Company, 1956.

————. *The Intelligent Woman's Guide to Conservatism*. New York: Devin-Adair Company, 1957.

————. *The American Cause*. Chicago: Henry Regnery Company, 1957.

————. *Old House of Fear*. New York: Fleet Publishing Corp., 1961.

————. *A Program for Conservatives*. Chicago: Henry Regnery Company, 1962.

————. *Confessions of a Bohemian Tory: Episodes and Reflections of a Vagrant Career*. New York: Fleet Publishing Corp., 1963.

————. *The Intemperate Professor and Other Cultural Splenetics*. Baton Rouge: Louisiana State University Press, 1965.

————. (with James McClellan), *The Political Principles of Robert A. Taft*. New York: Fleet Publishing Corp., 1967.

————. *Enemies of the Permanent Things: Observations of Abnormality in Literature and Politics*. New Rochelle, N.Y.: Arlington House, 1969.

————. *Eliot and His Age: T.S. Eliot's Moral Imagination in the Twentieth Century*. New York: Random House, 1971.

————. *The Roots of American Order*. LaSalle, Ill.: Open Court, 1974.

————. *Decadence and Renewal in the Higher Learning: An Episodic History of American University and College Since 1953*. South Bend, Ind.: Gateway Editions, 1978.

————. *Lord of the Hollow Dark*. New York: St. Martin's Press, 1979.

————. *The Portable Conservative Reader* (editor). New York: Penguin Books, 1982.

————. *Watchers at the Strait Gate: Mystical Tales*. Sauk City, Wisc.: Arkham House, 1984.

————. *The Assault on Religion: Commentaries on the Decline of Religious Liberty*. Lanham, Md.: University Press of America, Center for Judicial Studies, 1986.

————. *The Wise Men Know What Wicked Things Are Written on the Sky*. Washington, D.C.: Regnery Gateway, 1987.

————. *Edmund Burke: A Genius Reconsidered*. Peru, Ill.: Sherwood Sugden, 1988.

————. *The Conservative Constitution*. Washington, D.C.: Regnery Gateway, 1990.

————. *America's British Culture*. New Brunswick, N.J.: Transaction Publishers, 1993.

————. *The Politics of Prudence*. Bryn Mawr, Pa.: Intercollegiate Studies Institute, 1993.

————. *The Sword of Imagination: Memoirs of a Half-Century of Literary Conflict*. Grand Rapids, Mich.: William B. Eerdmans Publisher, 1995.

————. *Redeeming the Time*. Wilmington, Del.: Intercollegiate Studies Institute, 1997.

Rothbard, Murray. *The Panic of 1819: Reactions and Policies*. New York: Columbia University Press, 1962.

————. *Man, Economy and State: A Treatise on Economic Principles*. Princeton, N.J.: Van Nostrand, 1962.

————. *America's Great Depression*. Los Angeles, Cal.: Nash Publishers, 1972.

————. *For A New Liberty*. New York: Macmillan, 1973.

————. *Conceived in Liberty*, three volumes. New Rochelle, N.Y.: Arlington House, 1975–1979.

————. *Individualism and the Philosophy of Social Sciences*. San Francisco, Cal.: The Cato Institute, 1979.

————. (with Garet Garrett), *The Great Depression and New Deal Monetary Policy*. San Francisco, Cal.: Cato Institute, 1980.

————. *The Mystery of Banking*. New York: Richardson and Synder, 1983.

————. *The Case Against the Fed*. Auburn, Ala.: Ludwig von Mises Institute, 1994.

Scotchie, Joseph. *The Vision of Richard Weaver* (editor). New Brunswick, N.J.: Transaction Publishers, 1995.

————. *Barbarians in the Saddle: An Intellectual Biography of Richard M. Weaver*. New Brunswick, N.J.: Transaction Publishers, 1997.

Weaver, Richard. *Ideas Have Consequences*. Chicago: The University of Chicago Press, 1948.

————. *The Ethics of Rhetoric*. Chicago: Henry Regnery Company, 1953. Reissued by Hermagoras Press, Davis, Calif., 1985.

————. *Composition: A Course in Reading and Writing*. New York: Holt, Rinehart, and Winston, 1957. Revised with the assistance of Richard S. Beal and reissued as *Rhetoric and Composition*, 1967.

————. *Visions of Order: The Cultural Crisis of Our Time*. Baton Rouge: Louisiana State University Press, 1964. Reissued by Intercollegiate Studies Institute, 1995.

————. *Life Without Prejudice and Other Essays*. Chicago: Henry Regnery Company, 1965.

————. *The Southern Tradition at Bay: A Study of Postbellum Literature* (edited by M.E. Bradford and George Core). New Rochelle, N.Y.: Arlington House, 1968. Reissued by Regnery/Gateway, Washington, D.C., 1989.

————. *Language is Sermonic: Richard M. Weaver on the Nature of Rhetoric* (edited by Richard L. Johannesen, Rennard Strickland, and Ralph T. Eubanks). Baton Rouge: Louisiana State University Press, 1970.

————. *The Southern Essays of Richard M. Weaver* (edited by George M. Curtis III and James J. Thompson). Indianapolis: Liberty Press, 1987.

Williamson, Chilton. *Saltbound: A Block Island Winter*. New York: Methuen, 1980.

————. *Roughnecking It: Or, Life in the Overthrust*. New York: Simon and Schuster, 1982.

————. *Desert Light*. New York: St. Martin's Press, 1987.

————. *The Homestead*. New York: Grove Weidenfeld, 1990.

————. *The Immigration Mystique: America's False Conscience*. New York: Basic Books, 1996.

Wilson, Clyde. *Why the South Will Survive: Fifteen Southerners Look at Their Region a Half Century After I'll Take My Stand* (editor). Athens: University of Georgia Press, 1980.

———. *American Historians, 1607–1865* (editor). Detroit: Gale Research Company, 1984.

———. *American Historians, 1866–1912* (editor). Detroit: Gale Research Company, 1986.

———. *Carolina Cavalier: The Life and Mind of James Johnston Pettigrew.* Athens: University of Georgia Press, 1990.

———. *John C. Calhoun: A Bibliography.* Westport: Meckler Press, 1990.

———. *The Meaning of South Carolina History: Essays in Honor of George C. Rogers, Jr.* (edited with David R. Chesnutt). Columbia: University of South Carolina Press, 1991.

———. *The Essential Calhoun: Selections from Writings, Speeches, and Letters* (editor). New Brunswick, N.J.: Transaction Publishers, 1992.

———. *A Defender of Southern Conservatism: M.E. Bradford and His Achievements* (editor). Columbia: University of Missouri Press, 1999.

Index of Names

Abbey, Edward, 2, 100–101, 186
Acheson, Dean, 22
Ames, Fisher, 3, 153
Angell, Norman, 119
Aristophanes, 67, 86
Aristotle, 1, 158, 169, 174
Arnold, Matthew, 157
Aurelius, Marcus, 69

Babeuf, Francois, 85
Bach, Johann Sebastian, 161
Bailyn, Bernard, 146–47
Baker, James, 5, 128–29
Baldwin, James, 156
Barnes, Harry Elmer, 22
Barnett, Corelli, 114
Bastiat, Frederic, 108, 118
Beard, Charles, A., 22
Becker, Gary, 137
Bellah, Robert, 148
Bennett, William, 5, 169
Bentham, Jeremy, 117
Berger, Brigitte, 5
Berkeley, George, 156
Berns, Walter, 164
Berry, Wendell, 131, 142
Bloom, Allan, 164
Bohannan, Paul, 157–58
Bonaparte, Napoleon, 113
Boone, Pat, 154
Boorstin, Daniel, 150
Borah, William, P., 2, 22, 171
Borsodi, Ralph, 136
Boswell, James, 83, 111
Bowlby, John, 138
Bradford, M.E., 1, 14, 5, 8, 10–11, 196
Brennan, William, 173
Bricker, John, 28
Bright, John, 173
Broder, David, 174
Bromfield, Louis, 2
Bryan, William Jennings, 2, 171

Buchanan, Patrick, 4–5, 10, 12–14
Buckley, William, F., 5–6, 13
Buffet, Howard, 21, 27, 29
Burke, Edmund, 1, 61, 66–67, 70, 184, 190
Burnham, James, 9, 104
Burns, Ken, 5
Bush, George, 4, 98

Calhoun, Arthur, 136
Calhoun, John C., 2–3, 183, 190
Carlson, Allan, 8, 12–13
Carlson, "John Roy," 28
Carnegie, Andrew, 154
Carson, Johnny, 155
Carter, Jimmy, 12
Chappell, Fred, 162
Chaucer, Geoffrey, 86
Chesterton, G.K., 2, 141
Chodorov, Frank, 8–9, 12, 26, 29
Cicero, 60
Clayton, William C., 22
Cobden, Richard, 108, 119, 173
Cohen, Stephen, 115
Colbert, Jean-Baptiste, 121, 125
Columbus, Christopher, 109
Costello, John, 140
Croly, Herbert, 136

Dante, 161
Davidson, Donald, 2
Dawson, Christopher, 69
de Castro, Alfonso Nunez, 110
de Coulanges, Numa Denis Fustel, 164
de Maistre, Joseph, 2
de Melia, Vazquez, 61
Doenecke, Justus, 171
Doran, Charles, F., 125–26
Douglas, Lewis, 22

East, John, 151

Elders, Joycelen, 170
Eliot, T. S., 2, 66, 90–92
Emerson, Ralph Waldo, 102
Evans, M. Stanton, 4

Faulkner, William, 2, 156
Feulner, Edwin, 5
Fitzgerald, F. Scott, 156
Fleming, Thomas, 2–4, 6, 8, 13, 21, 143
Florida, Richard, 115
Flynn, John T., 22, 26
Fortunatus, Venantius, 160
Francis, Samuel, 4, 8, 13, 167, 175
Franklin, Benjamin, 164, 181
Frost, Robert, 2
Fulbright, William J., 2

Galbraith, John Kenneth, 105
Garrett, Garet, 20, 26
Geyer, Georgie Ann, 99, 104
Gilman, Charlotte Perkins, 133
Gingrich, Newt, 13
Gold, Mike, 156
Goldwater, Barry, 12
Gorbachev, Mikhail, 153
Gore, Tipper, 156
Gottfried, Paul, 4, 13–14
Gramsci Antonio, 156
Guttman, Amy, 171

Habermas, Jurgen, 171, 173
Hamilton, Alexander, 38, 108, 120–22,
    164, 189, 195
Harrigan, Anthony, 12
Hawkins, William, 12
Hayek, Friedrich, 2
Hazlitt, Henry, 2
Hegel, Georg Wilhelm Friedrich, 169
Helms, Jesse, 190
Hemingway, Ernest, 156
Henry, Patrick, 8
Hitler, Adolf, 54, 85, 124, 169, 181
Hobbes, Thomas, 163
Hocking, W.E., 89
Hofstadter, Richard, 170
Holmes, Stephen, 173
Holt, John, 142
Hoover, Herbert, 20, 189
Howe, Irving, 22–23
Huddle, Donald, 98
Hume, David, 109–110
Hunt, Al, 174

Jackson, Andrew, 108
Jackson, Jesse, 103
Jaffa, Henry, 164, 196
Jay, John, 164, 174
Jeffers, Robinson, 155
Jefferson, Thomas, 2, 102, 122–23, 160,
    164, 173–74, 182
Johnson, Lyndon, 66, 189
Johnson, Samuel, 83
Joyce, James, 92

Kant, Immanuel, 113, 160
Kazin, Alfred, 22–23
Keenan, George, 167
Kenny, Martin, 115
Ketcham, Ralph, 190
King, Martin Luther, 169
Kinsey, Alfred, 140
Kirk, Russell, 1, 14, 8–10, 150
Kitazawa, Yoko, 127
Kristol, Irving, 5, 22–23

Lady Bracknell, 153
LaGuardia, Fiorello, 25
Landess, Thomas, 4
Lane, Rose Wilder, 20
Lasch, Christopher, 166–68
Lauter, David, 19
Lenin, V.I., 51, 169
Lewis, C.S., 89, 161, 183
Lewis, Wyndham, 74
Lincoln, Abraham, 9, 102, 196
Lincoln, Edward, P., 126
Lindberg, Charles, 190
List, Friedrich, 107, 116, 121
Locke, John, 155, 160, 165, 173–74
Lodge, Henry, Cabot, 123
Lord Falkland, 64
Lord Halifax, 84
Luce, Clare Booth, 22
Luther, Martin, 166
Lytle, Andrew, 2

Machiavelli, 84, 189
Madison, James, 108, 121, 164, 183
Madonna, 13, 102, 153, 162
Mailer, Norman, 4
Mann, Horace, 134
Marcel, Gabriel, 66
Marcus, Bernard, 25
Marcus, Lloyd, 25
Marshall, John, 20

Marty, Martin, 148
Mathissen, F. O., 92
McCormick, Robert, 26, 29
McDonald, Forrest, 122, 195
McKibben, Bill, 99
Mencken, H. L., 20, 26
Meyer, Frank, 9
Miglio, Gianfranco, 163, 173
Mill, James, 117
Miller, Henry, 154
Miller, John, C., 196
Moore, Raymond, 142
Morris, Richard, B., 122

Neuhaus, Richard, John, 6, 169
Neusner, Jacob, 161
Nisbet, Robert, 143, 169
Nixon, Richard, 12
Nock, Albert, J., 20, 26
Novak, Michael, 169
Nye, Gerald, 22

Paine, Thomas, 67, 118
Parsons, Talcott, 138
Paul, Ron, 3
Penn, William, 150
Percy, Walker, 2
Perot, Ross, 12, 14
Piccone, Paul, 167
Pickney, Charles, 151
Plato, 1
Podhoretz, Norman, 6
Prangle, Thomas, 164

Rahe, Paul, 164
Randolph, John, 2, 190
Reagan, Ronald, 4, 12, 118, 151
Reed, James, 20
Reisman, David, 7
Riccardo, David, 112–13, 116
Ritchie, Albert, 20
Rockwell, Llewellyn, 3–4, 7, 172
Rosseau, Jean-Jacques, 165
Roosevelt, Franklin, 9, 189
Roosevelt, Theodore, 123
Rosen, Charles, 25
Rothbard, Murray, 4, 8–9, 12, 172
Ryder, Norman, 164

Saint Augustine, 169
Saint Luke, 160
Saint Paul, 98, 160

Saint Thomas, 155
Santayana, George, 73
Savile, George, 84
Savonarla, Girolamo, 170
Say, Jean-Baptiste, 107, 117, 123
Schaeffer, Francis, 161
Schmitt, Carl, 163
Schumpeter, Joseph, 132
Semmel, Bernard, 117
Seneca, 69
Shakespeare, William, 86
Sholokov, Mikhail, 85
Shultz, George, 128–29
Simon, Julian, 98
Smith, Adam, 113–14, 122, 143, 190
Smith, Frederick, C., 21
Smith, John, 147
Snopes, Flem, 153
Sophocles, 156
Spender, Stephen, 166
Stalin, Joseph, 54, 181
Steele, Danielle, 155
Strauss, Leo, 164
Strout, Cushing, 148

Taft, Robert, A., 4, 9, 27–29
Taguieff, Pierre-Andre, 170, 172, 174
Tapie, Bernard, 172
Tate, Allen, 10, 186
Terrill, Tom, E., 123
Thomas, Clarence, 153
Thoreau, Henry David, 59
Thucydides, 84
Thurmond, Strom, 4, 28
Trollope, Anthony, 155
Trotsky, Leon, 51, 156
Truman, Harry, 27
Tucker, Jeffrey, 172
Tylor, E.B., 157
Tyrmand, Leopold, 3

Vandenberg, Arthur, 27
Vargas, Getulio, 170
Vidal, Gore, 6, 167
Vives, Jaime Vicens, 111
Voegelin, Eric, 169
Voltaire, 110
Von Mises, Ludwig, 2

Wallace, George, 5
Wallace, Henry, 28
Washington, George, 1, 120

Wattenberg, Ben, 97
Weaver, Richard, 1, 18, 10, 149
Weber, Max, 170
Westcott, Glenway, 2
Wheatley, Phyllis, 156
Whitehead, A.N., 62
Whitman, Walt, 88
Wieseltier, Leon, 166
Will, George, 5
William of Ockham, 169

Williamson, Chilton, Jr., 4, 11
Willis, Ellen, 175–76
Wilson, Charles, 112, 124
Wilson, Clyde, 3–4, 8, 13
Wilson, Woodrow, 2, 123, 189
Wright, Fielding, 28
Wright, Louis, B., 146

Yeats, William Butler, 91–92

Zysman, John, 115